Women and the Business Game

Strategies for

Successful Ownership

Charlotte Taylor

VENTURE CONCEPTS PRESS

To my mother, who gave me
my entrepreneurial spirit,
and to my father,
who taught me that
business sense is good sense.

Published by Venture Concepts Press
1111 19th Street, NW, 1050
Washington, DC 20036

Designed by Irving Perkins
Manufactured in the United States of America
10 9 8 7 6 5 4 3 2 1

Library of Congress Cataloging in Publication Data

Taylor, Charlotte.
   Women and the business game.

   Bibliography: p.
   Includes index.
   1. Women-owned business enterprises—United
States. 2. Women in business—United States.
I. Title.
HF5500.3.U54T39   658.1'141'024042   79-17119

ISBN 0-9611214-0-8

Contents

FOREWORD 9

ACKNOWLEDGMENTS 11

INTRODUCTION: Women as Entrepreneurs 13

CHAPTER 1: Women: The New Immigrants 19

CHAPTER 2: The Entrepreneurial Game 29

CHAPTER 3: Getting into the Game 51

CHAPTER 4: Building Your Entrepreneurial Team 79

CHAPTER 5: Financing Your Business 93

CHAPTER 6: Developing Your Marketing Strategy 125

CHAPTER 7: Staffing Your Organization 149

CHAPTER 8: Controlling Your Company 171

CHAPTER 9: The Final Move: Playing the Game 191

EPILOGUE 213

APPENDIX 1. Scoring Sheet and Answer Interpretation: Do You Have What It Takes to Start Your Own Business? 217

APPENDIX 2. Tools for Financial Analysis 221

APPENDIX 3. Resources 229

BIBLIOGRAPHY 243

NOTES 251

INDEX 255

Foreword

A decade ago I wrote a small book entitled *Sex in the Marketplace: American Women at Work*. After reviewing the role of women in the labor force, I noted that the rhetoric of the era threatened to obscure the overwhelming economic significance of women's underutilization in the marketplace.

Events of the 1970s have helped me to worry less about sex discrimination in the job market, but only slightly less. The critical question of how the society can effectively use women's talents in and outside the labor force continues to be an issue of major importance not only to women but also to their male employers, colleagues, families, and the society. Nations striving to increase productivity cannot afford to underutilize vital economic resources—male or female—and the women-part of the dilemma grows as women become better educated, better trained, and more committed to careers outside their homes.

The dramatic reordering in the composition of the work force and in women's professional aspirations since the Second World War means that women are now routinely doing things seldom allowed in earlier times. They lead major corporations, fly commercial airplanes, attend military academies, and hold high positions in government. Two of the largest cities in the country, Chicago and San Francisco, have female mayors, and a female governor is no longer unique. Today's employment trends show more and more women entering and staying in the work force, despite marriage and child rearing. There is little doubt that this pattern will change. The steady postwar climb in work-force participation by women, the decline in the birth rates, the rapid growth in the number of single and divorced women, and a growing interest among women in lifetime careers suggest that a basic change has occurred in the attitudes and expectations of both sexes toward work roles.

But while the statistics show that the total volume of market work in the United States is coming to be more evenly divided between men and women, the positions held by most women follow the traditional patterns; the vast majority of women still labor in low-paying "female" occupations. They continue to staff the clerical jobs, the elementary classrooms, and the salesrooms; to make lower wages and own only a small proportion of the capital assets of this country.

Entrepreneurship as a career option for women, however, could become more popular in the 1980s. Just as immigrants have looked to business ownership as a way to increase their economic base and power in our society, women, too, are beginning to use this track. The President's Task Force on Women Business Owners found that the American dream of owning one's own business was not dead, but had become a dream of women, as well as of men. The Task Force found a growing interest in business ownership among women and an increased sophistication among those women who were already owners.

The Task Force report and subsequent actions by President Carter to establish a National Women's Business Enterprise Policy has left little doubt that women will, in time, take their place among the great business leaders of our country. How soon this change will occur depends on how quickly society removes the remaining discriminatory barriers and how rapidly women train themselves for the complex problems facing today's business leaders. Unfortunately, the discriminatory barriers will take time to erode. In the meantime, *Women and the Business Game* is designed to help women master some of the basic business principles needed to run a business.

To Sigmund Freud's plaintive query, "What does woman want? Dear God! What does she want?" there is, of course, no single answer. But as we enter the 1980s one thing that women want is to enter the economic mainstream of our society, not only as workers with responsible and equal positions but also as owners of their own businesses. This book and President Carter's initiatives in behalf of women business owners should help some women to achieve their goals.

Juanita M. Kreps
former Secretary of Commerce

Acknowledgments

I would like to express my gratitude to Juanita Weaver, whose work was an integral part of this book and whose long hours of interviewing caught the spirit of the entrepreneurial woman, and to Judi Aboud, Nancy Beard, Mary Bolton, and Amy Heyman for their assistance.

In addition, I would like to thank the following women and men, who shared their insight and experience, and who gave freely of their time and expertise. The information gained during interviews with them made a valuable contribution to this book:

Arlene Alligood, The Women's Information Institute, Washington, D.C.; Marjorie O'Connell Amey, O'Connell-Amey & Associates, Washington, D.C.; Joan Attianese, Elm Medical Laboratories, Inc., Boston, Mass.; Luke Bandle, Luketon Ltd., Washington, D.C.; Judith Barnett, free-lance writer, Washington, D.C.; Fay Bedard, Atlantic Railway Consultants, Inc., Drexel Hill, Pa.; Sharron Egan Belson, Belson/St. Louis, Inc., St. Louis, Mo.; Henry Bender, American Management Associations, New York, N.Y.; Evelyn Berezin, Redactron, New York, N.Y.; Aline Berman, Court of the Mandarins Restaurant, Washington, D.C.; Patricia Bissell, Bissell and Associates, Rockville, Md.; Juanita Burks, City Plaza Personnel Consultant Service, Louisville, Ky.; Denise Cavanaugh, Cook/Cavanaugh Associates, Washington, D.C.; Patricia Cloherty, Tessler & Cloherty, Inc., New York, N.Y.; Charlotte Cohen, Charlotte Cohen Stockbrokers, St. Louis, Mo.; Nona Cunane, Guardian Construction, Newark, Del.; Lynn Dearborn, Gallery 4, Alexandria, Va.; Janet Deming & Diane Olson, dor & associates, Inc., Minneapolis, Minn.; Alison & Paul Diamond, Diamond Paper Corporation, Silver Spring, Md.; Vicki Smith Downing, International Venture & Equity Capital, Dallas, Tex.; Kandra Driggs, Wing Conferences, Burlingame, Calif.; Peggy Dwyier, Dwyier Associates, Inc., Arlington, Va.; Pansy Essman, Pansy Ellen Products, Inc., San Jose, Calif.

Carrie L. Fair, Kendrick & Company, Washington, D.C.; Mary Farmer, Lammas, Washington, D.C.; Margaret Fenn, University of Washington, Seattle, Wash.; Beatrice Fitzpatrick, American Women's Economic Development Corporation, New York, N.Y.; Cynthia Gair & Helaine Harris, Women in Distribution, Washington,

D.C.; Eve Grover, First Women's Bank of Maryland, Rockville, Md.; Sandy Hancock, Sandy Hancock Enterprises, Inc., Dallas, Tex.; Cathy Hardwick, Cathy Hardwick & Friends, Ltd., New York, N.Y.; Elizabeth Haynes, Baltimore Rigging Company, Baltimore, Md.; Genie Hindall, Guide Service of Washington, Inc., Washington, D.C.; Pauline A. Hogan, Designs by Pauline's, Boston, Mass.; J. Herbert Hollomon, Center for Policy Alternatives, Massachusetts Institute of Technology, Cambridge, Mass.; Joyce Huber & Carla Massoni, Georgetown Employment Service, Washington, D.C.; Laurie Hutzler, Legal Management Services, Inc., New York, N.Y.; Carole S. Hyatt, Child Research Service, New York, N.Y.; Suzanne Ives, Ives & Associates, Washington, D.C.; Beverly Jackson & Sheila Summers, Jackson/Summers Associates, Inc., Washington, D.C.; Rene Jacoby, Amazon Hose & Rubber Company, Miami, Fla.

Constance Peet Kenney, Investment Counselor, Lexington, Mass.; Sarah Kovner & Barbara Handman, Arts, Letters, & Politics, Inc., New York, N.Y.; Nancy Lang, Lang Associates Realtors, Burlington, Vt.; Phyllis Linett, Andover Data Services, Inc., Gaithersburg, Md.; Lynn Lively, Management Consultant, Seattle, Wash.; Brooke Mahoney, Peter R.W. Bellerman, & Pamela Green, Volunteer Urban Consulting Group, New York, N.Y.; Virginia Mapel & Lynn Barnard, Virginia Mapel's Gazebo, Ltd., New York, N.Y.; Helen E. Marmoll, Esq., Attorney at Law, Arlington, Va.; Miriam Marshall, Port of Call Boutique, Bergdorf-Goodman, New York, N.Y.; Virginia Maynard, Citibank of New York, New York, N.Y.; William McCrea, The Entrepreneurship Institute, Worthington, Ohio; Suzanne Mendelssohn, Fundraising in the Public Interest, Inc., New York, N.Y.; Isabel Mitchell, Ambience Accessories, Inc., New York, N.Y.; James F. Molloy, TRAMCO, Cambridge, Mass.; Beth Myers, Alternative Development, Inc., Bethesda, Md.; June Myers & Cathy Irwin, Speaking of Women, Inc., Bethesda, Md.; Dona O'Bannon, Alcalde, Henderson, and O'Bannon, Rosslyn, Va.; Karen Olsen, New York Association of Women Business Owners, New York, N.Y.

Anne Pallie & Ila Gillaspie, Anne Pallie, Ltd., Washington, D.C.; Barbara Patinkin, Visual Concepts, New York, N.Y.; Mary Ann Petery, Selma Pressure Treating Co., Inc., Selma, Calif.; Diane Pingree, Paragon III Associates, Dallas, Tex.; Barbara Pinney, R.A. Pinney Company, Inc., Lincolnshire, Ill.; Joel Pitlor & Brian Haslett, Venture Founders, Belmont, Mass.; Jean Reid, formerly with American Women's Economic Development Corporation, New York, N.Y.; Lynn Salvage, formerly with First Women's Bank of New York, New York, N.Y.; Sandy & Mel Schifter, Le Sportsac, New York, N.Y.; Edith Schubert, The China Closet, Martin's, Chevy Chase, Md.; Margaret T. Shaffer, Paradigm, Inc., Potomac, Md.; Jayne Spain, Gulf Oil, Pittsburgh, Pa.; Ava Stern, *Enterprising Women: A Business Monthly for Entrepreneurial Women*, New York, N.Y.; Martha Stuart, Martha Stuart Communications, Inc., New York, N.Y.

Marie Tarvin, Sun City Delivery, El Paso, Tex.; Susan Thomas, formerly with Dub-L-Tape, Washington, D.C.; Jeffry A. Timmons, Northeastern University, Boston, Mass.; Corrine Travis, Rose Lash International, Ltd., New York, N.Y.; Rosemary Tucker, Tucker Tire Company, Covina, Calif.; Mary Vinton, Georgetown Leather Design, Alexandria, Va.; Eileen Weinberg & Christi Finch, Word of Mouth Caterers, New York, N.Y.; John Welsh, Caruth Institute of Owner-Managed Business, Southern Methodist University, Dallas, Tex.; Emily H. Womach, Women's National Bank, Washington, D.C.; Frances Young, DeForest Wood Products Company, St. Louis, Mo.; Carolyn Zaroff, Zaroff Communications, Inc., Rochester, N.Y.; Mary Zulalian, formerly with Holden & Company, Inc., Boston, Mass.

Introduction

Women as Entrepreneurs

The spirit of Horatio Alger is alive and well in America. Few people realize, however, that this spirit has been reincarnated in the body of a woman. A basic American dream, once primarily a male dream, has also become a female dream. That dream is the dream of owning your own business and reaping the economic and psychological benefits of hard work, determination, and perseverance.

There is a rekindling of the entrepreneurial spirit in women. It's a spirit that has always been present, imparted to us by our mothers and forebears, but which is being rechanneled from the traditional supporting role into a new economic endeavor for women: owning and operating their own companies. Today more and more women are beginning to view business ownership as a viable career option and as a means to achieve economic independence, upward mobility, and self-fulfillment.

You will see this new entrepreneurial spirit embodied in the women who were interviewed for this book. These women are not superwomen, but normal women who work hard at making their dreams become realities. These women will tell you that playing the entrepreneurial game is tough—you have to be willing to play with the boys and take the hard knocks and the heart-breaks along with the joys. They will tell you that you don't always win—you sometimes lose. Even so, they will tell you that the game is fun and satisfying and that they wouldn't do anything else.

Who is the new female entrepreneur? She is old; she is young; she is white; she is black; she is married; she is single; she is living in every village, town, and city in this country. She is like the women you will read about in this book. She is not unlike you and me. The common thread that binds these women together is the entrepreneurial spirit. That spirit is the ability to have the creativity, imagination, and drive to create something from nothing. It is a spirit that surfaces daily in every woman, from those who organize charities to those who make last year's dresses look like this year's fashion. It is a spirit we have seen in our pioneer foremothers and in our own mothers.

What is causing this revival of the entrepreneurial spirit? Part of it is being fired by the smoldering embers of the women's liberation movement. Many women feel that this movement has reached a new stage—a stage where economic power is becoming an important aspect of personal liberation. Money is power and independence and is necessary to achieve spiritual liberation as well.

If the consciousness raising of the 1960s made us realize that archaic sex stereotyping kept us from attaining our fullest potential, the consciousness raising of the 1970s is making us realize that economic freedom and power are fundamental to achieving equality. The recent growth in the number of women's banks across the country and the increasing numbers of women who want to learn to manage their own financial affairs are indications of this trend.

Women are suddenly realizing not only that they were deceived into accepting inadequate jobs or less pay than men for the same work but also that they have been neglecting to take advantage of what little money they have had. They have failed to take this money and make it work for them so that they could better their financial status and independence.

Lynn Salvage, formerly president of the First Women's Bank in New York, believes that American women are just beginning to understand that power is measured in dollars. This awareness, she thinks, will make a difference in the number of women owning businesses.

> It has taken years to raise the business consciousness of women. Even women who have had their consciousness raised and who believe in the Equal Rights Amendment, in equal pay, and in the need for more women politicians still don't realize the tremendous power the business owner has in this country. Power in America is dollars. It lies in the economy, not in politics. Take the Women's Bank for example: A bank equals power. Why? Because we control money and the power to finance companies.

Salvage points out that when the First Women's Bank of New York was in financial trouble, she had many sale offers from men to buy the bank charter. "Men realized the power of having a bank charter. Women just couldn't see the forest for the trees. They didn't realize the importance of economic power and why a bank that was concerned with women's economic interests needed to stay alive."

However, this trend is changing. Women are tired of thinking that equal opportunity for positions in companies and equal pay for equal work are enough. We also want equal access to equity, to ownership of the capital wealth in America. We are tired of the myths that have hampered us for generations: myths that we own most of the corporate stock in America, when such ownership is in name only for tax reasons and the wealth is actually controlled by husbands; myths that we control the wealth in America, when the poverty level for women is higher than it is for men; and myths that we can't or shouldn't manage money, that we can't balance checkbooks, that we are poor credit risks, and that we are "hobbiests" rather than serious businesswomen. All these myths continue to hamper us in the business environment. Yet women dream of making it big, just as men do. We also dream of being our own boss, of producing needed goods and services, and of reaping the economic benefits of those services.

Despite our desire for success, women are not making it big. The gap between what men and women earn in America has actually increased, rather than decreased, in the last ten years. Today women make only sixty cents for every dollar that men make. College-educated women still have lower incomes than men with only an elementary school education. We are still the nation's bank tellers, not bank presidents; bookkeepers, not accountants; teachers, not administrators; and secretaries, not executives. We are still clustered in low-paying jobs that offer us little opportunity for advancement.[1]

Yet, if work was ever optional for some, it is no longer. Rising inflation, changing social mores, and soaring divorce rates have made the two-income family as much an American norm in some cities as the two-car family once was. Only between 7 and 15 percent of the American families now conform to the so-called typical family model made up of a working husband and a housekeeping wife.[2] If a woman is not single now, experts say that four out of five women will be single again at some time in their lives through the death or divorce of a spouse.[3]

The old dichotomy of the terms *career woman* and *married woman,* which implied that work was an option for women, is passé. Today, the new term is *working woman,* and we are indeed working. The average American woman now spends twenty-three years of her life in the work force compared with twelve years in 1940. For single women, this average is much greater at forty-five years.[4] If today's woman isn't deadly serious about her economic future, she should be. It is a reality of life.

Labor force watchers say that there is little chance that today's woman will follow the pattern of World War II's Rosie the Riveter, who put down her hard hat and took up her apron when the boys came home. Today's working woman is increasingly serious about her career, no longer viewing it as a way station to marriage or a job she holds to pay children's college bills. She is taking a hard look at what jobs and careers offer her in terms of long-term employment and earning potential and is no longer bowing to social pressure that caused her to do traditional low-paying "women's work" in the past.

What does all this mean in terms of the future of entrepreneurship for women? It means that more and more bright, well-educated, and ambitious women will begin to beat their heads against the corporate barriers and work long hours but will see little chance for advancement; they, like male entrepreneurs in the past, will decide to take on the risk of business ownership for the potentially greater financial and personal rewards of fulfilled ambition. It also means that as more women whose careers have been raising families try to reenter the work place and find it closed, the entrepreneurial avenue will look increasingly attractive.

Although there are no current figures on the number of women entrepreneurs, statistics show that the rate of women choosing self-employment (either part-time, full-time, or moonlighting) as a career option is growing at three times the rate of men.[5] The President's Task Force on Women Business Owners predicted that when the results of the 1979 survey of women-owned businesses are in, the numbers of these businesses will have grown drastically since 1972, primarily because of the huge gap between the current level of women's aspirations and the career levels that they can realistically attain in corporations. Organizations are stiff and slow to adjust to societal changes; yet what is currently occurring in the work force—of which women now comprise almost half—has been compared by some to the impact that industrialization had on businesses in the Industrial Revolution.

The President's Task Force on Women Business Owners was established in November 1977 to see what this country could do to stimulate one of our greatly underutilized economic resources: women who are better educated, better trained, and more committed to careers than ever before but who are not being assimilated fast enough into our economic system. The Task Force found that women are no different than men in their entrepreneurial drive and their desire for the economic independence and personal self-fulfillment that business ownership can bring. However, there is a catch. It tends to be more difficult for women than for men to live out this drive. We have been made strangers to the business environment. From birth, we are told to sit still and be polite, whereas little boys are encouraged to excel and to be adventuresome. The subtle societal conditioning that started the moment the pink blanket was put on us and ended when we were pushed into typing and marriage, rather than business courses, creates a double-edged sword. We doubt our own ability to operate in this environment, and others doubt our ability to be competent in it.

There can be little doubt that the doors to a woman's opportunities begin to slam shut very young. The educational system carries on the work started at home as teachers, counselors, and peers diminish or discourage nontraditional aspirations and push us away from learning the very skills that we need to run a business. This fact is borne out by a study which found that 92 percent of the freshmen women at the University of California at Berkeley were unable to enter fifteen major fields of study because they lacked the advanced mathematics prerequisites for these fields.[6]

In general, women enter the entrepreneurial game with a handicap. We have been raised outside the mainstream of business and finance and have been steered away from the entrepreneurial playing arena. Our traditional position in society has kept us both off the playing field and out of the spectator stands. We have been too busy being daughters, wives, and mothers to view owning our own businesses as a viable career option. We have been inhibited and sometimes prohibited from taking courses and jobs that would have taught us the skills and enabled us to amass the money and the management track record that are the equipment of an entrepreneurial player.

The end result is that the average American woman trying to enter the entrepreneurial game faces additional obstacles that men do not face. Not only do we not know the rules of the game, but we don't know the jargon in which the signals are called or even who our opponents are. Most important, we do not know how to judge the realities of the game or ourselves to decide if we could be good players or if the game is worth winning. As a result, many women make mistakes when they go into business or shy away from the game altogether.

The impetus for writing this book came from talking to and receiving letters from hundreds of women during the time I was executive director of the President's Task Force on Women Business Owners. Over and over, pleas came for a simple how-to book that would explain the business basics to women. The seeds of the book, however, were planted much earlier. Like many women, I entered business school determined to get a passport to the business world, yet petrified by what I was sure were my inadequacies in anything related to business. That experience and an M.B.A. with honors smashed for me once and for all the mystery of business and taught me that it was our upbringing—the way we were educated from birth—that was inhibiting us.

I have often wished other women could have the experience, not for the knowledge gained so much as for the monsters slain. Since then, what I have learned from corporate life and as the owner of my own firm has convinced me that business ownership is a valuable career alternative women need to explore further.

Women can be among the great entrepreneurs of this country. We have the courage, the persistence, and ability. The only thing that has kept us from achieving this role in the past is the fact that we never learned (and were never taught) the rules of the game. As a result, we have been afraid to try to get in the game, or we have played badly when we do play.

The information in this book will help you understand the entrepreneurial game and enable you to assess whether you want to play it. It will not teach you everything you need to know, but it will tell you where to go for more information and how to deal with the problems and obstacles that could mar your chances of winning.

During the life of the Task Force and in writing this book, I have talked to hundreds of owners of both large and small businesses. I had thought that they would talk of their problems, pitfalls, and pains. They did not. Instead, they talked of the incredible sense of freedom and pride that owning their own business had given them. In talking to these women, there was an overbearing sense of the joy they felt in knowing that they controlled their own destiny, despite all obstacles.

These women are also, strangely enough, women who appear to have broken the mold of male entrepreneurs. Perhaps because women have had limited historical exposure to the business world, we are playing the game and winning by our own rules. Women tend to work not in order to have flashy red Cadillacs, as some male entrepreneurs do; they tend to work to achieve self-fulfillment. They also refuse to put their personal lives aside for their professional lives.

Displaced homemakers or corporate women who have reached career plateaus say the same thing: that they have found a place, at last, where their talents can be recognized and rewarded. They can now live to the limits of their potential and their dreams. How you decide to play the game is a very personal thing. There is no right or wrong way, only *your* way. That is what the women who participated in and worked on this book want you to know.

Women: The New Immigrants

Women are currently not among the major captains of industry in the United States. However, the time may come when they are—not because they have risen through the ranks to be nominated for chairman of the board but because they have struck out on their own and have started their own businesses.

Anne Wexler, who is now assistant to the president and who chaired the President's Task Force on Women Business Owners while she was under secretary for regional affairs in the United States Department of Commerce, believes that the inability of organizations to cope with the influx of women in the work force will spur the increase of business ownership by women.

The Task Force has found that there is an enormous gap between the reality of the changing composition of the work force and the ability of organizations to cope with this change. Although women are streaming into the work force better trained, more highly motivated, and more committed to careers than ever before, they are still clustered in low-paying jobs that offer little opportunity for upward mobility. There are still very few women at the top levels of the major corporations of this country. There's no question that women are an underutilized resource in the corporate structure.

Unless women really have the opportunity to become the "fair-haired boys" in corporations and gain true access to the executive suites, we suspect that more and more of them will choose to compete in the marketplace, rather than fight their way up the corporate ladder. They will choose to become suppliers and competitors, to build their own businesses, . . . industries, and, if you will . . . empires. Just as the immigrants at the turn of the century looked to business ownership when they could not be assimilated into the corporate system, women may prove to be the country's next wave of entrepreneurs.[1]

If historical trends are any indication, Wexler is probably right. Entrepreneurs traditionally have been born when there have been energy and ambition that were not being channeled. Many founders of some of America's greatest companies came from immigrant stock.

Another related hypothesis also applies to women: Those who are "strangers" or outsiders in a society will channel their energies into entrepreneurial endeavors because they have limited opportunities for conventional challenges. For instance, in Africa, the Indians are the merchants and entrepreneurs, and in Polynesia, the same is true of the Chinese.

The lack of access to traditional channels is also what caused the Irish, Italian, and Jewish immigrants to start their own businesses in this country. William Copulsky and Herbert McNulty in *Entrepreneurship and the Corporation* cited a study of 150 entrepreneurs in Michigan. According to that study, at a time when immigrants and second-generation Americans made up only 24 percent of the population, they made up 55 percent of the entrepreneurial respondents but only 25 percent of the nation's business executives.[2]

The women interviewed for this book also support these theories of entrepreneurship. Although the reasons why they started their businesses varied greatly, many indicated that they felt ownership was the only way that they could find an outlet for their creative intelligence, ambition, and drive. They felt that their sex made them outsiders in the traditional business structures and limited their opportunities for achievement.

One such woman is Martha Stuart, who owns Martha Stuart Communications—a business that produces videotapes on social issues. Stuart started her business in the basement of her house in St. Louis and has built it to the point where she now produces between eight and twelve videotapes a year, each costing between $75,000 and $100,000. She does work both in the United States and abroad, operating out of a brownstone in New York City. She gets a kick out of describing her business as a cottage industry, although the sophistication of her productions and her equipment places her in the big league as an independent producer. According to Stuart, the roadblocks, deadends, and lack of promise in the corporate environment pushed her into business ownership. "I was working for the networks and I woke up one day realizing that I wouldn't really be president of CBS . . . and I really like to run things. I love the exhilaration and the pain of it all. I wanted to be more, make more happen."

Martha Stuart is not alone. I have talked to hundreds of women who echo her feelings. Charlotte Cohen now owns a brokerage business in St. Louis with six branches and thirty-five employees, but she also faced roadblocks earlier in her career. Cohen got fed up and angry with the fact that she kept getting passed over for partnership, despite ten years of service and a good track record with a brokerage firm.

They finally admitted that I'd probably never make partner because I was a woman. I was angry. So I decided that if they wouldn't make me a partner, I'd start my own br kerage business. To my surprise, my former employer allowed me to continue working at the firm while I studied for my exams and got my license, primarily because he never thought I would pass. It was a big joke to them. My colleagues thought I'd never be able to fill out the forms, much less pass the exam. The day I passed the exam they were shocked. The only words out of my boss's mouth were "You did," and "We don't have any more room for you."

Cohen admits that her former employer's reaction hurt deeply. Her business has been a success from the beginning, even though she started it during the 1973 recession—a bad time for brokerage businesses. But starting up was not easy. While paying rent on an office, she waited months for federal and state approval only to discover that the application was held up not in Washington but in Missouri by a secretary who did not think that women should own businesses and kept putting her application at the bottom of the pile. Under state law she needed two people to start the brokerage business, and one of the biggest shocks was that she could find no one who wanted to work with her because she was a woman. She solved that problem by having her husband become certified as a broker and go into business with her, albeit primarily as a silent partner. Thus, she proved that the test of mettle for a successful entrepreneur is the ability not to get frustrated by obstacles, but to overcome them.

One woman attorney said that the thing that spurred her to take the leap to ownership was the fact that after four years with a law firm, she found that certain decisions were being made that were not the best for her career. She suddenly realized that she was being isolated from the best cases or the best clients. Knowing that it wouldn't solve things to switch firms because the same pattern would occur, she started her own firm. "You reach the point where you get sick and tired of arguing with people about why they should treat you equally. So, you decide to just go and show them that you are equal."

Today, women in corporations are judged on how well they perform tasks and are given more authority to do things, but they rarely have real power to make this authority work. Why does this occur? Women are perceived as powerless by subordinates because of their youth and sex. Such attitudes can be extremely frustrating. As one woman says: "You keep thinking that maybe if you could wait twenty years until you have grey hair, you will be awesome. But you can't wait."

Starting your own business can break the hierarchy that impedes most women in business. As an owner, you have both the authority and the power to carry through. Your clients and your colleagues know it because they know that you must be good if you can survive in the marketplace. More and more women are becoming aware of this possibility. Patricia Cloherty, a venture capitalist and former deputy administrator of the Small Business Administration, points out that entrepreneurship is still one of the major ways for a person to get assets under their belt and develop the economic power to enter the mainstream of our society.

Beatrice Fitzpatrick, founder and executive director of the American

Women's Economic Development Corporation in New York City, believes strongly that women will be the next great wave of entrepreneurs, not only because of their inherent talents but also because of the inability of the business environment to assimilate such women. Fitzpatrick feels that women have natural entrepreneurial qualities and are poised and ready to move in this direction. The only thing they lack is training, experience, and business contacts, something her organization is trying to help develop.

Fitzpatrick points out that women have always been entrepreneurial in their activities. We have always had to create something from nothing, even if it was just running the PTA. We are accustomed to being our own boss and managing ourselves, our kids, and our homes. We have just not been the boss in a work situation, nor have we been paid for our ability to be enterprising.

Fitzpatrick started the American Women's Economic Development Corporation because of her interest in the economic development issues. She was working as the director of a nonprofit research corporation and realized that women were talented, had a lot of good ideas, and were an underdeveloped economic resource. The assets they lacked were management training and experience. She founded a program that helps not only women but also the economy in that new businesses create new jobs. Fitzpatrick believes that the organization may have the lowest cost job-creation program in existence.

Started as a pilot program with funding from the Economic Development Administration of the United States Department of Commerce, the American Women's Economic Development Corporation is now in its third year and is growing strongly. Additional corporate donations and Small Business Administration funding have allowed it to expand its original program to provide both long-term and short-term training and counseling for would-be and existing women business owners. The organization has graduated seven groups of women through the training program and has counseled more than five hundred, helping to create a growing and vibrant force of women business owners in New York City.

The Impact of Corporate Mobility on Entrepreneurship

Entrepreneurship undoubtedly offers a great deal more promise for women who are committed to their careers and driven to excel than does the corporate environment. You have only to look at the realities of the work force to realize that. Between 1959 and 1977, the number of women in professional or highly technical jobs increased only 3.8 percentage points—to 15.9 percent of the total from 12.1 percent—while the number of managers and administrators increased less than 1.0 percentage point—to 5.9 percent from 5.1 percent. Men continue to far outnumber women in managerial and administrative jobs. While one in seven working men holds a managerial or administrative job, only one in twenty women holds such positions.[3]

Women, on the whole, are still clustered in low-paying jobs that offer little opportunity for advancement. Yet women are entering the work force in increasing numbers, drawn there not only by ambition and education but also by economic necessity. In 1977 more women were working or looking for work than were keeping house full time. Every other married woman worked, a staggering increase from the one in every six women who worked in 1960. In addition, the largest growth of women in the work force has been among women with young children, indicating that women not only are entering the work force in increased numbers but also are staying in despite marriage and children.[4]

Recent figures from the National Center for Educational Statistics show that in the five-year span between 1971 and 1976, the number of degrees awarded to women in education and social sciences decreased to 26.8 percent from 36.2 percent and to 11.4 percent from 15.7 percent, respectively. At the same time, women received 19.7 percent of all degrees awarded in business and management, doubling the 9.1 percent they received in 1971.[5] Although law and medical schools felt the onslaught of women's new aspirations earlier than business schools, business educators are now amazed at the increased interest of women in this profession. Yet despite the increasing career commitment and education of women, corporations have shown only a limited ability to assimilate women into positions of authority and promise.

THE NEW IMMIGRANTS

What does all this mean in terms of the future of entrepreneurship for women? It means that the number of women starting their own enterprises is growing daily. They are buying business franchises, starting manufacturing plants, constructing homes, and opening stores. They are inventing products and selling services. They are not only women like Diane von Furstenburg or Mary Wells Lawrence but also women like Juanita Burks. A black woman who started at the age of fifty-four, Burks now owns four businesses in Louisville, Kentucky, including City Plaza Personnel Consultant Service.

> It's always been a strong desire of mine to be a business person. And I got a lot of it from the encouragement from my mother and father. We were rural people and lived in a country town. I always had these aspirations and things that I wanted to do, but I never had the opportunity to do them, for many reasons. One was because I was socially deprived because of society, the white society. I did not have the money to do it because we were poor, my husband didn't have any, and my mother and father couldn't give me any. These are the reasons why I never got into it at an earlier age.

Or they are women like Elizabeth Haynes, of Baltimore Rigging Company in Baltimore, Maryland. She had only been working for her father a few months when he died and left her to run his rigging business and to take over the support of eleven children. "I just never had any self-doubt. I never entertained the idea of failure . . . I guess because I had to make the business succeed to take care of my mother, myself, and the children. I just went out and did it."

They are women like Rosemary Tucker, of Tucker Tire Company in Covina, California. Although she was a winner of the Small Business Administration's Small Business Person of the Year Award, Tucker had not intended to be a business owner originally. She was pushed into business by the fact that her husband left her with nothing but her wits to live by. When Tucker started out, she had six children and a tire company that was deeply in debt. Twenty years later she has a $2-million business.

Women are becoming a growing entrepreneurial force in America. However, there are those who feel that the entrepreneurial spirit is not new in women but that it has just lain dormant for a generation. Vicki Smith Downing, a Dallas woman who owns International Venture and Equity Capital, shares this view.

> Women—particularly Southwestern women—have always been entrepreneurial. Our grandmothers helped settle this section of the country. They were partners in development. Our mothers didn't have it, but our grandmothers did. Unfortunately, our mothers bit the whole feminine myth hook, line, and sinker and pushed us out on the debutante stage. However, the current struggle among women to find self-fulfillment is rekindling those fires.

Indeed, current labor statistics seem to support Downing's theory. The number of women choosing self-employment as a work option has been growing at a rate for women that is three times the rate for men. Between 1971 and 1977, the number of self-employed women jumped 25 percent.[6] In addition, most of the 3,400 women responding to the Task Force's inquiry became owners fairly recently. The majority (75 percent) had started their businesses in the last ten years, and 14 percent indicated that their businesses were only a year old.

These are women who are adding a new twist to the backbone of our free enterprise system. The "ma-and-pa" shops where Mom merely helped out with the books, or rang up the cash register while Dad owned and managed the business are now dead. Today, "mother" is not only running the show but is running it well. Women are creating vibrant and growing enterprises that are becoming an important part of our business environment.

In addition, there are those who think that women bring latent strengths to business that may ultimately make them better players than men in the entrepreneurial game if they can learn the rules of the game a little better. Ava Stern—the publisher of *Enterprising Women,* a monthly business magazine that reaches over twenty thousand women—feels that although women tend to be more conservative in their business behavior, primarily because they have not been used to playing the game, they are also creating more stable businesses that may grow slowly but very solidly. She recently recontacted two hundred women she had previously interviewed for her publication and found that only two were no longer in business—an amazing statistic given the volatility of the business environment and the high failure rate among small businesses. Part of this may be because women seem to give a great deal more thought to taking the entrepreneurial plunge than do men.

Dr. Henry Bender, who conducted the American Management Associations study of successful women entrepreneurs for the Task Force, points out that most of the women interviewed had made a profit in the first or second year, a time span that is shorter than is normally expected in a budding business. According to Bender:

> This may be attributed to the fact that women seemed to know up front that they had to be better than men to survive. They knew it was going to be tough and were willing to make the sacrifices that were necessary in the first few years, especially in terms of deferring income and putting it back in the business, so that it could grow. I don't think that they went into their businesses as naively as men. They seemed to enjoy the hell out of what they were doing and to think of their success in terms of the business and not the trappings of power or status that money can bring, which often motivates men in starting a business. They seemed to be a little more in tune with reality and the hardships involved, if not necessarily as familiar with the business world. They were realistic about the time it would take before the business could start earning them a healthy profit and were willing to stick to it. I think men, on the other hand, go into it much more for the money, or the power, and status that money can bring; and will drop out of the game earlier if the businesses aren't meeting their profit objectives.

Jeffry A. Timmons, a professor at Northeastern University who has done extensive work with entrepreneurs, echoes Bender's views on the positive aspects of women being oriented less toward the money aspects of business. He points out that the best entrepreneur is someone who really wants to implement an idea and who uses money only as a measure for keeping score, not as the goal of the business. Women, he feels, are avoiding the trap, which many men fall into, of making money too high a priority. If money is the priority, it makes a person go for the high-risk ventures that promise high payoffs, rather than more conservative ventures that could produce steady profits. Timmons, who also works with training programs of major corporations for goal setting, team building, and management, has found that an additional strength in women is that their cultural upbringing makes them better managers of people. He says that the women in his courses consistently earn higher marks in managing people than do the men—a factor he attributes to women having lesser needs of power, aggression, and ego relative to men. As a result, women are more flexible managers and entrepreneurs, and this flexibility is what makes or breaks most companies as they begin to grow and leave the entrepreneurial stage.

PROBLEMS WOMEN FACE

The only factor currently holding women back from becoming a major sector of our business economy is not our inherent abilities but our upbringing. Beatrice Fitzpatrick, of the American Women's Economic Development Corporation, points out that whereas men grow up thinking that they will help run this country, that they will be president, statesmen, financiers, policy-makers, women grow up thinking that all we will help run is our households. It's no wonder we often fail to see ourselves in leadership roles. However, Fitzpatrick feels women have a strength in that they are willing to admit what they don't know and are anxious to learn. They do not have ego problems in admitting their inadequacies, as men sometimes have; and once they begin to learn about business, the growth comes in a geometric, rather than an arithmetic, progression. Yet, the same source of strength is also a problem. Women have been taught how to intuit the needs of others. This makes women extremely ingenious in developing service businesses. They also tend to have an extreme sense of integrity about providing quality work and to cheat themselves, rather than the customer.

Fitzpatrick, who originally thought that all women needed to do was learn the basic business skills and most of the barriers would come tumbling down, now recognizes that there are also deep psychological barriers that a woman must lower before she can take her proper place in the business environment. Every little girl is taught that it is important to be nice, warm, and loving. But it's not "nice" to tell a customer you are going to take them to court if they don't pay up, and it's not "nice" to fire an employee, although it may be necessary. Fitzpatrick tries to show women that being tough doesn't mean you have to be nasty; it means you just have to be goal-directed. You have to know your goals and stick to them and stop wanting to be loved by everyone. Being nice, sweet, kind, and generous and reinforcing to people is fine, when it is appropriate behavior; but it isn't at all times.

Ava Stern of *Enterprising Women* feels that the self-made woman has four qualities: self-determination, self-discipline, self-interest, and self-reward.[7] But these qualities make it harder for women than for men. "It has only been recently, with the advent of the Women's Movement, that we have begun to realize that it is okay for us to think about ourselves, what pleases us—be it in sex or in anything else." While we have broken some of those old myths that our only interest lies in caring for others, accepting the fact that self-interest is not "selfish interest" is hard for many women and may fill them with guilt. Yet more and more women are choosing the entrepreneurial arena and are deciding that they want to learn the rules of the game so that they can be better players.

Indeed, women bring inherent strengths to the entrepreneurial game: We tend to be less hungry for power and money than are men; we tend to have more concern for people and to know how to work in groups better than men have; and we have not had our innovative and intuitive skills bred out of us by society. While these may not be "pluses" in the corporate world, they are in building a new company. Our only "minus" is that we have never learned the rules of the game or how it is played.

Dr. Henry Bender, who conducted the American Management Associations study, put it very succinctly: "It is not that the answers to questions don't exist or that women aren't just as resourceful as men in finding the answers. The problem is that women have never been taught the questions to ask, much less the answers." But when women learn the rules of the entrepreneurial game, they can be highly successful, as the women in this book illustrate.

CHAPTER 2

The Entrepreneurial Game

The question remains why women, if they have entrepreneurial strengths, do not currently number among the leaders of industry? Although there is nothing mysterious or difficult about the business game and women all over the country are illustrating that it is a game which women can win, women owning businesses currently make up only a small sector of our economy.

THE NATURE OF THE GAME

Women as Players

The only available statistics, which are from the Bureau of the Census' 1972 *Survey of Women-Owned Businesses*, show that women not only own a small proportion of the total businesses in America, but these businesses have an extraordinarily low level of earnings. According to these figures, women owned less than 5 percent of the businesses and earned less than 0.3 percent of all the gross business receipts in America.[1] In addition, they tended to be clustered in those industries that offer players the least promise for winning big in the entrepreneurial game. The majority (71 percent) of the businesses were in retail trade and selected services[2]—industries known for their lower than average rates of earnings and returns on investment.[3]

Just as women make low wages in the work force because of their job positions, they also tend to reap fewer financial benefits from business ownership because of the industries into which they choose to enter. The ten types of businesses earning the most receipts for women, according to the 1972 survey, are shown in the table on page 28. However, the majority of the

**AVERAGE RECEIPTS BY INDUSTRY OF ALL UNITED STATES
SMALL BUSINESS AND WOMEN-OWNED FIRMS, 1972**

	Small Business Firms, thousands			Receipts, amounts in billions		
	Total	Women-Owned	Percentage of Total	Total	Women-Owned	Percentage of Total
Construction	895	15	1.7%	$48	$0.5	1.0%
Manufacturing	263	8	3.0	25	0.3	1.2
Transportation, Public utilities	370	7	1.9	12	0.1	0.8
Wholesale trade	415	5	1.2	66	0.6	0.9
Retail trade	2,062	133	6.5	145	4.2	2.9
Selected services	1,973	151	7.7	26	1.5	5.8
Financial, Insurance, Real estate	828	37	4.5	23	0.5	2.2
Other	289	45	15.6	6	0.4	6.7
All industries	7,095	402	5.7	$351	$8.1	2.3

NOTE: Excludes corporations with more than 10 stockholders.

SOURCE: *The Bottom Line: (Un)Equal Enterprise in America*. Report of the President's Task Force on Women Business Owners. Washington, D.C.: U.S. Government Printing Office, 1978, p. 173.

women were in retail trade, where sales averaged only $32,000, or selected services, where sales averaged only $10,000.[4] These figures are hardly impressive. Although there are women who have started major businesses, such as Betty Graham of Liquid Paper, Anne Person of Stretch and Sew, and Mary Kay Ash of Mary Kay Cosmetics, for the most part the businesses started by women appear to be struggling businesses that began and stayed small. Ninety-eight percent of the firms were operated as sole proprietorships and only 13 percent of the businesses had paid employees, the majority (73 percent) of which had fewer than five employees.[5]

The fact that women were having problems playing the business game was brought home by the women I met and letters I received during the time I was executive director of the President's Task Force on Women Business Owners. There were women who were willing and ready to play the entrepreneurial game but who did not know how to play it. There were also bright, ambitious women with good business ideas, yet they could not get past "go" on the game board because they lacked the business know-how to implement their ideas. Most tragic, however, were those women already in business who had picked the wrong business because they did not know how to analyze business opportunities rationally; they did not realize that you work just as hard but make less money in slow-growth fields as you do in fast-growth fields.

On the Task Force we were concerned that the same systematic discrimination that hurt women in the work force was also harming them in the entrepreneurial environment. Women seem caught in a vicious circle. The fact that women have for years been relegated to lower-paying "women's jobs" meant that most of their experience is in these areas. Therefore, these were the types of businesses that they started despite the fact that these businesses offer limited opportunities for earnings and growth. Just as the majority of women now moving up in corporate organizations are going into positions that are out of the mainstream of top management, such as public relations or personnel management, the majority of women starting businesses do so in traditional female fields, such as retail trade and selected services.

It is impossible to pinpoint why women gravitate toward these low-paying industries. It may be because these are the industries we know the most about, or it may be because these are the industries in which we find the least resistance to our entry. A woman seeking to raise capital for a boutique will have better luck than a woman seeking to capitalize a cement factory; since the cement factory is a nontraditional business for a woman, that woman will be perceived as a greater business risk in this field by investors and bankers. Another reason women may go into traditional "women's" industries is because their capital requirements are relatively low; with neither the savings nor the knowledge of capital markets to capitalize bigger ventures, that is all that is left open to us.

Joyce Huber chose a service business, employment, because it required little capital. Huber and a friend started the Georgetown Employment Service in Washington, D.C., twelve years ago on a $250 loan. They worked at it on their lunch hour until they had enough business to quit their other jobs. Today, this business has grown to the point where it has two locations. In addition, Huber has opened another employment agency called the Employment Agency and has also started Georgetown Secretarial College. She turned her $250 investment into a half-million-dollar business.

Other women echo Huber's reasons for going into service industries. However, whatever the reasons, the reality is that most women are currently relatively small players in the business game. We are not a major sector of the business economy, either by the number of our businesses or their size. But a new breed of female entrepreneurs may change these statistics in the future. These are the women who are learning how to remove one of their major business handicaps—the lack of knowledge—by learning the rules of the entrepreneurial game. They are finding out how to assess bona-fide business opportunities before risking their savings and energies.

Learning the Business Game

Learning the business game is not difficult. It is basically a game of common sense and strategy, yet for some reason most women think it is highly complicated. If you can get over the feeling that you need a master's degree to play, you have a head start. It is only our upbringing that makes business seem alien. For some women, business is cloaked in mystery, appears extremely risky, and is thought of as being not altogether feminine. We tend to think of business women as gutsy, dehumanized women, not like ourselves. Even corporate women say that business education has not totally erased their feelings of insecurity about being intruders in alien territory.

Business is a game like any other game: There are rules, players, plays, and strategies. Strategies create winners, and it takes playing the game to develop the skills of a star. The entrepreneurial game is a wide-open opportunity, as it does not require the fancy credentials and higher education that you might need to move up the corporate career ladder. Anyone can play, and anyone can win. To enter the game, there are no requirements of age, education, or even money if you are resourceful enough, have a winning business idea, and can find people to back your entrepreneurial team.

Playing the game is not for the weakhearted. Although amateurs can play and win, it is a tough, grueling exercise. Yet just as any sport can give you a sense of exhilaration, so can business.

If you ask any woman who is running her own business what it is like, she will probably respond "tough." She will say that if she knew then what she knows now, she would probably never have had the nerve to do it. However, in the next breath, she will tell you she could never do anything else. She will speak of the joy and sense of well-being that comes with knowing you can beat the odds and control your own destiny. She will tell you that being boss can be bad. It entails hard work, responsibilities, and more daily ups and downs than most thought were imaginable. It is a lonely, stressful, and demanding job. However, she will also tell you that being boss can be rewarding. It means making decisions, taking responsibility, and reaping rewards. It means learning you can play as well as any of the "guys" and knowing that you can survive by your own wits in a highly competitive world.

Assessing If You Want to Play

Not everyone should play the entrepreneurial game. Business failure is a chronic disease in America. Dun & Bradstreet estimate that one out of three businesses will fail in their first three years. If you can survive five years, experts say that you have a chance of growing into a viable business.

The reasons for these failures hinge on a variety of factors. One set of factors are the general business conditions in the country, which have caused business failures to be high since 1955. These include the increased diversification of big business, the drying up of capital markets, and the general state of the United States economy. Another set of factors are management mistakes that can sap your playing strength and team resources. Although external competitive conditions also play a part in deciding whether you win or lose, it is usually poor management that rings the death knell for most firms. The last set of factors are the personal characteristics of the owner. Dun & Bradstreet, which tracks such matters, points out that a person who thinks that being in business will give her the freedom to take off anytime she wants and provide her with a fancy office and a high salary is not going to stay in business long.

Owning your own business means being able to live with worries, uncertainty, irregular income, debts, responsibility, and long hours of work. This is why you need to assess if you really want to play. Not everyone has either the physical or psychological makeup to be a player. Winning takes more than ambition and imagination; it also takes stamina, perseverance, and guts. You will be competing against both big and small companies for scarce resources of money, material, and manpower, as well as for markets. As a new and struggling company, you will feel disadvantaged in this competitive environment because you will have neither the money nor the business volume to attract competent staff, get lenient terms from suppliers, or find creditors. The game will never stay the same. Just when you think you are winning, something will happen that will make you think you are losing.

Business is a dynamic game that involves the interplay of resources, competitors, and the business environment. You have to be able to live with putting your savings, security, and home on the line because you think your chances of winning are good; but you have to realize that you can also lose. There is no guarantee that even learning the rules of the game will make you win, although this can improve your chances. J. Herbert Holloman, who has had years of experience with entrepreneurial ventures and who now directs the Center for Policy Alternatives at the Massachusetts Institute of Technology, points out that you can never hope to control whether you win or lose in the entrepreneurial game. There are just too many players and too many variables in the game. "When you get right down to it, it's like a crap game. There's a lot of luck involved in having the right idea at the right time. The best you can hope for is that the table is level and the dice aren't loaded."

There is no such thing as a "sure thing" that will reap you instant profits and success, as anyone who has ever watched the fluctuations of the stock market can tell you. The nature of the business environment is dynamic and changing, with ups and downs. This element of risk is something that inhibits many women from taking the plunge into ownership. Many women shy away from ownership or are frightened of it, primarily because they have never learned how to analyze risks. They either jump into the fire without assessing their odds for winning or losing, or shy away from it altogether and never win.

Ava Stern of *Enterprising Women* feels that what she calls the three r's of the entrepreneurial decision are particularly hard psychological barriers for women to overcome: the *risk* of, or the lack of, security that is involved in ownership; the fear that the *responsibility* will be all theirs and that they will have to do everything in the business; and the fear of *reward*, or of making money, particularly more than the spouse—a fear women often have since they are not accustomed to being the money-maker in the family.

These are all real risks, and you should look at them closely. It is important, however, to remember that there are positive sides to risk. Nothing is ever stable, and everything involves risk. Even standing still is a risk because everything may change around you. Unless we take risks, we live a static existence. Risk is no monster. By definition, risk taking involves the ability to deal with uncertainty, and uncertainty can be minimized by knowledge. The important thing is to assess risks well.

Dr. Margaret Fenn, a professor at the University of Washington School of Business and the author of *Making It in Management: A Behavioral Approach for Women*, believes women have never been taught how to analyze risk. "A little girl is told not to climb a tree because it is dangerous. Therefore, the whole tree is dangerous to us. A little boy, on the other hand, has probably learned through experience how high he can climb before he gets into serious danger. For him, the tree represents graduated danger he can calculate, while for us the whole tree is dangerous." Fenn also feels that another factor which enters into our fear of risks is the fact that little boys have learned how to bear the responsibilities of failures more than little girls.

> If a little boy is told not to throw rocks in the yard, but does it anyway and breaks a neighbor's window, he is usually made to face the consequences of the neighbor's ire. Little girls on the other hand, are reprimanded, but protected by the parents from all the consequences. This makes us have less experience at judging consequences. Since we are protected rather than encouraged to explore, we grow up with less experiential knowledge on which to judge risk.

Yet it is indeed possible to judge risk. Even in gambling, where winning is based on pure probabilities and luck, there are people who will tell you that they have learned how to beat the odds. But business risk is not pure risk; the risk in any business opportunity is tempered by your skill, your resources, and the conditions of the marketplace. You can increase your odds of winning if you learn how to take risks in a rational way and learn to analyze the market situation and your odds of winning before you make your moves. The secret is to know your personal limits: what you can afford to lose financially, professionally, and personally. Never risk more than you can afford to lose. Never risk a lot for an opportunity that offers little return.

You should ask yourself some hard questions. Are the rewards commensurate with the risks? How hard do you work now? If you already put in long hours for an employer, chances are you will not mind the commitment necessary for owning your own business. What will you lose if you fail? For example, you may think that if you start a business and it fails, you will never be able to find another job or you will lose all your savings. These are your apparent risks, but are they your *real* risks? What are the odds of your staying unemployed if the business fails? Won't you be able to rebuild your savings if you fail? Aren't your real risks less than your apparent risks?

Real risks are what you should use in making your business judgment, and being able to judge your real versus your apparent risks is especially important for women. As women have never been expected to succeed anyway, the negative aspects of failure may be less, and the positive aspects of the experience greater, than they are for a man.

Indeed, starting a business may help break the mold of stereotypical perceptions that hamper your career path. Owning a business gives you valuable experience in that it allows you to act as chief executive officer of your own organization—an opportunity women rarely encounter in large organizations. It also shows that you are committed to your career and ambition, both of which would be important to prospective employers should you decide to reenter the work force.

Certain personal risks for women may be greater in that they take on an added role to their already heavy responsibilities of family and home. Although some women point out that being the boss makes it easier to structure your time so that you can take your daughter to ballet class or the doctor, it also creates a tremendous drain on your energies because you can never leave your business the way you could a nine-to-five job. There is no denying that female entrepreneurs have a more difficult time than males because they also still maintain major responsibility for the home.

The important thing is to learn how to assess a business opportunity rationally, rather than emotionally. What may be a high risk to someone who has limited monetary resources may be a marginal risk to someone who does not have to worry about money. Remember, if you ask any owner of a business if she or he has made mistakes, they will undoubtedly give you a laundry list of what they should have done as opposed to what they did.. Everyone has had some losses among the wins. That's the nature of the game. What counts is that you make mistakes wisely, rather than foolishly, and that you end up winning overall. Joyce Huber of Georgetown Employment Service offers some good advice:

> It's like in a game of tennis. If you make a bad decision and you concentrate on the bad decision, you're never going to get beyond that. . . . You have to put it behind you very quickly. . . . If I make a bad decision in business, I never internalize it. It doesn't occur to me. Not that I don't realize I made a bad decision, but it doesn't bother me at all. Women sometimes think that when they make a bad decision they are failures, they internalize it and view it as the whole self. If I make a bad business decision it doesn't mean anything about me personally.

UNDERSTANDING THE GAME

The Basic Principles

To play the entrepreneurial game, you should understand certain basic principles. There are a lot of players and variables, and they change constantly. To win, you must stay alert and be prepared for your opponent's plays.

The game basically consists of strategies by which a player tries to outmaneuver her opponents, and keep the spectators rooting for her. Some people play a defensive game—trying to satisfy existing market demand while fending off competitors—so that they maintain their market share. Others play an offensive game—creating demand with a new product or service—and hope they can outrun their opponents by staying one step ahead of them.

The strategy you choose is up to you. You will find that your particular business situation will dictate your strategy. There is no tried and true formula for winning, as the women in this book will tell you. There are only basic principles you need to know for building your strategy.

The playing field, which is your business environment, is the first thing you need to know. It can be your neighborhood or the world, depending on the scope of the game you choose to play. The playing field is dynamic and changing, and you will have to bear in mind its condition in planning your playing strategy. Just as rain, mud, or snow may change the playing conditions of most other games, economic factors, such as oil embargos, minimum wage hikes, and trade regulations, can impact the business game.

The key player in this game will be you and your entrepreneurial team. I include the concept of an entrepreneurial team because one of the biggest mistakes a lot of players make is to think that they can win the game all by themselves. As a business owner, you may be the captain, but you will also need a team. It is the rare individual who can excel at all the skills needed in the business game. Just as the football player who is the superb runner is probably not the best tackle, the entrepreneur whose strength lies in marketing may not excel in financial management. It's important to realize your strengths and weaknesses and build your team carefully. How to do this will be discussed in chapter 4, "Building Your Entrepreneurial Team."

Your opponents in this game are your business competitors. These opponents will come in all sizes and shapes. They may be large corporations or small businesses. They may be the industry standard bearers or ambitious newcomers. The only thing certain about your opponents is that they will be constantly changing and continually developing new strategies to try to knock you out of the game, so that they can have the playing field to themselves. That is what they are saying when they politely talk to you about "building their market share."

There are also referees in this game to keep competition polite and make sure that there is no foul play, market gouging, or ganging up on the little guys. These referees are the federal, state, and local governments, who will regulate your business and grant your licenses. They will also take part of your winnings as taxes to pay for their services. They are the people who try to keep the business game clean by prohibiting price fixing, collusion, and other unfair competitive and labor practices. You will also find that these referees are not the most popular people among entrepreneurial players. Like all referees, they have a lot of rules that appear senseless and inhibiting.

Last, but certainly not least, there are your spectators. These are the customers you must have rooting for your team if you are to stay in the entrepreneurial game. Their purchasing dollars are what will make you win and are what you and your opponents are struggling over. How you get and keep these spectators is dealt with in chapter 6, "Developing Your Marketing Strategy."

The Goal of the Game

The goal of the business game is really quite simple, but some people get confused about it. Many people make the mistake of thinking that the goal in business is to make money. However, winning is not measured in cash in the business game; it is measured in assets. The real goal is to increase your net worth. Dollars are merely the denomination in which the score is kept.

Your net worth is the amount of assets you own once you have paid off all your creditors. The business terminology for net worth is the amount of assets you have once your liabilities are deducted. Assets are more than cash; they can include real estate, equipment, or even intangible things, such as the goodwill of your firm. Goodwill can increase your net worth if someone will pay you cash for it. Your balance sheet is the scorecard that allows you to keep track of your net worth and, over several years, how well a business is doing in the business game. Balance sheets, together with profit and loss statements, provide a tracking system by which to gauge success. How to use these scorecards will be explained in chapter 8, "Controlling Your Company."

For the most part, your net worth is a paper score. The entrepreneurial game is a little like poker. The only time you really cash in your chips is when you decide to leave the game. As long as you are in business, your assets and liabilities will fluctuate as you borrow money to buy inventory or finance expansion. These fluctuations are the only thing that will enable you to build your business and steadily increase your net worth. Without debts or liabilities you cannot buy the assets you will need—merchandise or products—to get your customers and produce the cash to buy back your debt. This is the basic formula of business—using someone else's money to make more money. It is what is meant in financial circles when they talk about *leveraging*. Using your money as collateral to borrow more money to increase sales leverages up the worth of your firm.

However, this basic business formula has a delicate balance, making both your balance sheet and your profit and loss scorecard extremely important. These financial statements are the scorecards bankers use when they pull out published financial ratios, like doctors use stethoscopes, to check the health of your organization against industry standards and to judge the odds of your winning the entrepreneurial game. You should learn how to use these scorecards and ratios to judge your own chances of winning.

Strategy—The Winning Ingredient

The entrepreneurial game is not a game of strength, but a game of strategy. It takes brains, not brawn, to win. Intuitive judgment, creativity, stamina, and common sense, as well as a basic knowledge of the rules of the game, are what is needed to make you a star in the business game. What makes the business game difficult is the fact that there is nothing stable. As a business person, your opponents (competitors), and spectators (customers) can change without notice, and your playing field can alter with a flip of a coin or a dip in the economy.

The fact that business is a game of strategy sometimes makes it difficult for women. Denise Cavanaugh, who is co-owner of Cook/Cavanaugh Associates, and who teaches a management course for women, feels that on the whole women tend to be poor strategists.

> When generalizing, I'd say that most women as a group are not very effective strategists. We have never learned the skills. A strategic person has a sense of priorities within a large framework; she knows what her first objective is and what her second, third, and fourth objectives are. She understands the compromises and trade-offs that are necessary to reach these objectives. A woman who sees the context of where she lives and sees the political ambience can put together a plan to achieve her objectives. She must be willing to juggle and trade off and adapt her strategy based on what is going on in the wider world. Women tend to fix on a goal and go after it directly. They are not aware of what *else* is going on around them. As the circumstances shift, they appear unwilling to make the compromises and trade-offs necessary to win the game and not just this play.

Cavanaugh feels women will develop this capacity to strategize as they have more exposure to the business world:

> Strategizing is not an overwhelming task. . . . When you are playing the game you simply look up and your eyes dart around the field and sidelines; you notice who is where and doing what. You go back to your position with this information and revise your plans as necessary. You don't have to go up to every player and get to know them, finding out what their mother-in-law is like and how their kids are doing, or what their personal goals are . . . I'm talking about surveying the situation in terms of who has the balance of power, who has the money, where are the openings, what are the barriers so you can focus on your goal and know where to move next. Each move is not based on an intensive thorough study; it's simply a quick glance to survey the field and go back to your work. That's the skill we have got to develop.

The first step to take in learning how to develop your strategy skills will be learning to view your business in the perspective that it really is: one player in a larger business game. Although the women in this book will show you that there are an infinite variety of business strategies that can work, you must recognize the basic principles and realities of the game.

Vicki Smith Downing, owner of International Venture and Equity Capital, believes that women are bringing a new dimension to business, but she still thinks that women need to realize they can't play their game in isolation. Downing further feels that because women are entering the entrepreneurial arena later than men, they have to work harder at learning the things they need to know to be good players. However, she is not convinced that we have to follow the same historical patterns in gaining this knowledge as have men. She points out that there are an infinite number of sources of tutors, from retired executives to professors to other businesswomen. Downing makes a conscious effort to find women role models who can symbolize or actually be mentors for her. She has also found that you can gain a lot of knowledge by having skill-trading sessions in which you share your professional knowledge with others and they share theirs with you. Finally, Downing believes you must be patient and persistent.

Suzanne Ives—owner of Ives and Associates, a firm specializing in marketing communications and publications, primarily for the real estate industry in Washington, D.C.—stresses learning as much as you can. "One of the keys to success in business is ASK QUESTIONS. . . . Ask questions of everybody. I think it is wrong to make assumptions. You can make a judgment, but confirm it with an expert. Ask the same question of five people, and then decide. When we get hung up on a creative problem for a client, we sit down together and throw it out; and it is astonishing what a different perspective you can get."

However, whatever you do before you decide to play, you need to look carefully at your personal motives and goals and at the realities of the game. You need to assess if you have what it takes to be a player and if you really want to play in this game. You must assess your personal motives, your life-style, and work goals, as well as your entrepreneurial strengths and weaknesses. People who have watched the steady stream of small businesses come and go all say that it is the entrepreneur, along with her or his ability to build the right kind of team to play the game, that is the critical factor in business success.

ARE YOU A PLAYER?

What Motivates an Entrepreneur?

True entrepreneurs are a strange breed. They are economic innovators, impresarios, and promoters. Although there have been many studies on entrepreneurial characteristics, no one really knows what makes entrepreneurs tick. Typically, a person is defined as an entrepreneur because of something she or he has done in terms of a function, rather than what she or he is.[6] Although there is no set pattern, people who have done research in this area can give you some clues as to whether you have some of the personality characteristics they feel are important in successful entrepreneurs.

One of these researchers is David McClelland of Harvard University. He has spent years testing and developing a theory of individual motivation, particularly in its application to management and entrepreneurship. McClelland has found that the entrepreneurial personality is one in which the individual has a high need for achievement and is a calculated risk taker. According to McClelland, an entrepreneur is a person who wants to operate in a situation where she can get a sense of personal achievement. The entrepreneur tends to be conservative in games of chance and more daring in games of skill, overestimates her chances of doing well, and works hard under competition.[7] He points out that the thing that characterizes entrepreneurs is a recurring pattern of thought that keeps them thinking at all times about doing something better and improving their performance.[8] Entrepreneurs tend to have higher need for achievement and lower needs for affiliation or power— the three needs behind McClelland's theory of motivation.

The need for achievement is the need to excel and do a job well. It makes you seek challenging and competitive situations and set goals that are both realistic and achievable. A person with a high need for achievement is competitive not because she or he wants to beat someone, but because she or he likes to do better. Such individuals compete against a self-imposed standard of excellence and like to do new and different tasks, to see if they can figure out a way to do them better. They need feedback on how well they do. They set realistic and challenging goals (usually long-term goals), work hard at achieving these goals, and plan carefully to overcome obstacles.[9]

A person with a high need for affiliation, on the other hand, likes to work because of the relationships and friendships involved. A person who is concerned with being liked, accepted, befriended, who tends to see gatherings as social situations, and who is concerned about the disruption of a positive personal relationship probably has a high need for affiliation.[10]

People with a high need for power are concerned with reputation, status, and their ability to influence situations and outperform others. A person who likes to outperform someone else, irrespective of any objective or self-imposed standard, who shows strong concern through powerful actions, who does things that arouse strong positive and negative emotions in others, and who is concerned about her or his reputation or position is probably a person with a high need for power.[11]

McClelland has found that what drives entrepreneurs most is a high need for achievement. Although they are concerned with profits, they are concerned with them primarily as a measure of their own personal performance, rather than as money. His studies have shown that high achievers actually fare worse when working for money than when working for personal achievement.

Gamblers or Calculated Risk Takers?

Many people think you have to be a gambler or an extreme risk taker to be an entrepreneur. This is not true. Although playing in the entrepreneurial game involves risks, one of the key characteristics that distinguish successful entrepreneurs, is the fact that they are not gamblers. Entrepreneurs are people who take calculated and moderate risks in which they bet on their skill, rather than on luck, to win against the odds. In experiments in which potential entrepreneurs participated using a ring toss game as an experiment, McClelland found that people with a high need for achievement would not stand either too close or too far from the peg. Instead, they would stand at a moderate distance from the peg—where their skill, rather than luck, was most likely to make them win.[12] He concluded that people with a strong achievement motive are drawn to a task only when winning at the task can be interpreted as a personal achievement, rather than luck as in a gambling situation.

Other Characteristics

Other people who have worked with entrepreneurs substantiate McClelland's findings. Some of the traits that they have identified among successful entrepreneurs, in addition to a high need for achievement, are the ability to turn problems into opportunities, the ability to set realistic goals, and the ability to bounce back quickly from failure. Others point to the fact that most entrepreneurs have a low level of pessimism and a high level of tolerance for rejection. For them a no will mean maybe, and a maybe will mean yes. They are also not easily discouraged and can put yesterday's nos behind them and move on. They are willing to take risks, willing to fail, and willing to do whatever is necessary to succeed.

Joel Pitlor, who works at Venture Founders—an organization in Belmont, Massachusetts, that assesses both the feasibility of business concepts and the personality and potential of individuals in an effort to lower the odds of business failure for investors—says that the best definition of an entrepreneur that he has ever heard of came from a participant in one of his organization's entrepreneurial workshops. This person described an entrepreneur as "someone who had a big enough ego to think that she (he) could do anything, and a small enough ego to do anything to accomplish that goal." Although having an unrealistic opinion of your abilities can be a negative factor if it makes you shoot for the stars, rather than realistic odds, this definition seems to sum up the combination of optimism and persistence that is necessary to win at the entrepreneurial game. It also seems to embody the entrepreneurial spirit found in the women interviewed for this book. They all seemed to have an amazing ability to see life not as a series of problems to cope with but as opportunities to be seized. In addition, they were persistent in figuring out how to turn these problems into opportunities.

Cathy Hardwick, a woman who has been recognized as one of the rising stars in American dress design and who owns Cathy Hardwick and Friends, Ltd., is a good example of this. Hardwick, who had no schooling in design, started out as a housewife in San Francisco. She points out that her business really evolved from opportunities that presented themselves to her, rather than from a plan. "I never try to force things, things just happen." She did not like the fashions in the United States and started making her own clothes. One day she decided she would try to sell them to department stores. She called up the buyer at a major San Francisco store, made an appointment, and took in her homemade designs. The buyer liked them and ordered eight thousand. Hardwick remembers the time humorously. "Can you imagine? Eight thousand. Then I had to figure out how to make eight thousand items of clothing. I certainly couldn't sit there at home and do it by myself. Since I'm Oriental, and I knew the Oriental community, I decided to find women who would help me out of their homes. I spent the entire time driving from house to house, picking up clothes, until I had eight thousand dresses I could deliver."

Hardwick took the money she made from that sale and opened a boutique, where she sold her designs. From there she went on to design for other fashion manufacturers until she made the decision to start her own firm. Today, she has both a design studio and a manufacturing side of the business and licenses her designs all over the world. She not only designs clothes but also creates designs for jewelry, china, and sheets. Last year sales from Cathy Hardwick designs amounted to $54 million. The other women interviewed for this book are not unlike Cathy Hardwick. They are women who saw opportunity and decided that they could figure out a way to make it happen.

Although it is difficult to generalize about what makes a successful entrepreneur, Jeffry A. Timmons, a professor at Northeastern University in Boston, and the staff of Venture Founders and its nonprofit licensee, the Institute for New Enterprise Development in Belmont, Massachusetts, have developed a list of fourteen personality characteristics and eight requirements that they feel individuals should possess to some degree in order to be entrepreneurs. These personality characteristics range from drive and energy to the ability to deal with failure, whereas the role characteristics range from knowing one's business to being able to be totally committed to the business venture. These entrepreneurial personality characteristics and role requirements are reproduced on pages 43-44, and a more complete explanation of them can be found in *New Venture Creation: A Guide to Small Business Development*, which Timmons wrote with Leonard Smollen and Alexander Dingee of Venture Founders. This book is a valuable investment for anyone considering taking the plunge into business ownership. It is written in a workbook fashion to help you identify the major characteristics of entrepreneurs, the demands of the entrepreneurial role, and your own strengths and weaknesses in this area.

Another aid for giving you insight into the profiles of entrepreneurial players is the questionnaire developed by the Entrepreneurship Institute in Worthington, Ohio. The institute is an independent nonprofit international organization assisting and encouraging entrepreneurship and new enterprise development. This institute conducts national seminars for existing and would-be entrepreneurs who are seeking to learn how to do business better. This questionnaire is also based on the existing research on entrepreneurship, and is reproduced on page 45.

Although no workbook or questionnaire can tell you if you should start a business, it can give you valuable clues as to whether you have what it takes to play in the entrepreneurial game. However, no one person will exhibit all of

ENTREPRENEURIAL PERSONALITY CHARACTERISTICS

1. **Drive and Energy Level.** Amount of personal energy; ability to work actively for long hours with less than normal sleep.
2. **Self-Confidence.** Level of one's self-confidence: A belief in yourself and your ability to achieve your goals and a sense that events in your life are self-determined.
3. **Long-Term Involvement.** Commitment to long-term, future projects and to working toward goals that may be quite distant in the future; implies a total immersion and concentration on the attainment of distant goals.
4. **Money as a Measure.** Money in the form of salary, profits, or capital gains viewed as the measure of what you have accomplished—as a way of keeping score—rather than the procurement of luxuries or the achievement of power.
5. **Persistent Problem Solving.** Intensive and determined desire to complete a task or solve a problem; a strong determination to get the job done.
6. **Goal Setting.** Ability and commitment to set clear goals and objectives that are high and challenging, but are realistic and attainable.
7. **Moderate Risk Taking.** Preference for taking moderate, calculated risks, where the chances of winning are not so small as to be a "gamble," or so large as to be a "sure thing," but provide a reasonable and challenging chance of success.
8. **Dealing with Failure.** One who is disappointed but not discouraged by failure; ability to use failures as learning experiences and to better understand your role in causing the failure in order to avoid similar problems in the future.
9. **Use of Feedback.** Demonstrated capacity to seek and use feedback on your performance in order to take corrective action and to improve.
10. **Taking Initiative and Seeking Personal Responsibility.** Desire to seek and take initiative and to put yourself in situations where you are personally responsible for the success or failure of the operation; one who takes the initiative to solve problems or fills leadership vacuums and who likes situations where one's impact on problems can be measured. A doer (self-reliant).
11. **Use of Resources.** Orientation which seeks to identify and obtain expertise and assistance that is needed in the accomplishment of your goals; not so involved in personal achievement of goals and independent accomplishment that you will not let anyone help you.
12. **Competing Against Self-Imposed Standards.** Desire and tendency to establish your own standard of performance which is high, yet realistic, and to compete with yourself.
13. **Internal Locus of Control.** The belief that one's accomplishments as well as failures lie within one's personal control and influence, rather than being determined by luck or other external, personally uncontrollable events and circumstances.
14. **Tolerance of Ambiguity.** Able to tolerate and live with modest to high levels of ambiguity and uncertainty concerning job and career security, and work-related events on a continuous basis. Sufficient self-confidence that job security and permanency are not important.

SOURCE: *New Venture Creation: A Guide to Small Business Development*. Jeffry A. Timmons, Leonard E. Smollen, and Alexander L. M. Dingee, Jr. Homewood, Ill.: Richard D. Irwin, 1977, pp. 121–122.

the traits thought to be helpful in entrepreneurship. Indeed, some combination of these traits is often more beneficial than just a high need for achievement. A high need for achievement seems to be the primary motive that encourages entrepreneurship, but it can also hinder people's ability to run a business if they are so independent and self-reliant that they will not seek advice or delegate authority or are such perfectionists that they are intolerant of others. Likewise, the need for power can contain seeds of self-destruction, such as clashes over authority or emphasis on status and getting rich that can be counterproductive to building a business.

Timmons feels that the affiliation motive—a motive at which women tend to rank high—can be an important asset, rather than a liability, for entrepreneurship. This is particularly true in the early stages of a venture, when the pressures of survival often make owners overlook the people problems in their organization. Timmons feels that a moderate to high level of affiliation motivation coupled with a high level of achievement motivation can be valuable because it eases the development of an entrepreneurial team that is crucial to business success.

ENTREPRENEURIAL ROLE REQUIREMENTS

1. **Accommodation to the Venture.** Extent to which the entrepreneur's career and venture are treated as the number one priority—above family, community, etc.
2. **Total Immersion.** Ability to become totally immersed in and committed to the building of the business; willing to invest life savings, reduce income as much as one-half in start-up, and early years; building the business seen as a way of life.
3. **Creativity and Innovation.** Extent to which one possesses an orientation and career anchor which places great value on creative, innovative work and which derives personal satisfaction from it; rather than doing the routine or merely doing a difficult task better.
4. **Knowledge of the Business One Wants to Start.** Extent to which one has thorough and proven operating knowledge of the business to be started.
5. **People and Team Building.** Extent to which one has demonstrated the capacity to attract, motivate, and build a high quality team whose capable management skills, know-how, and personal styles meet the needs of the venture.
6. **Economic Values.** Extent to which one believes in and is committed to the conventional economic and financial values of the American system of free enterprise, such as profits, capital gains, private ownership, earnings per share, etc.
7. **Ethics.** Extent to which one's business conduct tends to be defined and adaptive to the demands and needs of each situation, rather than by a rigid code of conduct applied uniformly, regardless of different conditions and circumstances.
8. **Integrity and Reliability.** Extent to which one is highly respected for dependability, reliability, and honest dealing.

Source: *New Venture Creation: A Guide to Small Business Development*. Jeffry A. Timmons, Leonard E. Smollen, and Alexander L. M. Dingee, Jr. Homewood, Ill.: Richard D. Irwin, 1977, pp. 125–126.

Who Are the Female Players?

Prior to the studies done by the Task Force, there had been relatively little research done into the nature of female entrepreneurship or the personality characteristics of those women who owned businesses. The Bureau of the Census' 1972 *Survey of Women-Owned Businesses* provided some benchmark data about the firms owned by women, but relatively little was known about the entrepreneurial woman herself.

The Task Force inquiry (to which 3,400 business owners responded), as well as the American Management Associations study conducted concurrently for the Task Force and incorporated into its report, provided a special look for the first time at women who start a business. Although both studies were statistically imperfect in that they did not use a random sample to find

---

DO YOU HAVE WHAT IT TAKES TO START YOUR OWN BUSINESS

Answer the questions for yourself. After you have finished the entire questionnaire, turn to appendix 1 (pages 217–220) for the scoring sheet and count your correct answers. An interpretation of each question also is provided.

		Yes	No
1.	Do I have a close relative that is or was in business for herself/himself?	—	—
2.	Have I ever worked for a small firm where I had close contact with the person who started it?	—	—
3.	Did I ever work for a small division of a larger firm where I had close contact with the top manager?	—	—
4.	Is my work experience in a variety of functional areas, such as marketing, finance and production?	—	—
5.	Have I ever had my employer reject my "better mousetrap" idea?	—	—
6.	Am I between the ages of 30 and 40?	—	—
7.	I like to *do* things, rather than plan things.	—	—
8.	I have lived in three or more cities in my life.	—	—
9.	I have been fired before.	—	—
10.	(If I am married) my spouse is supportive of my work.	—	—
11.	What generally happens to me is something I make happen, not something that is due to luck, good and otherwise.	—	—
12.	If I had to make a choice between working for a firm which I do not own for twice the money I make now and running my own firm at my present compensation, I would choose to start my own firm.	—	—
13.	When a problem comes up that everyone around me says is unsolvable, I usually try to figure out ways to solve it.	—	—
14.	As a child, I sold lemonade or had a paper route or similar activities.	—	—
15.	I get along well with other people.	—	—
16.	My subordinates respect me and work hard for me, even if they don't necessarily like me.	—	—

Copyright, Jeffrey C. Susbauer and the Entrepreneurship Institute, Worthington, Ohio, 1978.

participants, they did provide valuable insights into the nature of female entrepreneurship and the women who undertake it. Perhaps most important, they went far to explode some of the myths that have clung to women for years and have hampered them in their efforts to enter the mainstream of our business environment.

Myth Number 1: Women are not serious business owners, but are hobbiests seeking to capitalize on their free time. This myth is dead wrong. The Task Force found that the majority of women who responded to their questionnaire had been in the work force for several years prior to starting their venture. Although most of the respondents were first-time entrepreneurs, with only 9.6 percent owning more than one other business in the past, they were by no means newcomers to the labor force. Almost half (43 percent) had been working for at least twenty-one years, and only less than one-fourth (21.5 percent) had worked for less than ten years, although not all of these women had had managerial jobs. Only 13.4 percent had been managers for twenty-one years or more, and 39.5 percent reported having five or fewer years of managerial experience.[13]

Myth Number 2: Women get into business through inheritance or as part of a "ma-and-pa" business, rather than their own desire to do business. This myth is also wrong. The Task Force found that the women participating in its survey were classic entrepreneurs. Only 4 percent of the respondents had inherited their own business, while almost 80 percent were the original founders of their own business. Only 30 percent started the business with their spouse.[14]

Myth Number 3: Female entrepreneurs are motivated by different reasons than male entrepreneurs. Both the Task Force and the American Management Associations study found that women responding to their inquiry exemplified the traits that have been found in studies of male entrepreneurs. Most important, they are motivated by exactly the same factors that motivate male entrepreneurs—the desire to use a skill or talent they have, the desire for independence, and the desire for money.[15]

Myth Number 4: Entrepreneurship is incompatible with family life. Both the Task Force and the American Management Associations study showed that most of the respondents were married and had a supportive family—a factor which has been shown to be a key in business success. These women were able to manage both their business and their family life well. In addition, most had had entrepreneurial role models and had had working mothers.

The Task Force survey found that on the whole these women tended to own small, closely held businesses concentrated in the retail trade and selected service industries. They made relatively low gross receipts, had relatively few employees, and started their businesses from their personal savings.

The American Management Associations researchers looked at a different sector of female entrepreneurship in their study. They looked at those women who had been nominated by both the Small Business Administration and the

Department of Commerce field offices as being "successful." There was no attempt to define success in advance, since success, in terms of either gross revenues or numbers of employees, can be misleading due to industry and regional variations. However, their findings parallel those of the Task Force inquiry.

The American Management Associations profile of the successful woman entrepreneur indicated that she usually—

- came from a close, supportive family;
- was married to a supportive husband, who was either a business owner or professional;
- exhibited a strong entrepreneurial drive early in life, often during the elementary and high school years;
- tended to be highly educated;
- exhibited an inordinate capacity for hard work and dedication to her enterprise;
- was well informed concerning her business field;
- was persistent in her approach to work-related tasks;
- had an uncanny ability to redirect negative situations and attitudes to her advantage, much as a judo expert might apply the art of self-defense to the business environment. (This was perhaps the most important attribute.)[16]

Finally, this woman had the ability to juggle, yet integrate, the many diverse aspects of the different roles in her life. The dedication she applied to her business was equally applied to her husband and children.

The American Management Associations interviews made it clear that many of the women felt that early childhood experiences contributed significantly to their business aspirations. Said one: "I credit my success to my father. He never encouraged my sister or me just to work. He felt that you should have either a profession, so that you could go out on your own; or something that would put you into your own business, so that you would never have to be dependent on anyone else."[17] Another said: "My father always has been in business and my mother has been a housewife, but she worked with my father whenever it was necessary. My mother reinforced all three of her children; she taught us that we are individuals first. This is the way I always felt. Therefore, whatever I wanted to do, I felt I could accomplish."[18]

The American Management Associations interviews were particularly useful in articulating the problems of women as entrepreneurs. Women starting in business face their first obstacle in financing. The women reported that banks offered them their first major brush with discrimination. Many of the women interviewed found that obstacles dissolved when they came to the bank with a husband or male friend. Borrowing suddenly became possible.

Dealing with the financial establishment, the American Management Associations survey showed, was only one of many problems in discrimination. Among the others encountered were the perceptions men have of women business owners. Respondents indicated that men believe that women are intruding in a man's world, they are in business for fun, they have inadequate business experience, they cannot comprehend business intricacies, or they are overly emotional. Among the reports:

> Men don't take me seriously because they're not used to having women in executive capacities in a male-dominated business.
>
> You have to be better than men are, because you have to prove yourself all the time.
>
> If a woman asserts herself, it's not considered the same kind of positive behavior that it is if a man does. Assertive behavior in a man is much more acceptable; everybody admires it and thinks the man is going someplace. If a woman has the same kind of behavior, then she's considered a pushy broad and nobody really likes it. [19]

A particularly interesting reaction was the degree of difficulty the women reported in dealing with certain male colleagues. They listed in descending order of difficulty: bankers, suppliers, lawyers, customers, and accountants.

When these women were asked to what they attributed their success, the nature of their responses varied greatly. Obvious answers included knowledge of oneself, knowledge of the business area, educational attainment, hard work, aggressiveness, and good human relations skills. Some participants expressed the positive influence of being raised in a family which had business ownership. Other contributory factors to the success of these women included satisfaction with the work, enjoyment of the challenge, ability to set goals and priorities, ability to maintain self-discipline, and, in some cases, the realization that the individual was "driven." [20]

When American Management Associations interviewers questioned these successful women business owners about the type of advice they would give to other women going into business for themselves, the nature of the responses varied. Among the suggestions mentioned most often were thorough knowledge of the business (not only the product or service but also the market), sufficient capital, and the need for dedication and commitment. Many participants said that they would give the same advice to men who were starting a business; others said they would advise women differently than they would men because most women have not been raised to think they will own businesses and they have little experience in handling bank accounts and the day-to-day operations.

Deciding If You Really Want to Play

Entrepreneurs come in all shapes, sizes, sexes, and ages. There is no certain formula for determining whether you have what it takes to win in this game. The women interviewed for this book are living proof of this fact. Some, like Elizabeth Haynes of Baltimore Rigging, inherited their businesses and became owners out of circumstances.

Others followed the traditional displacement theory of business ownership, which maintains that you only start your own business when something happens to dislocate your life. These were the women who started their businesses because they could not cope with the bureaucracy of corporations, or were fired, laid off, or divorced. Carole Hyatt, owner of Child Research Services in New York, knew that she could not deal with the bureaucracy of NBC; Joyce Huber started Georgetown Employment Service in Washington, D.C., because she could not get along with bosses; and Beverly Jackson's pregnancy gave impetus to the formation of Jackson/Summers Associates, a public relations firm in Washington, D.C. There are also numerous incidents of divorce pushing women into entrepreneurship because of the need to support their children.

There are many reasons for women to decide that they want to play the entrepreneurial game. You may have also decided you want to play. However, it is important to make this decision carefully. You need to ask yourself who you are, where your motivation comes from, and how intense your drive is. The women interviewed for this book all say that it takes intense commitment, drive, dedication, and perseverance to make it as a business owner. As one woman said, "You have to want it so badly, you can taste it."

Vicki Smith Downing, owner of International Venture and Equity Capital, has talked to a lot of women about setting their life goals and perhaps choosing business ownership. Downing thinks it takes the same kind of close scrutiny of your life, in terms of both personal and business goals, that you should be doing no matter what your career objectives. "You have to look inward and outward, but in the final analysis you have to listen to yourself. It took me a long time to learn not to poll the neighborhood about my ideas. You have to listen to that resolute inner voice inside you. I think women are late to wake up to this voice, but when it screams loudly enough, you begin to listen to it."

Downing feels that the first step in making this personal scrutiny is to come to a rational recognition of how much time you have left to live and to determine what you want to be, do, and have in that time frame. "This first step is the hardest. It's hard to admit that your family trend has been to die at fifty or seventy or ninety, and that that is probably about how long you might have to do all you want to do. But once you know this, you can then work backwards, setting long-range, short-range, and intermediate goals; and establishing priorities and timetables to try to achieve them." Once you have done such a personal scrutiny, you will know if you want to play in the entrepreneurial game.

As Downing puts it, you only need two ingredients to be an entrepreneur: "It involves making both a rational choice and taking a leap of faith. It's that ability to believe in yourself and take that leap. That is the cutting edge that divides a would-be owner and an existing owner."

CHAPTER 3

Getting into
the Game

You now understand the nature of the entrepreneurial game and can assess whether you want to play this game. You know the players, the goal, and some of the odds. You also know how to assess whether you have what it takes to play in this game. You are now ready to enter the game.

To play the entrepreneurial game you need only five things: the motivation to play, a winning business concept, an entrepreneurial team, money to equip and pay this team, and the markets to support your business. How you can find these resources will be explained in the succeeding chapters. In chapter 2, you assessed whether you have the first requirement, the motivation to play. The second step is to find a winning business concept—that is, picking the game you want to play.

PICKING THE GAME

If you already have an idea for a business, picking the game may seem like a superfluous step; however, it is not. This second step is one of the most critical moves in the entrepreneurial game, yet most people forget to take it seriously. This step enables you to size up your odds before you bet your money, and as in all games, it can make the difference between winning and losing.

Most entrepreneurs, be they male or female, start their businesses without giving a great deal of thought to their rational chances of winning. It is only after the fact, after thousands of dollars and hundreds of hours of hard work have been invested and the owner is still eking out a modest wage, that they begin to wonder if the whole thing was a bad idea. Yet making so little money does not necessarily mean that they are poor players in the entrepreneurial game. It may mean that they merely entered the wrong game—one in which their chances of winning were marginal.

Therefore, if you have an idea for a business, put it aside, step back, and take a hard look at it for a moment. Don't let your love for an idea cloud your vision to the point that you can't be rational and realistic about its business potential. Remember that no matter how much you love doing something, the passion can wear off quickly when it fails to live up to your expectations.

The key is to avoid diving into a venture without assessing whether the business has the potential to generate the kind of return on the money, time, and energy invested to make it worthwhile.

What Does Winning Mean to You?

To avoid choosing the wrong business game, you should first define what winning means to you and then assess whether the business concept you have in mind will let you win. Winning is a very subjective and personal thing. For one person winning is being her or his own boss and earning an adequate but not luxurious standard of living. For another person, winning may mean earning a million dollars and building a business into an industry leader. What you may think is winning, I might think is losing. The difference in our opinion doesn't really matter. What does matter is that *you* have a firm concept of what winning means to you.

Defining what winning means to you will enable you to set both the financial and personal goals you have for yourself in running a business. Unless you have a firm grip on your financial and psychological goals in business ownership, you will soon find yourself getting lost in the entrepreneurial game. A firm concept of both your short- and long-range goals will help you devise the type of business strategies you will need in this game.

"It's working towards goals that make you a success and happy, not the money. I figure that's what makes me different from friends I have who have a lot of money or movie stars who commit suicide. I know what I'm working for, and it feels good when you make it," says one business owner whose original goal was simply to get out of a back alley garage and into a filling station on Main Street. Now that his first goal has been met, he wants to own more filling stations.

The filling station owner shows that winning in the entrepreneurial game involves personal as well as financial goals. This factor is highlighted by the American Management Associations study of successful women business owners. The women interviewed rarely relied only on financial criteria to measure their success. Success for them was measured in terms of their total lives. For them, success was like happiness—a by-product of reaching a goal and not the goal in itself.

Thus, one of the most important moves you can make in the entrepreneurial game is to nail down in the beginning what winning means to you in terms of both financial and personal goals. For example, if you are in love with making macrame and think that starting a macrame shop will make you a million dollars, you should forget it. Why? Because your personal and financial goals are not compatible. You are going to have to decide which is most important— macrame or the million dollars. A macrame shop is unlikely to also make you a million dollars unless you have invented a new way to make and merchandise the product on a large scale.

Don't get me wrong. There is nothing wrong with owning a relatively modest business if that is what will make you happy and if that is what you have defined as winning. However, there *is* something wrong if you go into a business without knowing your goal or without analyzing the odds. There is also something wrong if you set your business sights low, rather than high, because you think that it is easier or less risky to own a small, rather than large, business. Beatrice Fitzpatrick, director of the American Women's Economic Development Corporation, believes that women need to learn that it takes just as much energy to run a small business as it does to run a large one.

Indeed, your chances of success as the owner of a larger enterprise may be even greater than those of a small enterprise. Although the dollar amount of the risk may be higher, the probability of failure may be lower. You will find that being the owner of an enterprise that offers substantial growth potential increases your flexibility with bankers, investors, and suppliers. Suppliers like volume customers and are often willing to negotiate more favorable arrangements with such businesses. Investors, on the other hand, are looking for businesses that offer a high return on investment, whereas bankers are concerned both with the rate at which the business will repay its loan and the potential the business offers as a customer for future bank services.

Women rarely go into businesses that are either of the size or the character to give them such flexibility. The only available statistics show that women tend to go into businesses characterized by a low return on investment, a slow rate of debt repayment, a low growth rate, and small amounts of initial capital. This puts women in a curious "Catch-22" position in the business game, since all these factors decrease the attractiveness of their firms to lenders or investors.

The Task Force found that some of the problems women had in the financial arena were directly linked to the size and nature of their businesses. Traditionally, banks are loath to make loans for small amounts and investors look for businesses that offer a high return on their investment. The Task Force concluded that women were truly at the low end of the totem pole in our business environment. Both systematic discrimination, which puts them at a competitive disadvantage, and the low scale of their businesses inhibit their ability to maneuver in the business environment.

The banking, finance, and venture-capital companies surveyed by the Task Force indicated that administrative costs made small loans unprofitable; however, the women surveyed indicated that these were the types of loans that they sought. Eighty-two percent of the women responding to the Task Force inquiry indicated that they were initially capitalized at under $50,000, whereas 14 percent indicated that they were capitalized at between $1,000 and

$5,000. Yet banks view loans for under $50,000 as unprofitable, and venture-capital firms normally invest no less than $150,000 in ventures—hardly the scale of the typical woman-owned venture.

Therefore, before you leap automatically into a business you love, you should look carefully at the potential it offers you—both in terms of meeting your own goals for winning and in attracting investors and lenders. You may find a variation on the idea that could meet your goals easier.

Although no one would think of playing in a sports game unless they knew what it took to win and what their odds to win were, few people take the time to define their financial or personal goals for winning or to assess their odds before entering the business game. Many people seem to *fall* into business, rather than making rational decisions to *go* into business. Some make their first mistake because they start their businesses for the wrong reasons, as discovered by Kandra Driggs, owner of Wing Conferences—a San Francisco management consulting firm that specializes in small business management, management training, and employee development. Driggs has found that many people tend to be driven into business by exterior needs, such as getting away from a boss they disliked or frustrated career aspirations, rather than by their interior (personal) needs for business ownership. This pattern is particularly true for women, since the chances of our being stymied in a male-dominated organization are greater. As a result, women choose ownership out of frustration, rather than real entrepreneurial enthusiasm or a rational assessment of their chances of winning.

According to Driggs, women tend to run *from* something, rather than *to* business ownership—which obviously can be a mistake. Driggs believes it is important for any woman thinking about going into business to take the time to define her personal, or interior, needs and to make sure she is making her business choices for the right, and not the wrong, reasons. The right reason is picking something that will enable you to meet your personal goal for winning. The wrong reason is picking something without thinking about these goals.

Vicki Smith Downing, owner of International Venture and Equity Capital, shares Driggs's views. Downing spends a lot of time training and talking to women business owners. She has found that one of the most helpful things that she can teach a woman is how to sit back, put some distance between herself and her business concept, and rationally set out goals for herself. Downing's own business story is interesting in that she is the classic example of an entrepreneurially spirited woman who was able to transfer the volunteer skills of fund raising for charities in Dallas into money-making skills as a venture capitalist. "An M.B.A. and the fact that I had raised hundreds of thousands of dollars for charities made me realize that I could do the same thing for businesses that were seeking capital as I'd been doing for charities." This was the impetus for her current business, International Venture and Equity Capital, which tries to match international business ventures with venture capital.

Driggs and Downing agree that women may be more prone than men to fall into businesses, rather than judge their business decisions carefully, primarily because women have never known enough about the business game to know how to analyze business opportunities and are novices at this aspect of business. This factor may be one reason for the dismal picture presented by the only available statistics on women-owned businesses. According to the Bureau of the Census' *Survey of Women-Owned Businesses,* women owned less than 5 percent of all the businesses and earned less than 0.3 percent of all United States business receipts in 1972. Even more depressing is the extremely low figure for average gross revenues of these businesses. However, since this survey was drawn from tax records and includes both full- and part-time workers, it does not provide a true picture of the average earnings of bona fide full-time businesses. What these figures do show is that the businesses owned by women are clustered for the most part in industries that offer relatively little growth potential and low returns on investment: the personal service and retail trade industries.

The findings of the special inquiry conducted by the Task Force mirrored the Census Bureau's 1972 survey. Although the women responding to the Task Force inquiry appeared to operate slightly larger businesses than those in the 1972 survey, their businesses were still relatively small and were concentrated in the same industries. Only 5 percent of these women had gross receipts in 1976 in excess of $100,000, and the bulk of the respondents had sales that hovered around the $50,000 mark. Nineteen percent of the respondents reported sales of less than $10,000 in 1976. Although the outlook in terms of employees was also brighter than reported by the 1972 statistics, these women owned relatively tiny businesses. The majority had less than nine full-time people, although seventy percent reported having at least one full-time employee.

The bottom line of both studies shows that women, by and large, are not entering lucrative businesses. We tend to be the owners of small, closely held, and marginally profitable enterprises. Why this relatively bleak economic picture exists is not known. One can only surmise that the forces that have historically kept us out of the mainstream of political and financial matters continue to impact our business choices. The fact that we are still not readily accepted in some industries, do not know how to assess business opportunities, and have difficulty in raising capital may cause women to gravitate to the service and retail trades. These businesses have a lower return on investment and have lower capital requirements, but they are fields in which a woman's expertise is more readily accepted.

However, we do not have to stay in these industries. Today, more and more women are beginning to set their sights higher and to move into industries that offer greater growth potential, such as manufacturing and wholesaling. Therefore, one of the basic rules of the entrepreneurial game is to choose a business that will meet both your personal and profit goals. You can do this by first defining what winning is for you and then assessing the business opportunities available to you.

Sizing Up the Business Opportunities

A lot of people play the business game as if it were blind man's bluff. However, there are better methods for sizing up a business game. One of the easiest ways is to use the same tools that bankers do. Bankers must make daily decisions about the businesses for which they will approve loans, using as tools various published financial ratios. These ratios provide a yardstick for measuring the performance and potential of a business.

Ratio analysis has been used since 1913, when the Bureau of Business Research of Harvard University conducted a study of the expenses of shoe stores.[1] Today there are several sources of financial and operating ratios that provide yardsticks for measuring the performance and potential of businesses. They will help you not only assess a business opportunity but also manage and control your business. The use of these ratios will be discussed more fully in chapter 8, "Controlling Your Company." These ratios can provide you with a wealth of information about the profit potential and cost of doing business in particular industries. The main sources of these ratios are Dun & Bradstreet and Robert Morris Associates, although trade associations often develop their own ratios for their particular industries.

Dun & Bradstreet publishes "Key Business Ratios" in its monthly *Dun's Review*. These financial ratios cover 22 retail, 32 wholesale, and 71 industrial lines of business. Dun & Bradstreet also annually compiles *Cost of Doing Business*—a special pamphlet that includes operating ratios for 120 lines of business extracted from data in the Internal Revenue Service's *Statistics of Income*. These ratios can tell you such things as the average for these industries in terms of profits on business receipts, bad debts, salary and other operating expenses, cost of goods sold, and the gross margin on sales. For example, if you are interested in going into a personal service industry, this publication will show you that barber shops make a higher profit than beauty shops. Another publication that will be of interest to you in deciding on the type of business to go into is Dun & Bradstreet's *Business Failure Record*. This booklet gives general failure trends in terms of the geographic distribution and causes of bankruptcy, as well as the failure rate for specific industries. For example, if you are interested in retailing, this publication will show you that sporting goods companies have a higher incidence of failure than automobile outlets. These publications are available from Dun & Bradstreet, Public Relations Department, 99 Church Street, New York, New York 10007 or at any of the company's branches.

Robert Morris Associates, a national association of bank loan and credit officers, is the major source of business ratios used by banks. This organization has developed ratio studies for over 350 lines of business, ranging from casket manufacturers to vending machine companies. You can get copies of these studies in most libraries, your local bank, or by writing to Robert Morris Associates, Philadelphia National Bank Building, Philadelphia, Pennsylvania 19107. The National Cash Register Company also publishes an annual booklet,

Expenses in Retailing, that examines the cost of operation in about 40 lines of business from apparel stores to variety shops.

Other sources also may provide the information you need. The Bank of America periodically issues detailed studies of problems in opening a business. The Internal Revenue Service annually publishes *Statistics of Income*, which contains income-statement and balance-sheet data compiled from federal income tax returns. The Census Bureau publishes every five years its *Census of Business*, which provides some financial information.

These financial statistics will help you take the blindfold off when you are choosing a business venture and develop your business expense projection to determine how much money you will need to capitalize your firm. Many trade associations provide information on the breakdown of expenses in the average business in their trade, which can be invaluable; for example, the table on page 58 shows operating ratios of high-profit hardware stores. How to develop the formal business plan you will need to show bankers and investors when you start to capitalize your business will be discussed in chapter 5, "Financing Your Business."

Although opinions vary as to the operating ratios a business owner should know, ten key ratios are suggested in the Small Business Administration's booklet, *Ratio Analysis for Small Business* (SBMS No. 20).

1. Current assets to current liabilities
2. Current liabilities to tangible net worth
3. Net sales to tangible net worth
4. Net sales to working capital
5. Net profits to tangible net worth
6. Average collection period of receivables
7. Net sales to inventory
8. Fixed assets to tangible net worth
9. Total debt to tangible net worth
10. Net profit on net sales

This excellent booklet, which explains to business novices the ratios and their uses, can be obtained from the United States Government Printing Office in Washington, D.C. A brief description of these ratios excerpted from the booklet can be found in appendix 2. (See appendix 3 for other useful publications.)

However, the best way to find out which ratios your bankers use most often in judging loan applications is to ask your banker. Such a fishing expedition can prove beneficial in more ways than one. Not only will it teach you about financial ratios, but it will also allow you to bounce your business idea off the banker, who knows a lot about the marketplace in which you will be operating. You can also find out in advance the kind of things she or he will be looking for when it comes time to make your formal loan application, but be sure to explain to the banker that this visit is exploratory. Tell the banker that you want to find out what services the bank might be able to offer you as a potential

SUMMARY OF OPERATING RATIOS
OF 350 HIGH-PROFIT HARDWARE STORES

	Percentage of Sales
Net sales	100.00%
Cost of goods sold	64.92
Margin	35.08%
Expenses	
Payroll and other employee expenses	16.23%
Occupancy expense	3.23
Office supplies and postage	0.40
Advertising	1.49
Donations	0.08
Telephone and telegraph	0.24
Bad debts	0.30
Delivery	0.47
Insurance	0.66
Taxes (other than real estate and payroll)	0.46
Interest	0.61
Depreciation (other than real estate)	0.57
Supplies	0.37
Legal and accounting expenses	0.31
Dues and subscriptions	0.08
Travel, buying, and entertainment	0.19
Unclassified expenses	0.64
Total operating expense	26.33%
Net operating profit	8.75%
Other income	1.65
Net profit before income taxes	10.40%

Source: *Ratio Analysis for Small Business*. Small Business Management Series No. 20. Washington, D.C.: Small Business Administration.

business owner and that you will provide them with a formal business plan and projections when you have finished your research. Use the time wisely to make a good initial impression with the banker and to develop a friendly relationship.

A strategy one business owner used was to drop in frequently on her banker with questions in order to develop a relationship and get the banker in her corner prior to applying for the loan. Asking questions is another way to assess whether your business idea is viable. You will be surprised at the amount of advice and information other small business people will give a person interested in starting a business. Even people in competitive businesses will often provide you with information, since they rarely see a newcomer as a real competitor.

Another factor to consider in picking your business game is whether you know anything about the business. Dun & Bradstreet's *Business Failure Record* ranks lack of experience in the particular industry behind only incompetence and unbalanced experience in all aspects of basic business functions (sales, finance, purchasing, and production) as a major cause of business failures.[2] You will up your odds of winning if you go into a business you know something about. Brian Haslett, who works with entrepreneurs at Venture Founders in Belmont, Massachusetts, points out that a person needs to possess three characteristics to succeed in a new venture: the personality characteristics of an entrepreneur, some experience in at least one of the functional areas of management (finance, marketing, etc.), and knowledge of the industry in which the person is entering. Therefore, you should look long and hard at whether your greenness in a new industry will place you at a competitive disadvantage, before you throw away the years of experience you may have in one industry.

But you are not necessarily locked into doing the same kind of work you have always done, particularly if this business offers little growth potential. Two ways to alleviate the greenness are to take a job for a while in the new industry or to find the required skills in other members of your entrepreneurial team, either as partners or as employees. Many people advise prospective business owners to work in a business similar to the one in which they want to start for two to three years before going out on their own, but this experience is usually enough to destroy the enthusiasm of any true entrepreneur. However, there are alternatives for gaining the experience you will need.

Perhaps the best way to gain experience is to find a business owner who will let you be an apprentice for a month or two and teach you the ropes. You'd be surprised how many owners will be willing to take in a bright, ambitious person who can help fill their employee gaps at a nominal wage. Another way you can learn is to take jobs in the area in which you need experience, ask a lot of questions, and then quit when you have learned enough. Eileen Weinberg followed the latter course. Weinberg is co-owner, with Christi Finch, of Word of Mouth Caterers, a small catering firm located on the bottom floor of a New York City brownstone.

Weinberg and Finch, who were both hospital administrators, originally began their business on a part-time basis, cooking on weekends while still holding their full-time jobs. They did this for three years and had a few regular clients before they took the leap into full-fledged business ownership. However, prior to opening their business, Weinberg took a job as a restaurant cook in order to learn about the business side of cooking. She feels that the restaurant job taught her the kinds of things she needed to know for the business, such as how to purchase ingredients, cook in quantities, and produce under pressure. She advises women to take such jobs for a month or so until they have learned what they need to know.

The last factor you should consider in sizing up your business game is whether there is a genuine market potential for your business. Too many people make the mistake of thinking that a business idea, ambition, and drive are all that is needed to win in the entrepreneurial game. They forget the key ingredient: There must be a real market need for the idea, and that need must be great enough to generate the sales volume necessary for operating at a profit. How to test the winds to see if your business idea will fly will be explained more fully in chapter 6, "Developing Your Marketing Strategy." For further assistance in picking a business game, consult appendix 3, "Resources," which provides an overview of the many types of aid available.

GETTING IN THE GAME

There are more ways than one to enter the entrepreneurial game. The three basic ways are acquiring an existing business, buying a franchise, and starting your own business from scratch. While the rest of this book concentrates on starting a new business, do not overlook these important options. Most women make the mistake of thinking that the only way to get into business is to start a new business. If this describes your situation, think again. The easiest way to get into business is by acquiring an existing business or a franchise. These are also the safest ways to go into business. An existing business has already weathered many of the initial crises associated with starting a business from scratch, and a franchise can offer immediate customers and some management assistance from the parent company.

The difference between acquiring an existing business or a franchise and starting your own business is a little like the difference between buying a ticket to get into the entrepreneurial game and trying to climb over the fence. The first method is easier and less painful, if sometimes a little more costly. Yet most women tend to overlook this avenue. Very few of the women responding to the Task Force inquiry took this route to business ownership: 80 percent indicated that they were the original founders of their companies, whereas 16 percent had bought a company and 4 percent had inherited their businesses. Why so few women buy existing businesses or franchises is unclear. However, women who deal daily with women business owners feel that it hinges on our cultural upbringing. Our unfamiliarity with, and sometimes fear of, the business environment and money markets make it difficult for us to identify and negotiate a good acquisition deal.

Yet buying into business has its advantages. You can get involved in bigger businesses that have a greater growth potential and you won't experience the normal lag time in reaping profits that occurs in business start-ups. It is also often easier to capitalize an acquisition than a start-up. Although the downhill side of buying a business is that you inherit some initial management problems, the uphill side is that you also inherit a stream of existing customers and a track record of sales and profits. The latter can give bankers that nice, warm, secure feeling that makes them more prone to make loans.

An important rule of the entrepreneurial game that Lynn Salvage, former president of the First Women's Bank in New York City, feels women need to learn is that you don't have to do it the hard way.

> Acquisition is the way a lot of men make the jump from corporate employment to ownership. For example, I know a fellow who went from being an officer at a very large company to owning one by buying out the original owners. He has since bought into a chain of beauty shops, an executive search firm, and any number of other businesses. Women just don't think that way. When a woman thinks about entrepreneurship, even if she is with a large corporation and has experience and a good salary, she usually thinks about starting something from scratch instead of buying somebody else out. I think it is important to condition women into awareness about acquisitions.

Salvage believes that cultural conditioning keeps women from dealing in the marketplace, with an impact both on the way women enter the entrepreneurial game and on the limited growth plans they tend to hold for their businesses. She points out that women rarely think about buying a business or selling one business for another one, yet such a move is a normal business procedure for many men.

> Men are deal-oriented. I see that in our financing. They are deal-oriented in closing, opening, selling, and buying. Women are not. Even if they make a loan, they don't realize the big picture of finance. If a person or a business is a good credit risk, we do not want another bank to get their business and are willing to negotiate and deal with them. Women don't think in terms of deals. They don't think about acquiring, and they also don't think about selling for the same reasons. Yet selling out can give you capital to buy a bigger business. If you sell out for $2 million and put that $2 million together with some financing, and then buy something for $10 million, you can begin to build a series of businesses faster than you can by starting from scratch.

Another reason women don't acquire businesses is because we tend to see our businesses as an extension of ourselves—an ego extension, if you will— rather than the nonemotional game that business really is. Virginia Maynard— who has worked in the financial arena for more than thirty years—points out that the same pattern that women exhibit in other financial markets also holds true in the area of business ownership. Maynard was a vice president of Citibank and is now at the First Women's Bank of New York. "When women buy stocks they hold onto those stocks. They become their babies. Men are less sentimental. They buy, trade, make a few dollars. They then buy something else and make a few more dollars. Women think of stock as ownership in a company, not as a paper you can trade to make money. They don't watch the stock market, and they don't trade because to them the stock becomes a possession."

Beatrice Fitzpatrick of the American Women's Economic Development Corporation, agrees with Salvage and Maynard. Fitzpatrick feels that while women have raw entrepreneurial talent, there are big differences between men and women in the way women view the marketplace and the reasons they go into business. If you look at entrepreneurial motivation as a spectrum between achieving personal satisfaction and making money, women tend to lean toward the personal satisfaction end of this spectrum. A man will ask the question, How can I make some money and still like what I do? A woman will tend to ask, How can I do what I love and still make some money? When your emphasis is on doing something you love, rather than on something that will make you money, it makes acquiring a business difficult.

Other women business owners feel that a major reason women pick their business game poorly and don't think of acquiring businesses is because it is hard for them to admit that making money is a legitimate goal. Vicki Smith Downing hid the *Feminine Mystique* in a bottom drawer when she was first married because it was considered so revolutionary. As a cofounder of one of the first women's credit unions, she still manages to attend to both her budding business and her family equally well. Downing feels that women have a lot of latent guilt about making money. "Women need to learn to say money out loud and realize that it is not a four-letter word, especially Southern women. We are raised to feel that somehow something is wrong if you have to make money. It is unladylike. Money is okay if it comes from daddy or a husband; but it's not okay in your mind if you make it yourself. And God forbid you should *enjoy* making it!"

Constance Kenney, who owns an investment management company in Lexington, Massachusetts, has found that this guilt is not just a Southern phenomenon. She is currently teaching a continuing education course entitled "Women, Money, and Investing" and is also writing a book on the language of money and wealth for women. Kenney feels that women often have difficulty coping with the idea of profits and that money can be a harsh reality to them. She remembers one woman potter who had convinced herself that she was running her business for the sake of her art. This woman told her, "It was hard for me to come to terms with it, but I now realize that what I *really* want to do is to make money."

Money is the name of the game in business. Business failure, by definition, is when you run out of money to keep operating. Therefore, it's important to look at all the possible options available to you and their profit possibilities in picking the business in which you want to invest your money, time, and energy. Although the other chapters of this book will deal primarily with the moves you will have to make in a business start-up, don't overlook the possibility that you might be able to acquire a business or franchise as alternatives to business ownership.

Acquiring an Existing Business

Acquiring a business that is already in operation can be one of the quickest and best ways to get into business, particularly if you think you have a better chance of succeeding than the previous owners. You will find that it is easier to raise capital for an acquisition because you have an existing track record of sales and will see an immediate return on your investment. The time saved in setting up equipment, building inventories, and creating customers can mean immediate money in your pocket.

Finding a company to acquire is not hard, once you start looking. In your local newspaper or the *Wall Street Journal* you will see listings under "business opportunities." Your local banker, lawyer, and accountant are also good sources. They often have an intimate knowledge about businesses that may be seeking to liquidate in order to bail out of trouble. They also hear about owners who have grown tired of their business and want to move to other ventures. Other sources are those business "watering holes" such as Chamber of Commerce meetings or any other business networks.

Not all these businesses are losers. Business turnovers are a reality of business life, especially since the bulk of all small businesses are sole proprietorships or family held businesses. The owner will have to sell out if she or he wants to retire and does not have a relative that wants to carry on the family business. Such an owner will often make it easy for you to purchase the business by allowing you to string out your payments, particularly if she or he is looking for retirement income. This arrangement gives tax benefits to the owner by providing a staggered income from the business.

Genie Hindall followed the above route to business ownership. Hindall is president and general manager of Guide Service of Washington, a business that provides trained tour guides for out-of-town tour buses that visit Washington, D.C. A telephone survey of existing businesses led Hindall to Guide Service of Washington, where she went to work as a guide to gain experience. Four years later she took over the business, rather than starting a new company, when the owners decided to retire. For tax reasons the owners agreed to allow her to pay for the company over three years.

Hindall believes that acquisition can be a good business route for women, especially if the previous owner will help teach them the ropes of the business. As an employee, the previous owners trained Hindall in all aspects of the business prior to her acquisition in January 1977. Although she comes from a family of small business owners and is married to an owner of two businesses, she found her work experience invaluable. In addition, she kept the previous owners involved for the first year on a contract basis for counsel. She thinks this decision helped her avoid many initial mistakes and allowed for a smooth transition of the business from one owner to the other.

The key to making a good acquisition is to look carefully before you leap. Not only will you be taking on the existing customers of the business, but you will also be inheriting its existing inventory, staff, and perhaps some of its liabilities and management problems. Even if you find a business is making only marginal profits, it may be a better deal than starting your own company from scratch, if you think you have the capability to turn the company around. However, you need to make a careful analysis of all aspects of the firm to make sure that the business is inherently sound and that the conditions contributing to the marginal profitability do not have a lasting or permanent effect. No prospective seller is going to tell you that the reason for the sale is that the company is losing money. They'll blame retirement or family reasons, but never business failure. This factor makes negotiating a purchase agreement complicated. The advice of a competent attorney and an accountant is absolutely essential if you want to avoid getting burned badly in an acquisition deal.

Luckily, you can tell a great deal about a potential company from its books. Just as any good doctor can tell you a lot about the health of a person by looking at past medical records and X rays, business financial records enable you, with an accountant's help, to piece together a picture of the firm's health. You should also check with bankers and suppliers about their dealings with the owner. Having a competent attorney to take a look at the legal implications of the deal is equally important.

Remember that the idea is to piece together as complete a picture of the firm as you can from all available materials. What you will be looking for is information about the nature of the business in the past, the present condition of the business, and the relationship of the past and present to what you can expect the business to produce in the future. You will need three types of information: financial, market, and legal.

The financial information on the firm is the most critical piece of information that you will need, since cash is the lifeblood of any company. This information will enable you to figure out how viable the firm has been in the past, and what its current financial status is in terms of its assets and liabilities. It will show the patterns of growth or decline in both sales and profits, as well as the patterns of success or failure of past business strategies. You should ask to see financial statements of the firm for at least three years and preferably for ten years; including balance sheets, income statements, cash-flow statements, and income tax returns, as well as any other records that analyze selected accounts on these statements. For example, the owner may have analyzed sales by customer or product, inventory turnover, or the average age of accounts payable. All of these records will be of interest to you. They can provide you with vital information about the health of the company, since they are tangible evidence of the success of the management decisions of the company.

The relationship of the assets of the firm to its liabilities is the key factor you will be gauging from this information. Scrutinize these liabilities carefully, since the liabilities are the only thing that are absolutely certain. You want to be extremely careful that you do not get stuck with the previous owner's debts and liabilities. Generally, it is wise to try to buy the assets of the business, rather than the stock. In an asset transaction, the legal continuity of the seller's business is broken, and the liabilities are not usually carried over to you, unless you agree to assume them. Buying assets also protects you from hidden liabilities, such as lawsuits from customers or employees, penalties for the previous sale of defective products, or back taxes. If you do purchase the stock of the company, you should take precautions against these unknown liabilities by getting an indemnity from the seller or holding part of the purchase price in escrow as a contingency for such liabilities.

Market and legal data on the firm are also important. Market information will give you a picture of the firm's past performance and an assessment of its future performance. You will need to see historical records on factors such as sales, the cost of goods sold, and average rate of stock turnover, as well as a market analysis of where you think the firm can go in terms of the existing competition and market for its product. You will want to ask about past marketing and sales strategies to assess whether you think another strategy would increase sales. Since any acquisition involves the transfer of ownership, title to property, and responsibilities for liabilities, you should examine all legal information, including copies of contracts with customers, suppliers, and employees and all evidence of ownership and organizational documents. You should also check external sources of legal information, such as public records and the records of third parties with whom the seller has had dealings. Be sure to look at the firm's tax payments carefully. The last thing you want to do is to inherit a liability for the back payment of taxes.

Paper records, however, cannot tell you everything about a business. You will also want to spend some time observing the actual operations of the firm. Although paper records track the success of the firm, only personal observation can tell you about employee morale, efficiency, and general attitudes toward the business. A common mistake made in acquisitions is to think that simply putting up a sign that says "under new management" will change things overnight. Personal observation is the only way you will be able to gauge whether you think implementing the changes you desire in the business will be relatively easy or difficult.

Once you have analyzed all available information, the next step is to decide the value of the business and how much you will pay for it. It is important to separate value from price. *Value* refers to what the business is worth, whereas *price* refers to the amount of money for which ownership will be transferred. You may think that a business is worth a great deal in terms of its future potential but be willing to pay only its present value.

You and the seller will undoubtedly have different opinions about the value of the business. The seller will probably think in terms of all the money she or he has invested through the years, but you will be measuring the value of tangible items, such as equipment and inventory. Thus, determining the value of the business is one of the most difficult steps in the acquisition process. Two methods can be used as bases for determining value: expectations of future profits and return on investment or the appraised value of the assets at the time of negotiation. The first method is preferred, as it forces both you and the seller to pay attention to the future profit performance of the business. However, the second method is the one most commonly used, simply because it is the easiest. Some bankers refer to the latter method as determining the "bone power" of the company. These "bones" are the accounts receivable, inventory, and other assets that will keep a company alive, even if the change in ownership creates a heavy slump in sales. For example, the new owners of an old-line retail store indicated that they could have survived on just the outstanding accounts receivable for the first several months without a single new sale.

How you value the business will depend on your business goals. For example, one person may consider a business worth buying only at the liquidation value of the assets, whereas another prospective buyer may view the same business as the answer to a lifetime dream. Or some aspects of the company you are thinking of buying may be key to your future plans, thereby causing you to put a higher value than would be otherwise justified by the worth of its tangible assets alone. For example, a large company recently paid a high price for a small company that had a relatively low value of tangible assets because the company acquired had a key intangible asset sought by the larger company. This key asset was an existing home marketing system (such as the kind used by Tupperware or Stanley Products), which the larger company had decided to institute to expand sales, and acquiring the existing network was easier than building one from scratch.

The key is to know *what* you are buying, particularly if the company is in a service industry, and whether the intangible assets have a value to you. For example, most sellers will assign a price tag to existing goodwill. You should take a hard look to make sure that the goodwill is indeed attached to the firm and not to the individual. In some cases, especially in service businesses— where there are few tangible assets and where goodwill and existing client base are the key things you are purchasing—you may want to stipulate in the purchase contract that the owner cannot establish a similar business in the same location for a period of time. Such a clause would protect you from paying a high price for an empty shell.

Once you have answered the question of what you are actually buying—a lifetime dream, existing assets, or some feature of the business—the last step is determining what return you think you will get from the investment and deciding if it is adequate or if you could get a better return if you invested the money elsewhere, either in another business or in stocks and bonds. Remember that no matter how excited you are about the prospect of owning a particular business, the dream can turn into both a headache and a heartache if you find that the return on both your money, time, and energy is not enough to keep you happy.

Mary Zulalian, who looked at several businesses before acquiring a brokerage house, points out that the key thing to remember in both acquiring or starting a business is to stay objective about the business and to scrutinize it carefully. "There is plenty of time to get excited after you're in business. You have to remember to keep your head and your objectives straight while you are looking. Once you have put your foot in the water, be emotional . . . not before."

Zulalian was one of the first graduates from M.I.T.'s prestigious Sloan Fellows Management Program, and she got this graduate degree without ever having finished college. The business she acquired was Holden and Company, located in Boston. Zulalian decided on acquiring a brokerage house after looking at three companies, including a soap manufacturing business. "I chose the brokerage firm because I knew that I didn't know the first thing about making soap, but I did know a little about the stock market and thought a discount brokerage firm was a good option. I knew it was a business I could learn about fairly easily." She points out that the investment and lead time needed to get a brokerage house licensed made the acquisition route even more attractive.

The key problem you will find in taking the acquisition route is the fact that you inherit more than the profit potential of a business. You also inherit its image, existing staff, and management problems. It is also not unusual for you to inherit the former owner, who may want an employment contract with the firm for the first several years. You may find that it is not always so easy to implement the policy decisions you want when you put up that sign that says "under new management."

Zulalian found that her main problem was changing the image of the firm from a traditional brokerage house to a discount brokerage house. Unlike traditional firms, discount brokers do not manage client stock portfolios. Instead, they take and place stock orders from sophisticated investors who watch the market for themselves and like the lower brokerage fees that discount brokers charge because they do not offer other client services. Zulalian points out that it was difficult to wean former customers away from wanting the kind of service they once had to accepting that offered by a discount brokerage firm. An additional problem was getting her colleagues in the brokerage business to accept her new management role. Although she purchased a seat on the stock exchange, it took a while to gain acceptance— both as an innovator in a conservative field and as a woman.

Edith Schubert's problem was that she inherited a business format of many years standing and the period of adjustment was frustrating. The firm she acquired was Martin's, a prestigious old-line firm dealing in the finest china, sterling, crystal, and antiques. Fourteen years earlier, she had started her own business, the China Closet, which now has three locations in the Washington, D.C., metropolitan area. This firm specializes in mass merchandising of tabletop wares. Although she thinks that acquisition is a good route for a novice business owner because it provides a little breathing room for getting one's feet on the ground, with ready-made customers and an experienced staff, she found the switch between business start-up and acquisition difficult in her case.

Schubert had great trepidation about starting her original business, the China Closet, and was actually pushed into it by her husband, who thought it would make her happy. Although the first years of the business were difficult for her, particularly coping with the problem of learning to be a boss, she is now a businesswoman par excellence. She owns five stores in the Washington, D.C., area: three China Closet outlets and two Martin's—which gross well over $3 million annually.

Schubert, Zulalian, and Hindall—all feel that acquiring a business offers an important business option for women getting into the business game. For further information, refer to *Buying and Selling a Small Business*, published by the Small Business Administration. That booklet outlines the kind of questions you should ask in negotiating a purchase to help you decide if this is a business route you want to investigate further.

Buying a Franchise

A route to owning your own business midway between acquiring an existing business and starting one from scratch is to buy a franchise. By purchasing a franchise, you essentially purchase the right to sell a known product of an existing business under its franchise distribution network. Franchises vary from dealerships that make you the sole distributor of the product within an area to franchises that provide the buyer with an entire support system business format, including training and headquarters support. Dealerships are an arrangement found frequently among manufacturers of automobiles, gasoline, and appliances. The entire business franchise is used by many fast-food restaurants, motels, car rentals, and service businesses. The latter type is the most attractive for women, since such franchises can provide you with a blueprint for running a business and training. Although people sometimes laugh that part of the agreement in purchasing a McDonald's franchise is that you will have to go to "Hamburger College," such training has proven a boon to the business and has made McDonald's one of the most sought-after fast-food franchises.

If you decide to buy an entire business type of franchise, you will normally pay an initial franchise or license fee, as well as periodic royalties or service fees—which are often based on a percentage of sales. You may also be asked to pay charges for on-the-site start-up aid and promotion and a continuing percentage of advertising or centralized administrative costs. In return, the franchiser typically gives you goodwill, know-how, and contractually limited use of a trademark. Support services may also include use of trade services and copyrights and access to system-wide promotion, standardized operating procedures, product and service research, and group purchasing power.

The key thing you will want to look for in finding a good franchise deal is a company that is well known, well managed, and financially strong; has a good sales record; and is interested in finding buyers who will not only pay the price but also add to the overall distribution system. You want to avoid fly-by-night franchisers who promise high profits but offer no substantial support services in terms of national marketing plans, advertising, or training. The major advantage of purchasing a franchise over starting your own business from scratch is the profit benefits that the tie-in with a large company will make. You should investigate the franchise carefully before you make your decision. In general, you should shy away from franchisers who promise high profits in return for minimum effort and who refuse to give you specific examples of the training and management assistance they offer, along with a list of references.

The Federal Trade Commission (FTC) receives thousands of letters every year from people who feel deceived by franchise operators. Most of the complaints involve small, little-known franchisers, although a few also touch on the big chains. The major problems cited included the following: the franchiser falsified the profit potential; supplies were overpriced; more competitors were allowed in the area than the franchisee had expected; the franchisee received less training than was promised; and promised technical assistance failed to materialize.

You should be aware of a new FTC rule that requires franchise operators to give the following information to potential investors:

- A list of all key executives in the franchise operation and their employment background
- Disclosure of all lawsuits and bankruptcies in which the company has been involved
- Disclosure of all suppliers that the franchisee has to do business with and the amounts of money these suppliers pay to the franchise operator
- A full description of any financial assistance given by the franchiser to the franchisee
- Disclosure of all money the franchisee has to pay at the start and during the life of the business
- A clear explanation of the terms under which the franchise may be revoked

Fifteen states have franchise-disclosure laws similar to the FTC regulation. Two excellent pamphlets will help you learn how to assess the deal offered you: *Investigate Before Investing: Guidance for Prospective Franchisees*, published by the International Franchise Association, and *Franchise Index/ Profile: A Franchise Evaluation Process* (SBMS No. 35), published by the Small Business Administration. It is also a good idea to visit one of the existing outlets of the company and ask the owner what her or his experience has been with the franchiser. She or he will have learned a lot about the franchise market the hard way and will probably be willing to share this knowledge.

In general, you will want to know about the company's product and its market potential; the number and the success rate of existing franchises; the company's plans for expansion, in terms of both projected franchises and an expanded product line; the total cost of the franchise and how it will be financed; the financial and legal stability of the parent company; and the support services the franchiser offers in terms of marketing, training, consultants, service departments, and field support. You should also be sure that the following details are covered in the written franchise contract: franchise fee, termination, selling and renewal, advertising and promotion, patent and liability protection, home-office services, commissions and royalties, training (initial and continued), financing, territory, and exclusive versus nonexclusive rights. Also, check the terms under which the franchiser can revoke your contract or fail to renew the agreement.

In figuring the total franchise cost, be sure to include not only the purchase cost for the franchise but also the amount of money you think you will need during the first year for start-up and operation. You should be sure you understand what is included in the franchiser's stated initial fees. This may include just the cost of the franchise fee, and you may have to pay fees for services, inventory, equipment, and real estate on top of that.

The kinds of franchises that you can buy are almost endless, ranging from the woman-owned firm of Rent-a-Yenta, which is an international service franchise offering to do anything that is "legal and kind" for clients, to hamburger and donut shops and diet workshops. Prices can vary from several thousand to hundreds of thousands of dollars. The International Franchise Association has more than 150 members, and their membership list is a good source for finding franchise opportunities. Write to International Franchise Association, 1025 Connecticut Avenue NW, Washington, D.C. 20036. The United States Department of Commerce also publishes *Franchise Opportunities Handbook,* which is available through the many libraries or through the United States Government Printing Office, Washington, D.C. 20402.

DECIDING WHAT TYPE OF PLAYER YOU WANT TO BE

Once you have decided the game or business you want to play and how you want to enter the game, the last step is deciding what type of player you want to be. There are basically three types of players in any business game: sole proprietorships, partnerships, and corporations. Sole proprietorships are by far the most common, especially among women. The Census Bureau's 1972 *Survey of Women-Owned Businesses* found that 98 percent of the firms owned by women were sole proprietorships. Although the pattern was different among the women who responded to the Task Force survey, this was still the predominant form of business organization. Almost one half (49 percent) of the firms were sole proprietorships, whereas 28 percent indicated they were partnerships and 25 percent were corporations. The main reason sole proprietorships are popular is because this type of organization is not only the least expensive but also the easiest form of business to choose. Usually all you need is an occupational license and an employer's identification number for tax purposes to start business.

It is often wiser to start out as a sole proprietorship or partnership and move to a corporation when the business conditions in your firm indicate that this way would be the most beneficial. Whatever you do, be sure and get the advice of a competent legal adviser. Attorneys point out that it is a lot easier and less expensive to get legal advice before you make a mistake than to pay the cost of litigation to get you out of a mistake. Although there are books on the market that will tell you how to incorporate your business by yourself, such action can be risky. As one attorney put it, "If I needed surgery, I sure wouldn't try to become a doctor. I'd go to one."

A consideration that will influence the type of business organization you choose is whether you want to share the responsibility of running a business with someone else. However, this reason is not the best for choosing a partnership. There should be only two reasons to form a partnership. The first and most important is if you think the other person can bring a talent or skill to the business that will broaden your own. The second is if you think that you will work better as a team, rather than alone. The importance of picking the right partner will be discussed in the next chapter (4), "Building Your Entrepreneurial Team."

What type of business organization is best for you will depend on the specifics of your business. Every business situation is different, and the type of organization best for you should be decided only in consultation with an attorney. The decision should be based on five factors: how the business organization will affect the *control* of the business, the ability to raise capital (the *financial* factor), the personal *liability* of the owners, *taxes*, and the *continuity* of the business in the event of death or disability of the owners.

THE CONTROL FACTOR.   In general, a sole proprietorship is the best form if you want absolute authority over all business decisions. In a partnership, control of the business is shared with your partners, and you and your partners may not always agree. In addition, you are legally responsible for both your partners' personal and business actions—an important factor many people overlook. Control in a corporation will depend on your stock ownership. If you own 51 percent of the stock, you will be able to control policy decisions, though this control will be exercised through regular board of directors' meetings and annual stockholders' meetings. Although small, closely held corporations can operate more informally than large corporations, recordkeeping cannot be eliminated entirely, and you must be able to document decisions made by the board of directors. It is also important to remember that officers of a corporation are liable to stockholders for improper actions.

THE FINANCIAL FACTOR.   It is sometimes easier to raise capital with a corporation than with a partnership, since a corporation can theoretically sell stock to raise capital. In addition, there is a special tax incentive to outside investors of small businesses that allows an investor in a business with five initial investors to deduct his or her losses directly from income, rather than having the losses offset capital gains, if the business fails. Generally, however, the major market for stock in small corporations is through friends and relatives, rather than the public at large. A private offering in which you approach no more than thirty-five people does not have to be registered with the Securities and Exchange Commission (SEC), but a public offering must be registered. This can be an expensive and time-consuming matter.

In a sole proprietorship or partnership, your ability to raise capital is limited to your personal assets, the soundness of your business venture, and the personal and financial reputations of the proprietor or partners. You can bring in *limited* partners, however, in order to raise money. These partners do not have the same rights and responsibilities as the general partners and are only liable if the firm has debts for the amount of money that they put into the firm. Nevertheless, limited partners do have some rights in your firm, such as the ability to find fault with your management of the firm.

Sole proprietors seeking investment money should not overlook the option of a joint-venture arrangement, as is frequently used for Broadway productions. Under such an arrangement, one person may contribute the play, another the money for the production, and another the expertise to put the play on. The specifics of joint-venture arrangements will vary with each business deal, but all will agree among themselves as to how they will split the profits and the arrangement will be valid only for the specific business transaction.

THE LIABILITY FACTOR.   The liability factor is one of the major reasons that many new businesses choose to incorporate. A corporation is an entity created by the state with a life of its own, independent of its stockholders. It offers limited liability to investors in that only the amount of money invested can be lost. Creditors of the corporation cannot reach your personal assets for corporate debts, unless you have agreēd to use these personal assets to secure business loans.

Many people select the corporate route because of the liability factor, since in a sole proprietorship all personal assets are available to creditors to satisfy claims against you. The added danger in partnerships is that you are also responsible for your partners' debts. If you have more money than your partner, you may have to bear the brunt of the business debts even though the partnership agreement says that you split debts fifty-fifty because your written partnership agreement cannot bind third parties. Ultimately you may be liable for all debts if your partner defaults. However, choosing to form a corporation solely for the liability reason is not always the right move to make.

Helen E. Marmoll, an Arlington, Virginia, attorney who owns a firm specializing in tax law and has many small business clients, feels that people can make a mistake by rushing into a corporation too soon. "You can always switch from a sole proprietorship to a corporation, but dismantling a corporation can be a lengthy and expensive task." Corporations, like marriages, are easy to get into but hard to get out of.

Marmoll points out that many people choose to incorporate to protect their personal assets from business liabilities. This reason can, however, prove to be a hollow one, since most lenders will nevertheless require you either to secure a loan with both a personal signature and personal assets, such as a house or car—at the least—or to sign personally on the loan without using specific personal assets. The corporation itself has to be well established, with sufficient assets on which a lender can draw for repayment of the debt, before such personal commitments are waived.

Regarding liability, there are many things you need to look out for if you are married. For example, in a sole proprietorship, your spouse may be liable for your business. If you borrow money from your spouse, he may have a legal claim for an equity interest, rather than a debtor's interest, in your business if there is a divorce and you do not have documentation of the loan. In some states it may be a disadvantage to locate your business in your home if you are married, since the profits may be assessed as part of the husband's income. It is also a good idea for a married woman to secure a written agreement regarding the distribution of the profits and ownership of the business if any part of her funding involves property owned solely by or jointly with her husband. This might prove necessary even if it is only that part of the collateral for a loan that includes a second mortgage on a jointly owned house. Such an agreement would prove her claim to the business and its profits in case of her husband's death or a divorce.

THE TAX FACTOR. Taxes are a critical factor in deciding what type of business organization you need. For this reason, you should be sure that the attorney you pick has a sound base in tax law. If cash is the lifeblood of your company and the area in which you will experience the most painful problems, taxes are the leech that can kill you unless you have competent advice on how to structure your business to get the maximum advantage from existing tax laws.

Marjorie O'Connell Amey—owner of O'Connell Amey and Associates, a Washington, D.C. firm that specializes in tax law—points out that many of the provisions in the tax code were written specifically to encourage business enterprises, and a new and budding owner to take advantage of these rules and regulations.

Taxes are one of the reasons many businesses start out as a sole proprietorship. Corporate earnings are taxed twice—once as corporate profit and again when the profit is paid out in dividends to investors. On the other hand, earnings of partnerships and sole proprietorships are simply treated as the individual's taxable income. However, forming a Subchapter S corporation is one way to get around this double taxation. Under Subchapter S, the corporation does not pay corporate tax on its income; instead, the stockholders pay taxes on it, even if the profit is not physically distributed.

If you are a Subchapter S corporation, you are taxed in the same way as a sole proprietorship or partnership. To qualify as a Subchapter S corporation, you must meet the following requirements:

- Have individual shareholders
- Have no more than ten shareholders
- Have no shareholders who are nonresident aliens
- Have only one class of stock
- Have not more than 80 percent of gross receipts from outside the United States
- Have not more than 20 percent of the corporation's gross receipts from royalties, rents, dividends, interest, annuities, and gains on sales or exchange of stock or securities

As a straight corporation, profits are taxed at corporate rates, which graduate from 17 percent for the first $25,000 net profit, 20 percent for income between $25,001 and $50,000, 30 percent for net profit between $50,001 and $75,000, 40 percent for net profit between $75,001 and $100,000, and 46 percent for all profit over $100,000. Salaries of officers are deductible expenses and therefore reduce corporate profit subject to income tax. However, salaries of officers are also subject to individual income tax. If salaries become too high, the Internal Revenue Service (IRS) may treat the excess as a dividend, resulting in double taxation because the same money is taxed both as part of corporate profits and as individual income.

If you own a sole proprietorship or partnership, all net income is taxable according to each person's share of ownership, and your tax rate depends on your income bracket. You may be able to deduct from your gross income some personal expenses that are directly related to your business, such as business use of your personal car or home. You should check with the IRS regarding current regulations and with an attorney, particularly if you are married.

THE CONTINUITY FACTOR.   The last factor you should consider in drawing up any kind of business organization agreement is what will happen to the business in the event of your, or one of the key partner's or stockholder's, death or disability. Corporations, which are a separate legal entity, are not affected by the death or disability of shareholders in the same way a sole proprietorship or partnership is affected. In the case of a corporation, shares of stock can be sold if one owner wants to leave the business, and in the event of a shareholder's death, the stock goes to the heirs. Shares in a partnership cannot be sold without the consent of the partners; if either a partner or a sole proprietor dies, the business dissolves and the heirs inherit the assets of the business.

This aspect of planning for the future of the business in the event of death or disability is one of the most frequently overlooked but one of the most serious aspects of business planning. Karen Olsen, who owns her own business as an insurance broker in New York City, points out that it is not unusual for an owner to be forced to liquidate a growing company if a partner dies because the partners failed to make provisions for the continuation of the business in the event of death. Even those partners who have the foresight to draw up agreements that will give the surviving partner the right to buy the partner's shares from the heirs often find themselves in a bind because they didn't take out life insurance, which would have provided the money necessary for carrying out the agreement.

Olsen advises that you think carefully about whether you really want your partner's spouse or child as your new partner in the event of death or disability. If not, your best bet is to draw up a partnership agreement that will give you the right to purchase your partner's interest in the business for cash and then to have either you or the business take out insurance on all partners' lives so that you will have the cash available to execute your agreement. You should also be sure that this insurance is continually upgraded to cover the value of the partners' shares as the firm grows. Thus, the cash value of the insurance will actually cover the cost of purchasing the shares in the event of death.

THE PLAYING REGULATIONS

It is not as easy to enter the entrepreneurial game as it was in the olden days. The days when all you had to do was hang out a shingle, sit back, and wait for the customers to beat a path to your door went out with the horse and buggy. Today, federal, state, and local governments impose requirements on a new business person. The major types of federal and state regulations revolve around making sure that you are meeting your employee and tax obligations and are not violating fair trade practices. In other words, they govern those three basic resources you have to manage daily—money, manpower, and markets—and their specific regulations will be discussed in the chapters dealing with these resources. However, there are some regulations you should be aware of before you open shop: You are properly licensed to do business in your location; you are complying with all local ordinances for your industry; you are operating under a name that has not been taken previously; and you have registered with the IRS for your employer identification number. This latter regulation is one that many business owners who begin their operations as free-lance or part-time sole proprietors working out of their homes often overlook. Although once you have employees you are made painfully aware of federal requirements, many sole proprietors do not realize that getting your employer identification number has its advantages.

Marjorie O'Connell Amey, a tax attorney, points out that getting this identification number early can be important in allowing you to deduct many of the start-up costs of your business by putting the date you began your business on record with the IRS. It is simple to file, like a social security number. Even if you decide not to carry through with your plans, you will not be required to file any other forms or notifications.

Your state's department of commerce and local city hall are the best sources of information about licensing requirements. Licensing is required for many businesses, such as restaurants, public vehicles, and other types of public vendors, but not all businesses must be licensed. Some of these licenses require fees, examinations, and specific renewal requirements for protection of the public. Others merely help the local authorities keep track of the businesses in operation. In addition to licenses, you may have to file additional papers with your local government. The extent of these legal requirements will vary with both the state you live in and the form of business organization you choose. Although meeting the legal requirements for a corporation requires an attorney, those involved in establishing a sole proprietorship or partnership are usually minimal. Unless you plan to do business under a trade or service name, rather than your own name, there is usually no formal requirement for sole proprietorships or partnerships other than obtaining the appropriate licensing and registering the business or partnership with the county clerk.

If you use a trade name for your business, you must conduct a name search to be sure that the name is not already in use, and you must then file a "certificate of doing business under an assumed name" with your county courthouse, so that there is an official record of the proprietors. Some states will assist, or even conduct, the name search for you for free. If you produce a product, you must also make sure there is not a trade name or service mark that has already been taken. Owners often overlook the importance of conducting this name search and then find that the money invested in advertising to create a public awareness of that firm's existence is wasted when they are forced to withdraw the product name from the marketplace because it is a part of the name that belongs to someone else.

Pansy Essman, the inventor and manufacturer of a unique baby bathing device, found out that even with a name search you may not be able to use the name you choose if another company wants to take issue with it and insists you drop the name, as did Procter & Gamble when Pansy called her infant bathing pillow "Pamperette." Procter & Gamble had trademarked the name Pamper for disposable diapers and would not let anyone use Pamper in any part of a product name, even though the products were unrelated. Essman found herself faced with the dilemma of having to change the name of her product when Procter & Gamble asked the patent office to rescind their decision to allow her to use the name Pamperette. The company stated that it spent millions of dollars each year on advertising the name Pamper. The name Pamperette was disallowed to Essman, causing her delays and loss of money spent on printed bags and advertising.

Essman then used her own name and called her product Pansy-Ette. Unlike most people who figuratively dream of being a business owner, Essman never thought of going into business for herself. Yet it was a real-life dream that put her into business.

> The product I produce came from a dream and an experience I had trying to bathe my new granddaughter, Letha, who was extremely difficult at bath time when I put her into the cold hard tub. For some reason, my own babies didn't present the problem Letha did. However, this baby was different; she disliked her bath. I thought that there must be a better way to bathe babies. It worried me. That night, I went to bed and dreamed of the product I now produce. It is a sponge bathing pillow with a cavity cut in it to hold the baby, while it is being bathed, in a comfortable reclining position, leaving mother with two free hands for the washing process.

Essman, a grandmother with an eighth-grade education, worked in the electronic industry for some twenty years. She is a classic example that age or education is no barrier when you have a viable idea that fills a need. "Once you have found a good product, then you need a combination of self-reliance, common sense, enthusiasm, positive mental attitude, and a sense of humor to step out in front and say I will do it."

Convinced her product was needed, Essman worked hard to make her dream a reality. Essman wrote to the companies who manufactured the kind of sponge material she needed and they sent her samples for experimental purposes. Her next problem was figuring out how to cut the cavity she wanted in the soft sponge material. She solved the cutting problem in another dream, and she then built the necessary machinery for production, which she began in an old chicken coop in back of her mother's house. Essman now has fourteen employees, produces thousands of bathing aids and toys a year, has a factory space of 25,000 square feet, and distributes her products nationally to stores ranging in size from department stores to grocery stores. She is diversifying her product line to include sponge toys and an adult-size bathing aid. Pansy Ellen Products, Inc., is proof that it is never too late to start a business.

CHAPTER 4

Building Your Entrepreneurial Team

Business is a team, not an individual, sport. No one can win at the entrepreneurial game without a good team, yet many people forget to consider this factor. Unfortunately, the strong individualistic characteristics that lead a person to start a business may hamper her or his ability to build a business. Although the entrepreneurial spirit is needed for start-up, team building and leadership skills are needed for growth.

Although the entrepreneurial game may be lonely, you should not try to play it alone. You will find that the ability to build an effective entrepreneurial team that adds needed business skills and understands your business goals will be a key to your success. Thus, the next move in the entrepreneurial game—building your playing team—is critical. However, people often leave it to the forces of fate, friendship, or accidents of timing or geography.

No one, not even the best entrepreneur, has the capability to play all positions necessary in the entrepreneurial game. Just as someone whose talent is in passing a ball may not be good at tackling, every entrepreneurial player will possess strengths in one area and weaknesses in another. You will therefore need other players to help you win. The major components of your entrepreneurial team will be your employees—which will be discussed in chapter 7, "Staffing Your Organization"—and your partners, advisers, and business colleagues. It does not matter where your players come from; what does matter is that they bring skills to your team that you do not possess.

Building a good entrepreneurial team requires a look at the requirements for success in your business and deciding whether you think you can fulfill all of these requirements alone. You must take a hard look not only at your capabilities but also at your limitations. Although this process can be painful to the ego, you should do it before you go any further in your business game. Brian Haslett of Venture Founders points out that the persons who think they

79

can do everything without admitting their own limitations usually bite off more than they can chew and fall flat on their faces in business.

Having only the strong individualistic characteristics of an entrepreneurial personality is not enough to ensure success. To be successful in a new venture, you should also have some experience in at least one of the functional areas of management (such as marketing or finance) and also in the line of business in which you are going. If you are a person who has all of these prerequisites for success, you are lucky. However, if you are missing some of them, you should not despair. The best way to fill these gaps in your business game is to find players—as employees, partners, or advisers—who will make up for the areas in which you are the weakest.

Finding these gaps in your business game takes asking yourself some hard questions. The first question you should ask yourself is, What skills are needed to make the business succeed and are these skills related to marketing or to production? The second question is, Do you have all the skills needed and sufficient time to perform all those skills? And the third question is, What do you want to do most in the organization? For example, are you a people or a numbers person? Do you like to market your product or do the administrative part of the business? Once you have identified what is needed for the long-term success of the business, what skills you bring to the business, and what you like to do, you are in a much better position to decide how to close any gaps in your business game.

The strategy you choose to close the gaps will depend largely on how critical the skills are to the firm's success, how much time you need them for, and how much money you have. For example, your periodic needs for accounting and bookkeeping may be met by hiring from outside your organization. However, certain skills deemed prerequisites for success, yet for which you do not have the money to hire, may call for finding a partner or offering an employee stock options in the firm. Moves such as these can only be measured by an assessment of how critical that person's talents are to the organization and how much they will increase your business. Unless you are going the partnership route, it is often best to offer employee stock options as a condition of employment only if the relationship works out and business results can be tied to employee performance.

THE FIRST STRING: PARTNERS

Many people are willing to take the plunge into business ownership only with a partner. It is undoubtedly scary to open a business, as the responsibility is awesome. You may think that it would be easier if you had someone to go into it with you. It's a little like the old saying that you really don't mind dying—you just wish you didn't have to do it alone. However, if this is your thinking and your main reason for choosing a partner, you should think twice.

Partnerships are a hard thing to make work, particularly if the partners are picked for the wrong reasons or if they go into a business with different expectations. Although you may think that you will work better as a part of a team, you should look carefully at the person you are counting on to carry half the load before you leap into a partnership. The best person to choose is someone who can bring a skill to the business you need, who has the same work values and goals for the business, and whom you have seen in a work situation but with whom you are not good friends. This advice was given by women who have seen good and bad partnerships.

Joyce Huber, co-owner of Georgetown Employment Service in Washington, D.C., knows about partnerships that don't work. Although Huber currently has a new partner, her first partnership did not last. She can attest to the fact that partnerships, like marriages, require a lot of work to keep together and are sometimes not what you thought they would be at first blush. Getting out of them can be difficult, painful, and disillusioning. "It is a very, very difficult thing to get out of a partnership. It certainly can be equated to a marriage. I was very close to my first partner and had a very close friendship with her." Huber started her business with a $250 investment as a part-time venture with a friend. Both had held several jobs and knew that they wanted to be their own boss. "I didn't know anything else about what I wanted to do, but I knew that there was no room for an employer in my future."

Huber and her friend came up with the idea of starting an employment agency partially because a typewriter, desk, telephone, and license were all that was required and partially because they knew that there was a market need. Their own experiences had taught them that there were very few employment agencies in the city that had a reputation for really caring about placing employees in jobs that they would like. "I had gotten my second job in Washington through an employment agency where the counselor called me 'honey' every other word and had broken fingernails that were taped together with Scotch tape to make them appear long. Although neither my partner nor I had graduated from college, we were going to school at night. We thought that there should be an employment agency that would help people who really wanted to have better jobs and would listen to people and try to find them jobs that fit their career needs."

Although they opened the agency on a part-time basis, operating it on their lunch hour while they both kept their other jobs, business was so good that they paid back their $250 loan in the first month. Huber quit her job three months later, and the other partner joined the agency soon after. Today, twelve years later, the firm has two locations, a new secretarial college, plus a third agency and grosses about a half million dollars a year.

Huber feels the personal problems of friends affect both the personal relationship and the business. "I would say that the most difficult years for Georgetown Employment Service were when the owners were having personal problems—and I don't mean marital problems, I mean self-identity problems. Problems with exactly where you wanted to be five years from then at age thirty, thirty-five, forty, and so on. Those kinds of discussions took away from the business tremendously. Those were the years in which we were indecisive about how professional we wanted to be and how serious." Huber now believes that any woman who wants to succeed in business must be committed to it 100 percent—a decision she made.

Huber is also a firm believer in the fact that you should choose someone as a partner who will bring skills that complement yours and whom you have seen in action. "It helps if you've seen them under pressure; how they solve a problem; how they handle criticism; how they manage their household; and how they feel about money. You could find a partner who in every area would be wonderful; but if she doesn't really care that much about money because her family or husband has it, it could be very damaging to business."

Carla Massoni, Huber's second and current partner, feels that after having gained the confidence to run a business, she might not choose the partnership route if she were to start another business; she now feels she knows enough to go it alone. However, she points out that having two people to share the responsibility can be a boon, in terms of energy, support, and comaraderie. "I think the thing that I would miss if I didn't have a partner would be that comraderie and having another person to back you up and give you the sense that you are equals. It's hard to bounce an idea off employees because there is a subtle tendency for them to agree with you."

Beverly Jackson—co-owner of a public relations and advertising management consulting firm, Jackson/Summers Associates, with Sheila Summers—expresses similar sentiments. She sought out a partner because she realized that she had no desire to be the type of sole proprietor who was a slave to the business, never being able to take a vacation or to be away from the business. She also knew that a partner could alleviate some of the day-to-day pressure of the work load without having to hire an employee. She first hired Sheila Summers as a subcontractor on several projects, and the relationship later grew into a full partnership. "It got to the point where Sheila was putting in forty hours a week, almost a full-time job. She was picking up a lot of experience in public relations, and it became clear that there was enough business to justify really looking forward to a company with a future. We just continued to work along the lines we were, but as partners."

Jackson and Summers admit that they were very lucky that their partnership worked out. They did two things that they would never counsel another woman to do: Enter an arrangement without a formal partnership agreement and go into business with a friend. They feel the reason the arrangement has worked out well is because they fill the gaps in each other's skills, experience, and personalities.

Sarah Kovner and Barbara Handman used their volunteer experience in political campaigns to start a business called Arts, Letters, and Politics in New York City. They had worked with each other enough before to know that their partnership would be a success. However, they feel the key to their success is the fact that they both have similar work ethics and goals. They point out that it is hard to keep a partnership going if one of the partners defines work as a nine-to-five day, while the other believes that it means working until the task is done. They also feel that their partnership's success was further aided by their both having good marriages, since both take understanding and compromise.

Kovner and Handman started their business when they got tired and angry because they were having to take money out of their cookie jars to pay for the expenses incurred doing volunteer political work, whereas a lot of other people were either being paid or were being supported by their businesses. Starting with a minimum investment out of Handman's apartment, they began to offer for a fee what they had formerly been doing for free: public relations and campaign organization for political candidates and nonprofit organizations. Their reputation in political camps led to a steady stream of clients and an office in downtown Manhattan.

Denise Cavanaugh also believes that compatible work values are important. When Cavanaugh met her future partner, Dottie Bruce Cook, they had a three-hour conversation and discovered they had compatible values even though they had very different skills. Cavanaugh had a community and organization development background, and Cook had a background in the personnel business. Cavanaugh explains that they got together again and wrote a twenty-page paper outlining what they could sell, whom they could sell it to, and how much they would charge. That was the start of Cook/Cavanaugh Associates, a consulting firm that does organizational diagnosis and establishes mechanisms to facilitate change. The firm works with organizations to diagnose problems and arrive at solutions in terms of their group process, conflict resolution, staff turnover, and other tensions that organizations may experience. "The twenty-page paper was a way for us to organize our values about work and what we thought organization life should be like."

Virginia Mapel and Lynn Barnard are examples of another ingredient needed to make a partnership work: mutual respect and the ability to let the other person carry out her or his role without interference. For Mapel and Barnard, this ability is complicated by the fact that they are a rare mother-and-daughter business in an environment where father-and-son is the norm. Mapel and Barnard own Gazebo, a retail store in New York City that specializes in home decorating items and art. The store, which is overflowing with silk flowers, quilts, needlecraft pillows, and wicker furniture, has been called the prettiest store in America by a Japanese publication.

But silk flowers and homemade crafts were not always Gazebo's markets. The store is a good example of how a business problem can become an opportunity. Originally, Mapel and Barnard had operated a traditional flower shop, which only carried a small line of silk flower arrangements. However, during the gas crisis their delivery truck had such difficulty getting gas and making deliveries before the flowers died that they decided to drop the fresh flower line and concentrate on the silk flower arrangements and mountain crafts—items that had always been a small but profitable sector of their sales. This move proved to be a boon to the business.

Both Mapel and Barnard think a mother-and-daughter relationship brings an even more complicated dimension to the partnership than the father-and-son norm. A customer—Nancy Friday, author of *My Mother; Myself*—was amazed to find that a mother-daughter business team could work. (Friday's book deals with the complexity of the mother-daughter relationship.) Mapel and Barnard attribute their success to the fact that they have a great deal of respect for each other as individuals, and can transcend their familial roles in the business relationship. In the daughter's view: "Of course you have to sacrifice the perfect mother-daughter relationship for the business relationship. You can no longer go to your mother for the kind of emotional support that you might normally do if you were not sharing your business lives." And the mother's side: "A mother has to learn not to consider herself superior to her daughter. She has to learn to deal as woman to woman, not mother to daughter, and let her handle her side of the partnership."

No matter how well you know someone, you still need a partnership agreement which spells out in advance how you will share management duties and responsibilities, arbitrate differences, and dissolve the partnership if necessary. Such agreements are required when you incorporate, but are often overlooked in starting a partnership. According to Joyce Huber of Georgetown Employment Service: "I think too many women make the mistake of saying, 'I trust her; I'm sensitive to her; I care about her. If we have a problem, we can settle it.' They think that if they have to put it down on paper, there must be something wrong; and they later learn that a written statement could have protected both of them." Huber points out that a partnership agreement is just a form of protection and does not imply that you don't trust the other person. "A lot of people make the mistake of not drawing up an agreement from the beginning." This won't work unless you are very unusual. It's just human nature to forget about it until the weather gets rough. Then it is usually too late to sit back rationally and think about the things you should have thought of when both partners were objective and optimistic about the business.

Helen E. Marmoll, a tax attorney who owns her own firm in Arlington, Virginia, has helped in numerous business start-ups. She feels that a formal agreement is the key to a good partnership. This agreement should try to iron out in advance what the financial, operating, and separation rules of your business will be; what you are going to do with the money; who is going to be the boss of what; and how differences will be settled. Marmoll also advises that the agreement should be drafted carefully to allow the partners to take advantage of the various factors in the tax code, so that no one loses in any decision to dissolve the partnership. "You don't want the partnership agreement drafted in such a manner that it is disadvantageous tax-wise and therefore impossible to admit that they [the partners] are at a point of irreconcilable difference." She believes that one of the goals behind a partnership agreement should be to make the decision to dissolve the partnership a financial decision and one based on common sense, rather than on emotional grounds.

THE SECOND STRING: ADVISERS

As no one can know everything that you will need to know in business, the use of advisers is crucial. One woman responding to the American Management Associations study of women entrepreneurs pointed out that advisers can help fill the gaps in business knowledge left by our upbringing. Thus, having competent advisers at your beck and call will be a significant part of your entrepreneurial team. Jean Reid, who once screened and counseled women for admittance to the American Women's Economic Development Corporation program, thinks that women need to learn this important rule of the entrepreneurial game. "We find that women tend to overlook this area. They either think that they can do it themselves, or they buy too cheap. They don't realize that it is a little like trying to be your own doctor, and just about as dangerous." This advice is particularly true in the case of accountants and lawyers. You should obtain good professional counsel in these areas, early on.

Patty Bissell—owner of Patricia Bissell and Associates, a certified public accounting (CPA) firm in Rockville, Maryland—has helped hundreds of women business owners start their own businesses. "I always say that if someone can't afford a CPA or a lawyer, then they can't afford to be in business. It is so critical. My most successful clients are the ones who have come in to see me before they started business, not three months down the line. We can tell you what to look out for so that you don't get hit unexpectedly and end up behind the eight ball." Coming to an accountant early can also be less costly in the long run. As Bissell puts it, trying to clean up a mess rings up accounting fees faster than starting off right with a clean slate.

Attorneys also believe that the time to see them is before starting a business. The job of a good lawyer is not to argue your case before a court of law but to keep you out of court. Don't make the mistake of thinking lawyers are needed only when you are in trouble, or in case of emergencies.

Suzanne Ives—owner of Ives and Associates, a public relations firm—points out that her CPA has been a valuable asset in all of her money matters.

> I have a very bad attitude about money. I am learning from my CPA how to manage the dollars that come in and how to work out your debt schedules so that you use money to your advantage. Basically, when bills come in I want to pay them all off at once. This isn't always wise. My CPA has also advised me on when and how to give raises. I made the mistake in the beginning of being too generous. I wanted to pay all my people a lot of money and I wanted to give them raises frequently. My CPA has made me realize that frequent raises make people expect them, and if your business falls off for a moment, you're in a bind.

However, just having competent advisers at your beck and call is not enough. You need to use these advisers effectively so that they will become true members of your entrepreneurial team, even if they are not full-time players. You need not only to seek and get adequate advice but also to know what this advice means and how to use it. Too many business owners make the mistake of thinking that hiring a legal or financial adviser is the same as hiring away a problem, and women seem especially prone to fall into this trap. Virginia Maynard of First Women's Bank in New York City sees women who are really the backbone of the business but who know nothing about the financial aspects of their business. "They turn all the financial aspects over to a male partner or an accountant, without developing an understanding for what it means."

Mary Vinton represents a success story par excellence, but she could have been a failure had she not eventually become aware of difficulties caused by her lack of financial knowledge. Vinton bought a sandal-making business for $40 in the flower-child era of the 1960s and turned it into a $4.5-million business called Georgetown Leather Design, which now has six branches in the Washington, D.C., metropolitan area. She attributes the most serious problems she faced in her business to neglecting financial planning and not being aware that the employee acting as controller was not throwing up red flags about potential financial problems along the way. "We were expanding, and of course this takes a great deal of capital, and we had not done adequate capital planning for the expansion. So there we were with a beautiful new store, but no money to pay any of our bills. We got very deeply into the situation before I even had any recognition of what was happening."

Ava Stern, publisher of *Enterprising Women*, also feels a lot of women make similar mistakes regarding financial matters. "For some reason, it seems to be easy for women to fall into a child-parent, rather than client-adviser, relationship with accountants and attorneys, particularly if the adviser is male. This can make us tend to shift the decision making onto the adviser, rather than just use the information for our own decisions. We forget that the adviser is working for us and that we are the bosses." The best way to avoid this problem is to remember that although you may hire advisers for their expertise, at least half of their job is to translate this experience in a way you can understand and use to make decisions. You don't need to *be* an accountant, or a lawyer; you just have to know enough to ask questions, understand what the experts are talking about, and use this information to make some wise business judgments.

You will find that good advisers are well worth their investment. They not only provide you with their professional skills and their accumulated business knowledge, but they also can be good sounding boards for business ideas. They enable you to spend your time building a growing business without diverting or fragmenting your energy into something someone else can do better and less expensively than you can.

Finding Advisers

The best way to find the two kinds of advisers you will need for your entrepreneurial team—accountants and attorneys—is through referrals. Your banker, trade association, and other accountants and attorneys are all good sources for referrals. Your local CPA or bar association can also provide you with names. For attorneys, you can consult *Martindale-Hubbell Law Directory*, a directory of attorneys that both rates and describes their services.

But just as you take the time to interview employees before you hire them for your business team, you should take the same strategy with advisers to ensure that you will work well together. The key to developing a good professional relationship is to find someone familiar with small businesses or businesses similar to yours and someone with whom you feel comfortable. You will want to develop an open and trusting relationship with your advisers. You should ask prospective advisers about their education, the type of clients they handle, the type of businesses they deal with, and their working procedures and rates.

You should also make sure that the person you are contemplating hiring does not harbor any latent difficulties in dealing with women. Women participating in the focus groups that the American Management Associations held as part of the Task Force study indicated that it is easy to run up against condescending bankers, lawyers, and accountants—particularly men—who are not used to the idea of women owning enterprises. Handling this can be tricky, but if you spell out expectations clearly in the beginning, maintain authority without being patronizing, and let the person know that her or his time has been bought and they are being tested as to how they can best serve you, you should be able to develop a good relationship. However, avoid at all costs anyone whom you feel is dealing with you in an overly simplistic, paternalistic manner, anyone who does not take your business problems seriously, or anyone who seems to resent your position. These attitudes can only spell disaster in any client-adviser relationship.

Most attorneys and accountants will talk to a prospective client without charging them prior to a formal engagement. They will then send an engagement letter to you outlining what they can provide and what they will charge for such services. A CPA's engagement letter usually will tell you exactly what they will and won't do, what services are covered, and what services are not covered. It will also usually state the maximum and minimum of service that they anticipate providing you for the next twelve months. If you come back to them for things not included in the original engagement letter, they will draw up a new estimate, which must be agreed to before the work begins for new services. Attorneys' engagement letters are usually more general and are sent to formalize the understanding. They may state the hourly rate charged or, if you ask them to do certain specific tasks, they may provide a "not to exceed" cost estimate for such tasks.

Marjorie O'Connell Amey, owner of a Washington, D.C., law firm, points out that it is unfortunate that a great deal of the owners' legal expenses occur when they are starting to organize their businesses, when cash is crucial; this factor may keep owners from seeking the kind of legal advice they need. Amey advises women to be aware that lawyers are as anxious to develop a good, ongoing relationship with a growing business as anyone else, and they often work out an arrangement that will allow an owner to schedule the payments for the legal services over a period of time, particularly if they think the owner will consistently use legal advice and will budget such advice into her or his business projections.

The key, according to Amey, is to find someone who is interested in your business and who, though a part-time adviser, will be a real part of your business team. Finding the appropriate adviser is therefore only half the game. The other half is developing with this person a good working relationship, which you can do if you follow three basic rules: (1) Bring up potential problems immediately, and not at the point when they have become emergencies; (2) pay your bills promptly and keep your appointments, remembering that time is money for professionals and that they have to make a living too; and (3) be absolutely honest and don't hold back any facts, as such action just makes the adviser's job more difficult and decreases your credibility. However, the third rule can be a difficult one for entrepreneurs, who traditionally like to play their cards close to their chests. Mary Vinton of Georgetown Leather Design says that when she first hired an accountant to help, she went through an emotional tug of war. "I'd ask myself, how much do I hand over to them? How much don't I hand over? How would I evaluate their capabilities because at some point it got beyond my knowledge without knowing accounting." But she now knows that having competent advisers as part of your team is critical to survival, especially as you begin to grow.

Your Financial Advisers

A good CPA will be your key financial adviser. CPAs can not only set up your books and recordkeeping system, but they can advise you on cash requirements, budget forecasts, borrowing, business organizations, licensing requirements, and taxes. They can also help you develop the financial statements you will need to attract financing and can advise about whether you should seek short-term or long-term funds. In many cases, they can even help you find financing since they work with banks and have existing relationships. Finally, she or he can raise red flags over danger spots.

Patty Bissell feels that many banks tend to listen more to a client who comes from a CPA, as the accountants wouldn't send them if they thought they were a really bad risk. She also points out that accountants traditionally have years of experience dealing with other people's businesses that can be useful to a new business. "A good CPA can usually look at a client and say, 'Hey, you have a good idea, but you are in the wrong location' or advise them to develop a better marketing plan to get their product to the customer." For example, Bissell once matched a client who was having marketing problems with another client who did direct mail advertising. "It sounds like simple advice, but the client called back to say that it had worked and they were having more business than they could handle."

Although the fees of a CPA may be a little higher than those of a noncertified accountant or bookkeeper, the range of services offered is much broader. The differences between CPAs, accountants, and bookkeepers is that

CPAs must have a business degree from an accredited university as well as a certain minimum number of hours in accounting. They must also pass a test for licensing and are governed by state regulations and the ethics of their professional association. Most CPA firms have departments in accounting, auditing, tax, and management assistance. Accountants, on the other hand, are not licensed, although they normally have an accounting degree but have not completed as much course work as have CPAs. Bookkeepers are schooled in posting ledgers and drawing up financial statements but are not usually educated in analyzing these statements for the purpose of providing business advice.

The basic services that you should seek from a CPA are assistance in getting your federal and state withholding numbers, instructions on where and when to file tax returns, and the design of a bookkeeping system. A good CPA will suggest that she or he monitor these systems for the first few months to make sure that you are keeping your records properly. It is a good idea to get semiannual financial statements, at least in the first two years of business. Quarterly statements are best but expensive. Patty Bissell notes that although some business people seem to operate out of their hip pockets and know their financial condition exactly, this practice can be dangerous for a novice. "Having and using up-to-date full financial statements, not just cash statements, is so critical. People think that they are doing well because they see money coming in, but two months later when a bill comes in, they may find that the cash isn't there."

Two areas where your CPA will also be of assistance to you are in capital and tax planning. In capital planning, the accountant will help you see how your business projections will impact your need for capital. This function includes helping you assess your probability of inventory requirements, outstanding receivables and payables, and develop a cash-flow plan and a strategy for finding the required capital.

Tax planning involves helping you assess your tax obligations and deductions and when you should pay your taxes. Your accountant can advise you whether certain business decisions will give you any tax advantages and at what point it becomes advantageous for you to switch from a sole proprietorship to a corporation for tax reasons. However, it is important to remember that although your accountant can advise you on many tax matters, some matters will require the advice of an attorney. You should learn when to draw the line between the advice of your accountant and that of your attorney.

Your Legal Advisers

The first thing that you learn in any beginning law course is that "ignorance is no defense" in a court of law. Therefore, acting as your own lawyer can be an extremely dangerous practice. Although a course in commercial law or books for the layman may provide you with some basic knowledge about how our commercial legal system works, they are no substitute for an attorney. A lawyer is necessary to give you assurance that you are complying with all the federal and state regulations applying to your business; to see that you have the best form of business organization to minimize both your tax bite and liabilities; and to help you negotiate partnership agreements, acquisition leases, contracts, title to merchandise, and a myriad of other business-related problems. As a business owner you will find that you will be involved in a number of relationships that can have legal ramifications, ranging from the rights of buyers and sellers, landlords and tenants, creditors and debtors, and employers and employees—not to mention the problems of liability if your product should poison someone or the customer in your shop should slip on a banana peel.

Although there are many types of attorneys, you should try to select an attorney who is experienced either in business start-ups or in acquisitions, depending on the route you are taking, and who has a strong grounding in tax law. Although taxes will not be your only legal problem, they will probably be your major one unless you are in a highly regulated industry, such as securities, land, or transportation. As most problems in the first year invariably deal with cash, tax management is an important aspect of staying financially healthy.

THE THIRD STRING: OTHER TEAM MEMBERS

Business Colleagues and Networks

Partners, advisers, and employees are not the only people who can help you win in the entrepreneurial game. Your business colleague can provide an important source of advice, as well as a cheering squad when the going gets rough. Owning a business can be a lonely undertaking, particularly for women. Although the Task Force found that the numbers of women business owners are growing, the breed is still relatively rare. What will this mean for you as a business owner? It will mean that unlike your male counterpart, who can run across the street to Joe, the liquor store owner, and inquire about how he handles a particular business problem, you may have to look a little harder for friendly advice. You'll also find that many of the traditional networks in the business environment used for trading information are closed to you. For example, both the International Rotary and the Junior Chamber of Commerce, two organizations whose purpose is to promote commerce, have consistently refused to admit women to membership, a position that has been upheld by the courts.

Unfair? Yes. Likely to change in the near future? No. So the best thing to do is not fret about these inequities, but to infiltrate your local business environment as best you can by developing your own networks and sources of business advice. At a regional meeting of the White House Small Business Conference in Boston last fall, a black woman succinctly stated the importance of building a network: "If you are male, you were taught the business environment as a part of mystical rites of passage between childhood and adulthood. You are introduced to your father's business contacts, taught the ropes of the system, and encouraged to join the Jaycees. Many of your friends grow from playmates to business colleagues. That doesn't happen for a woman."

Such isolation and the need for an informal information-sharing system has led to the formation of many organizations of women business owners. That was the genesis of the National Association of Women Business Owners, which now has ten affiliated chapters. The association started as an informal group that met to discuss mutual problems. Their numbers grew by such leaps and bounds that a formal organization was formed. You should check your local telephone directory or ask other women business owners to see if there is an existing organization in your area. Although a list of current women business associations is provided in appendix 3, new organizations are cropping up daily.

Just as women in corporations need mentors, a woman business owner is well advised to find a person who will provide her with informal advice. Isolation and loneliness are key complaints for many women business owners. Said one woman: "I sit at my desk daily and ask myself why in the hell am I doing this? I know I'd make the same decision over again, but that doesn't help assuage the fright or the loneliness you feel out on the limb, wondering where the money is going to come from to pay the bills. Also, so many people go around, shaking their heads, and saying things like 'What's a nice girl like you doing in business for herself?' and you dread hearing the 'I told you sos' if you should fail."

Therefore, taking the time and investing the money to be active in professional and trade associations is crucial. Not only will they provide you with an informal support system and source of information, but they can be a valuable marketing network. Ask any business owners where they get the bulk of their sales, and they will say word-of-mouth advertising. Most will also say that they receive advice on daily business problems from business colleagues. One of the unwritten rules of the business game is "you scratch my back and I'll scratch yours." There is nothing illegal or unethical about it. It merely means that if you refer a customer or client to me I will probably remember to return the favor some day. That is the spirit behind the downtown merchants associations, chambers of commerce, and organizations such as the Rotary and Junior Chamber of Commerce. They not only trade fellowship and friendship, but they also swap advice and business contacts.

Although you may find that you can't currently join all the business organizations in your community because you are a woman, you can join many. So join those, and worry about the others later. You will find that it can be money well invested. You may also, in the long run, hasten the day when those all-male networks are opened to women. For example, one Rotary chapter in California has already included women, and several Junior Chamber of Commerce chapters have voted to admit women, although their membership is not recognized by the national organization. It should be just a matter of time before men realize that admitting women members makes good business sense.

Your Bankers

Business networks are not your only source of business advice. An important source, often overlooked by women, is your banker. Your bankers are not a foe, but a friend, and they can become the best friends your business can have because your bankers, more than anyone else, will be your key to additional financing. Not only do they control the purse strings of their own institutional funds, but they also can be a channel to other sources of funds. They are an invaluable source of business advice, as they have years of experience with other businesses. They may be able to flag areas in your financial statement that appear weak and provide suggestions about how others have dealt with similar problems. They are also excellent sources of referrals and can put their network of contacts and status in the business community to work for you.

Women tend to forget that bankers have a vested interest in the success of their business. Your success ensures that you will both repay your loan, and make larger deposits—which is how banks make their money. Virginia Maynard, of the First Women's Bank in New York City, points out that a lot of women make the mistake of thinking that the only time they should see their bankers is when they are looking for loans. What they should try to do instead is develop a good working relationship with them. "We like to know how the business is going and to help out if we can. We don't want to see a business go under any more than the owner does. Our goal is to get our loan repaid and develop a good customer. Also, it is a lot easier to continue to get financing from a bank if you come in before you are in a bail-out situation. No bank likes to throw good money after bad." The importance of developing a good relationship with your banker cannot be underestimated. This topic is treated in more depth in the next chapter, "Financing Your Business."

CHAPTER 5

Financing Your Business

There is a golden rule in business: He who has the gold, makes the rules. There is also a corollary to this rule: He who has the gold, gets the gold. You will run into these golden rules time and time again as a new and untried business owner. You will find early in the game that trying to raise capital for your business will be one of your first stumbling blocks. Overcoming this obstacle is one of the hardest, but most important, tasks you will have to perform. So if you have read all those articles about how to start a business on little or no money, forget them. They are a little like all the magazine articles that tell you how you can beautifully redecorate your home for under $50. Such pictures are not only unrealistic, they are dead wrong, and they can also be dangerous.

Of course, there is no denying that there are rags-to-riches stories—like that of Mary Vinton, who bought a sandal shop for $40 and turned it into a $4.5-million business called Georgetown Leather Design, or that of Betty Graham, the Dallas woman who became a multimillionaire after inventing Liquid Paper in her garage. However, these cases represent the exception, rather than the rule. Undercapitalization is one of the biggest causes of business failure. Dun & Bradstreet, a firm that tracks causes of business failures, ranks the lack of sufficient capital second only to the lack of business experience as one of the nine major causes of business failure.[1]

What is undercapitalization? *Undercapitalization* is a term used to mean, simply put, starting a business on a shoestring and not having enough money to keep it operating. It means having inadequate financial resources at your disposal to meet financial obligations. Undercapitalization can kill your business faster than anything else, but it is a disease that the wise woman starting her own business does not have to suffer. Just remember that no business makes money the first day it opens its doors. You must therefore have enough cash to carry you through to the time that your incoming sales can pick

93

up the burden. This does not necessarily mean that you need to have those thousands of dollars in hard, cold cash stashed away under your mattress or in the piggy bank. Nor does it mean that you need to wait to own a business until you have saved the $50,000 you think you need for the first year. What you need to do is to plan your capital needs, identify sources of capital, learn enough about the money markets to maneuver in them, and raise the capital you need.

WOMEN AND THE MONEY GAME

If you are a woman whose dealings with banks have only been with tellers who handle your checking or savings accounts, suddenly attempting the capital markets for start-up or operating capital can seem like approaching an iceberg: You can see the tip—the money you need—but understanding how to get to it is hidden from us by the murky waters of years of training that has made being financially savvy "unfeminine." Women have been taught about dollies and scents, not dollars and cents—an educational slant that definitely places us at a disadvantage in competing for capital. Although anyone—man, woman, or child—with a million dollars to deposit is likely to get the red carpet rolled out for them, most women feel they get the cold shoulder from bankers. Part of this cold shoulder may be caused by subtle discrimination on the part of bankers who question "why a nice girl like you wants to go into a business like that," but a great deal of it is caused by the fact that women just don't understand the capital markets and how they work.

For most women, finance is as foreign as French and just about as comprehensible to the untrained ear. Terms bantered around by bankers and accountants—such as liquidity ratios, knockdown value of assets, and acid tests—fill us with fear and trepidation. Bankers tend to be those serious strangers fenced off from us when we go to deposit our paycheck with the teller. I've talked to women who dread a visit to a banker with the same dread that they hold for visiting the doctor or the dentist. It's almost as if they fear that the banker will pronounce their financial condition so serious as to be beyond redemption.

Our timidity in approaching banks is primarily because we have been steered away from the world of finance. We are raised in the realm of allowances rather than budgets and are brought up to believe that someone else will take care of financial matters. Beatrice Fitzpatrick, head of the American Women's Economic Development Corporation, believes that it's hard to change overnight when someone has told you all your life to not "bother your pretty little head with such things." It's not that we can't handle finances, it's just that we haven't learned about it before and therefore it seems like a mystery.

There's no doubt that this process of role separation begins at a very young age. How many of us remember the nursery rhyme that went: "The King is in the counting house, counting out the money; the Queen is in the pantry, eating bread and honey"? Studies have shown that although little girls tend to achieve high scores in math in their younger years, they develop "math avoidance" in adolescent years when sex-stereotypic roles begin to develop. Virginia Maynard, of the First Women's Bank in New York City, sees women daily who don't understand, or are afraid to understand, the financial aspects of their businesses, and many leave this aspect of the business exclusively to male partners. Although it is a bad business practice for any owner not to know all the aspects of her or his business—from finances to marketing—the fact that many women let male partners or accountants handle the financial aspects of their business because they are uncomfortable with it is a reality. It stems from a fear that is rooted in a lack of knowledge and the pattern by which we were educated. It begins with the pink blanket and ends when we are counseled into typing, rather than bookkeeping.

Examples of the fact that our prior education impacts our ability to understand, comprehend, and compete in the money markets run rampant. One of the best examples is the story of one woman who founded a high-technology firm that grew into a $20-million business and was later acquired by a large corporation. Although the woman had an impressive corporate track record and could both conceptualize a winning business and raise almost three-quarters of a million dollars from backers, she was still naive about the money markets. What this woman didn't realize was that with almost one million dollars in capital to deposit, most banks would bend over backward for her. Instead of meeting with the bank president to establish an ongoing relationship between her new firm and the bank, she just walked up to the teller and asked to open a regular account. With a capital base like that, she was a valuable customer of the bank and therefore had the leverage to negotiate lower interest rates on future loans or open a line of credit to help with any future cash-flow crises.

The woman in the above example was lucky. She did not have to borrow money, and her business was successful. However, the average woman enters the competition for that scarce resource in our economy called start-up capital several steps behind the average man.

Money—be it to start out, keep afloat, or finance expansion—is a key problem in running a business. The Task Force found the need for capital high on their list of problem areas facing women. Women, because of their traditional position in our society, wind up handicapped on two counts when competing in the marketplace for money. First, few women have held the kind of job that would allow them to develop either the type of management track record or amount of collateral that financiers look for as prerequisites for funding ventures. Women have been, and still are, traditionally clustered in low-paying, nonmanagerial jobs—a factor that has a residual effect on a woman's ability to raise capital. We tend to be secretaries, not executives;

bookkeepers, not accountants; nurses, not doctors; and tellers, not bankers. Most women therefore get low marks on the four factors by which creditors—be they bankers, venture capitalists, or suppliers—judge us: collateral, capability, character, and credit. These factors can be called the four c's of credit worthiness.

Second, women have never learned the mechanisms of the game well enough to maneuver effectively in money markets. Not only do we often not understand the game, but we also don't know the players and we certainly don't know the plays.

Yet learning the money game can be easy. It merely requires understanding the game, mastering a few basic rules, and becoming acquainted with some of the jargon, so that you can ask and answer questions. Armed with this knowledge, you should be able to learn to play with the pros, or at least well enough to finance your own business.

BASIC MOVES IN THE MONEY GAME

Understanding the Money Game

The first thing to realize is that there is nothing mysterious about money. It is merely a commodity that someone dreamed up to standardize bartering and make our lives simpler. Money has two basic values: consumption—you can use it to buy the products you need, or think you need, for your physical and psychic survival—and investment—or the value money has when someone uses it to make more money. What makes most women unfamiliar with the money game is that they have probably used money only for the first purpose, to buy goods and services. This makes us unsure of how to use it for the second purpose, to make money, because we have so little experience with it.

Constance Kenney—an investment counselor in Lexington, Massachusetts, who teaches a course on women, money, and investing—points out that although women know how to *spend* money, they have never learned how to *use* it to their advantage in an investment sense. "Women tend to hoard their money. They are very cautious about their investments and extremely insecure about dealing with money. They don't see money as a commodity whose only worth is how it is traded and used. Perhaps the years of having so little of it that you could call your own makes us hoard it."

The second value of money—money used to make money—is what you will be considering as a business owner. You will also be entering into the realm of debt, which can be frightening for women who have never handled more than their personal budgets. In business, you incur debts to use someone else's money to make money—and you hope to make more money than the cost of borrowing the money. Paula Nelson, in *The Joy of Money,* distinguishes between *constructive* and *destructive* debt. Destructive debt is being in debt because you spent too much money on purchases, whereas constructive debt is borrowing money in order to use the money on investments that will make you money.[2]

The goal of the money game is the same as that of the entrepreneurial game: to increase the net worth of the player. Net worth is the money at the player's disposal once she or he has paid all debts and has liquidated all assets. The money game is played by New York financiers, your local banker, and other individuals. It is a game played every day and it is a game at which some people win and some lose, whether they invest in real estate, business ventures, or stocks and bonds. It is also the game you will be playing in your business.

Money is the lifeblood of your business—the ingredient that will make it grow and increase its net worth. It is the critical factor to your success. The major source of this lifeblood, once a company is operating, is money generated by the sales of your product or service. A steady growth in the retained earnings—the amount left over after you pay all the operating expenses—is the sign of a healthy company. However, even the healthiest company sometimes needs to turn to the capital markets for fresh infusions of cash to get them over seasonal downturns in sales or to finance expansion. These capital markets are the sources you will turn to if you do not have enough personal savings to finance your business start-up.

Capital markets mean nothing more than those businesses or institutions that trade in the commodity of money. The only difference between your business and their business is that while you trade in the product or service you produce to make money, they trade in money to make money. They are therefore regulated more strenuously by the government than you are. People who deal in this commodity include international financiers, who make money on foreign exchange fluctuations, or your local banker, who uses the money deposited in checking accounts to lend to other businesses at an interest rate that creates profit for the bank.

The only difference between the various traders in the money market is the way they trade their money and the degree of risk involved in the trading. This degree of risk involved will impact not only the sources of capital that might be open to you as a new business person but also the jargon you hear spoken among the people in this industry. For example, venture capitalists, who tend to fund high-risk ventures for the promise of high returns, talk about "putting deals together"; whereas bankers, who must be cautious because they are using depositors' funds, talk about "funding business propositions."

Understanding this risk perspective will enable you to know what the people who work in the various sources of capital look for when they assess a business venture's proposal. It will also make you realize that there are different kinds of money available, and they have different conditions attached to them. For example, the cost attached to equity capital is giving up some of the ownership in your business and future revenues, whereas the cost attached to debt financing is the amount of interest you pay on your loan. If you are adding inventory that you can sell to repay a loan, you may want debt financing; if you are financing a major expansion, you may want to seek equity capital. The type of money you will need will depend on your particular business situation. You should therefore shop around for money like you shop for any other commodity you buy. The key is to determine the *amount* and *type* of money you need under conditions you can *afford*.

You can figure out the best type and source of money for your situation by following the four p's in the formula for finding money: preparation, presentation and pluck, and persistence.

PREPARATION.   The first p in the formula for raising money is preparation. Preparation will help you answer the basic money questions:

- How much money do you need?
- For how long do you need it?
- What kind of money do you need?
- What will the money be used for?
- How will the money generate revenues?
- How will it be repaid?

Although developing an initial estimate of how much money you will need to operate your business may sound difficult at first, you will be amazed at how easy it is to come up with it once you begin listing and projecting your expenses into component parts such as rent, salaries, and insurance. You can pick one of two starting points to make these estimates. One way is to estimate the level of sales you think you will make and then estimate the staff and operating expenses you think you will incur to make those sales. The other way is to estimate the profit you want to make and then determine the level of sales and expenses you will incur to generate these profits. The publications on existing financial ratios and the average expenses in industry lines mentioned in chapter 3, "Getting into the Game," will give you some good guidelines for estimating expenses.

The important thing is to be as thorough in estimating these costs as possible. An item left out can cause an adequately capitalized firm to become undercapitalized quickly. The number you choose for capitalizing your firm should not be picked out of your head, but carefully calculated. Janet Deming—who started a firm called DOR & Associates in Minneapolis, Minnesota, which specializes in drug and alcoholism counseling—is a woman who attests to the importance of this factor. She and her partner failed to figure the cost of professional liability insurance—a necessary ingredient in her business—into their business plan. "We had been insured previously through our professional association, but as business owners we were no longer eligible for this coverage. It was a big overhead item and an oversight that no one caught, not our accountant nor our banker." This oversight created a tremendous unexpected cash drain.

Sarah Kovner, co-owner of Arts, Letters, and Politics, with Barbara Handman, also found the everyday costs of doing business a shock when the business was moved out of Handman's home and into offices in midtown Manhattan. Starting out of their homes with only $2,000 in initial capitalization, they quickly learned what overhead means when they moved to an office. "It's what it takes to unlock the door every morning, irrespective of your business volume."

To determine how the money borrowed or invested generates revenues you must do a sales projection for your firm—that is, an estimate of what the sales volume for your business will be each month. You will probably make an educated guess based on your assessment of competitive conditions and the market's dollar potential, but beware of overestimating sales. Just as there is a tendency for parents to think their child will grow up to be President, there is also a tendency for business owners to overestimate sales in the initial months of operation.

As no one makes enough money the day they open doors to carry all their overhead costs, it is best to be conservative when preparing the sales projections for your first three to six months. Pamela Green—an adviser for minority business owners at the Volunteer Urban Consulting Group, a nonprofit organization that organizes and provides volunteer management assistance primarily to minority businesses and art organizations—points out that one of the biggest problems is that people inadequately estimate the amount of cash they will need in the first months to keep them operating. Green, who received an M.B.A. from the University of Chicago, was formerly a banker. She recommends that you be as conservative as possible, estimating zero sales for the first three months.

Jim Molloy—a professor at Northeastern University in Boston and owner of TRAMCO, which has worked with small businesses—echoes Green's view. Molloy feels that one of the major mistakes new businesses make in the first year of operation is to put too much money into fixed assets. They buy equipment, refurbish or decorate, and then don't have enough money left to do business. "It's a natural tendency. The business is your dream and you want it to look like your dream. The day-to-day operation can be more mundane and less exciting. But having a firm fix on your working capital needs—that money you need for day-to-day operations—is critical. It doesn't matter how attractive your store is if you can't afford to keep the lights on for people to see."

Once you have figured out what your costs of operation are and what your projected sales are going to be, you should determine how the money will be repaid. This last step requires assessing the break-even point of your business. Break-even is the point at which your costs of doing business exactly equal the amount of revenues coming in—that is, you are not making money but you are not losing money either. The break-even point gives you an idea of what your potential profit will be and how fast you can repay a loan. Figuring the break-even point is fairly simple and is explained in more detail in chapter 6, "Developing Your Marketing Strategy." It is probably a good idea to have your accountant help you with these calculations initially, although you should develop your own rough sketch of what capital you think you will need. She or he will have more experience in dealing with the fixed and variable costs of doing business. These fixed and variable costs are the two key components you examine when doing a break-even analysis. Fixed costs are costs that stay the same regardless of whether you make one sale or a hundred. Variable costs are those costs that vary with the business volume. Finally, remember that only *you* can answer the type of questions that need to be asked about your business.

PRESENTATION AND PLUCK. Once you know your costs and potential profits, you can then begin to try to sell your business concept to potential backers by developing the next two p's for success—presentation and pluck. Even the best preparation and the most dogged persistence will not accomplish your goal of capitalizing your business unless you have the ability to convince others to believe in your venture. This means that you not only have to have the pluck—that is, the spirit and determination that your business will succeed despite all odds—but you must have the know-how to make a strong presentation.

Your next step will be to develop a formal business plan which will communicate your idea and its potential. Although you may be able to trigger interest in your business ideas verbally, any prospective investor or bank will want something in writing when it gets down to the wire in making a financial decision. You will have to develop a document that can quickly and succinctly show interested parties not only your business concept but also your sales projections for the first year and how you plan to finance the business. They will also want to know not only something about you and your key partners so they can judge the merits of your idea but also your capacity to carry it through.

It is not important that your business plan be lengthy or fancy. What is important is that it be well thought out and include all the cost items you anticipate. Developing a written business plan forces you to take an objective, critical, and unemotional look at your future business. It provides you a valuable dry run at anticipating your business strategy, costs, and success. It not only helps you judge whether the risks and hard work are worth the remuneration offered but it also enables potential investors to look at the facts behind the business. Your business plan can serve as a tool both for generating start-up capital and for measuring your progress against these initial projections once you are started.

The major purpose of your business plan is to communicate: to yourself so that your dream becomes a reality and to others, so that they will have the information necessary to make their investment decision. Most business plans include four major sections:

• A general section allowing potential investors to judge the market viability of the business, with a description of the business concept or idea; its potential markets;

existing competition; and basic facts, such as organization, staffing, and planned location of the firm.

- A section allowing potential investors to judge the financial viability and stability of the business, including all available financial data and projections, such as sources and uses of funds, a balance sheet to show initial assets and liabilities, income projections to show the sales you project, a pro forma cash-flow statement to illustrate the projected flow of cash, and a break-even analysis to show at what point the sales will begin to carry the business. If it is an existing business and you are seeking funds for expansion, historical financial statements are usually included.
- A section allowing investors to judge the capability of the principals. Personal resumes, letters of reference, credit reports, and personal financial statements can be included.
- A final section for any other supporting documents that might be relevant to your business plan, such as leases, contracts, and legal documents.

There are many business service firms that specialize in helping small businesses develop these business plans. However, this route is often expensive and dangerous. A professionally prepared business plan won't do any good if you don't understand it thoroughly enough to answer a banker's or investor's questions or how to use it as a management tool. The best way to develop this understanding is to work out your own plan. A suggested outline of a business plan is provided in an excellent booklet—*Business Planning Guide*, by David H. Bangs, Jr. and William R. Osgood—available from the Upstart Publishing Company, Portsmouth, New Hampshire. That outline, which is reproduced on page 102, describes and gives examples of the planning steps that you need to take. The Small Business Administration also has a pamphlet, *Business Plan for Small Service Firms* (Small Marketers Aid No. 153), that details the questions you should ask yourself in developing a business plan, including the following:

- Why am I in business?
- What business am I in?
- Who are my competitors?
- What is my sales potential?
- How will I attract customers?
- How will I sell customers?
- What fixtures and equipment will I need and what will they cost?
- What parts and materials will I need and what will they cost?
- What will my general overhead be?
- How will I structure my organization?
- How will I staff it?
- What will I pay my staff?

The format of the Small Business Administration pamphlet is a workbook that enables you to work through the problems involved in answering the above questions. Armed with these pamphlets, all you need to do is ask the bankers you initially deal with what they normally like to receive in a business plan and

SUGGESTED OUTLINE OF BUSINESS PLAN

Cover Sheet: Name of business, names of principals, address and phone number of business

Statement of Purpose

Table of Contents

 I. The Business
  a. Description of business
  b. Market
  c. Competition
  d. Location of business
  e. Management
  f. Personnel
  g. Application and expected effect of loan (if needed)
  h. Summary

 II. Financial Data
  a. Sources and applications of funding
  b. Capital equipment list
  c. Balance sheet
  d. Break-even analysis
  e. Income projections (profit and loss statements)
   (1) 3-year summary
   (2) Detail by month for first year
   (3) Detail by quarter for second and third year
   (4) Notes of explanation
  f. Pro forma cash flow
   (1) Detail by month for first year
   (2) Detail by quarter for second and third year
   (3) Notes of explanation
  g. Deviation analysis
  h. Historical financial reports for existing business
   (1) Balance sheets for past 3 years
   (2) Income statements for past 3 years
   (3) Tax returns

III. Supporting Documents Personal resumes, job descriptions, personal financial statements, credit reports, letters of reference, letters of intent, copies of leases, contracts, legal documents, and anything else of relevance to the plan

SOURCE: *Business Planning Guide*. Rev. ed. David H. Bangs, Jr., and William R. Osgood. Business Assistance Monograph Series. Portsmouth, N.H.: Upstart Publishing Company, 1978, p. 3.

find an accountant who can help you develop the necessary financial projections. Then you can sit down and begin to crystallize your business dream into a business reality.

Nancy Lang is a woman who believes presentation and pluck pay off. Lang owns a major Burlington, Vermont, real estate firm Lang Associates Realtors, that has eighteen agents and grosses close to $20 million annually; she is also a partner in a sizable real estate development project. Her experience as both a business owner and as a member of the board of a local bank has made her believe that the proper presentation can, in many cases, dictate the outcome of a loan application. Although the product or project is important, it helps if the bankers have a concise presentation that makes economic sense and provides them with all the facts and figures they will need to make their decisions. Lang also feels that including reports from your accountant or lawyer can be helpful, since these people are usually known and respected and can add to your sphere of influence, thereby taking some of the pressure off the board members because the opinions of experts can be cited. She says that she has seen more than one case where an applicant's presentation and ability to convince a bank of the worth of a proposition has been the ingredient that tipped the decision in the applicant's favor.

Virginia Maynard, a banker at New York City's First Women's Bank, agrees that the attitude of the persons can make all the difference in the world. "What we are looking for is a winner, and you have to be able to project that positive attitude." Said another banker: "If you come into a bank not knowing how much money you need, or what you think your business can make, no bank will want to loan you money. We have to stay in business too—that means having only a few loan defaults in our loan portfolio. The best advice I can give a woman seeking bank funding is to do her homework."

This ability to understand and feel comfortable in the money game well enough to exude a self-confident attitude is often difficult for women and minorities. One person who has worked with the minority community points out that it is a difficult task to teach the subtleties of dealing with the business environment. "I don't know how to teach people how to 'con' a banker. The only thing you can do is teach them how the game is played and hope that they will learn the plays well enough to win."

PERSISTENCE.   Preparation, presentation, and pluck are not all that you will need to succeed. The final ingredient is persistence. You'd better steel yourself early on for the fact that getting capital is not going to be easy. You will discover that finding money is not only the first stumbling block you will come to but the first test of your mettle as a potential entrepreneur. It may also be your first brush with real discrimination.

The myth that women can't handle money continues to plague us. We tend to forget that it was only in 1974 that the Equal Credit Opportunity Act was passed to end arbitrary abuses that women often experienced because of their sex. Yet every lawyer knows that there is a big difference between a "right" and a "remedy." It often takes generations for prejudice and discriminatory practices to be erased. I am sure we have all heard horror stories about women trying to get credit or borrow money: women who were not allowed to have their incomes count on mortgages because they were "ripe" for childbearing, single women who couldn't get a department store credit card even though they had a job and no debts, divorced or widowed women who suddenly found themselves unable to get credit in their own names, or working women who were unable to get small loans without their husbands cosigning.

Although the Equal Credit Opportunity Act made it illegal for banks to discriminate on the basis of sex, age, race, or marital status, women writing to the Task Force still complained of discrimination, particularly in seeking loans for starting a business. Said one business owner: "There is still a tendency for the business community at large to view women business owners as 'hobbiests,' rather than serious business people. They think we were either put in business by our husbands to keep us busy and off the streets, or else that we are all part-timers, 'dabbling' in business out of our homes." And it doesn't matter whether you are the owner of a big business or a small business, the sex stereotyping persists.

Marie Tarvin started Sun City Transportation in El Paso, working out of a car with a two-way radio and two vans. She has built it into a $2.5-million business with a fleet of vans and six companies in three states and is now branching into warehousing and containerization. Tarvin believes the same sex stereotyping about women in corporations applies for women business owners. "If you are a man who is out there competing in the marketplace by running a business and buying companies, you are bright and ambitious and the head of a growing company. As a woman, you are that broad who is putting all of the little guys out of business."

Tarvin's story also illustrates that part of the entrepreneurial game is not following the rules or at least not what everyone else is doing. Rather than advertise, Tarvin found a gimmick to attract attention to her company when she first started. Each van was a different color with a color-coordinated ribbon painted on it. "All of a sudden there were these crazy-looking different-colored trucks with ribbons on them. Everyone thought we had twenty vans, rather than two, because they kept seeing different-colored ribbons." Feminine? Perhaps. Smart? Yes. Successful? Definitely.

Both the Task Force study and the special study of successful business owners done by the American Management Associations found that women felt they faced additional obstacles in ownership because of discrimination. These women described situations in which they were not treated in a professional manner by male accountants and lawyers and where their businesses were considered a joke, an indulgence, or a hobby. Yet most difficult, they felt, were bankers. Many felt that it was difficult for women to gain the confidence of banks and other financial institutions no matter how much expertise or how good they were. Many also expressed the feeling that bank rules and regulations were more stringently enforced with women than with men, and others found it difficult to convince bank officers of their capabilities in delivering an adequate return on the bank's investment.

Women responding to both the Task Force and American Management Associations studies indicated that banks often gave them the impression that women should not be operating a business. They felt they often got the runaround or unprofessional answers from bankers. "It's subtle, but you can tell when you aren't being taken seriously," said one woman business owner. One woman described her situation as follows:

> It was a very busy day for me and I couldn't afford the time to go over to the bank [to help correct an error that had been made in her account], but I agreed to do them this favor. When I got there the officer's secretary didn't seem to understand or take me seriously. She treated me like somebody else's secretary. Men arrived in the office who had no appointments and were ushered in to see the officer who had asked me to be there. I finally had to show myself into the office—really barge in.

Another stated that the only time she remembered prejudice against her was when she went to the first bank she approached on a loan. The justification given for turning her down was that she was a woman going into a man's field. One woman pointed out that although she was unable to get credit for herself, she was able to cosign for her eighteen-year-old son's loan.

Indeed, many women find it is easier to get a loan to buy a car or redecorate their homes than to get a loan to start a business. One woman who started a consulting firm calls the money that capitalized her firm her "carpet money" because the only way she could obtain funding was to borrow money to allegedly recarpet and redecorate her home. She found it easier to get a loan for this reason than to find a bank that would back a woman-owned firm.

And the story of discrimination is not limited to the new and the small. In fact, it rankles hardest at those who are established and know that they should be able to get the money but find financiers uninterested. Miriam Marshall, owner of the exclusive Port-of-Call boutique that occupies a street floor corner of the Bergdorf-Goodman Department Store in New York, has found financiers consistently unreceptive to her, despite the fact that her 100-square-foot boutique grosses $500,000 in sales annually and makes more per square foot than any other business in retailing. "Perhaps it's because I'm little and feminine, but they always treat me as though I was a daughter," she says, not without some anger.

Marshall points out that although her product—exquisite jewelry and other decorative items that she designs and manufactures abroad through cottage industries—has a higher profit margin than sugar, men don't understand it. Her items sell for prices that range from $6 to $6,000 and she counts Jackie Onassis, Rudolph Nureyev, and Martha Graham among her regular customers. Currently riding the crest of the fashion trend that is now making women less sheeplike and more desirous of individual and distinctive looks, she has plans on the drawing board to start franchising her business to other department stores under an arrangement that will allow them to purchase collections of her items under the Port-of-Call name.

Marshall was not always so successful. "When I first started out in the fur department at Bendel's, I had so few items that I had to be ingenious and create a display with packing crates and straw to make the product look bigger. I only grossed $10,000 in six months the first year." She is originally from

Australia and had done public relations and writing in the Orient before she started designing jewelry with an exotic Far Eastern character. Geraldine Stutz, president of Henri Bendel's gave Marshall her start. Stutz suggested that Marshall enter a sublease arrangement with the store. Under this arrangement, Marshall owns her own business and hires her own sales personnel but pays the department store a percentage of her sales in return for the space they provide her.

Today Marshall is highly successful, yet she still finds she has difficulty in getting financing on the merits of her business volume without a personal guarantee. She says that the only way she ever got a line of credit, which is critical in a business where she must finance the manufacture of inventory months in advance of sales, was when a woman banker went to bat for her. Marshall now banks with the First Women's Bank of New York because it was the only bank that would finance a second venture—Ports of Call, a travel agency in Saks Fifth Avenue, which specializes in first-class travel and grossed several million dollars last year. Marshall started the agency with three female and two male partners. She points out, with some bitterness, that although she was responsible for creating a cottage industry that produced $12 million in export revenues for Cambodia, she and a female partner were unable to get money for the travel agency, which was grossing $1.3 million at the time. "I am sure if my male partners had gone in and made the application, they would have been funded."

Marshall is like many women who have found prejudice in the banking community and who now patronize the women's banks that are cropping up all over the country. These banks are proving a valuable aid to removing some of the discriminatory obstacles that women have faced in the past. There are presently seven women's banks operating, in Richmond, Virginia; Denver, Colorado; Washington, D.C.; New York, New York; Los Angeles, California; Rockville, Maryland; San Francisco, California; and Greenwich, Connecticut.

Eve Grover, president of the First Women's Bank of Maryland, believes that as long as the banking industry is predominantly male and insensitive to the needs of women, there will be a need for such banks. Grover has been in banking for thirty years, starting at Citibank in New York City. She was formerly in charge of the State National Bank of Maryland's Women's Headquarters, a special branch and program that Grover initiated both to attract more women to the banks and to provide special services for them.

Grover points out that targeting a bank to a particular market segment is no different than the genesis of some of the other major banks in America. For example, Seaman's Bank for Savings in New York or the Farmers and Merchants National Bank are banks with names indicating their original market segments. And Bank of America initially started out to service the Italian immigrant population in San Francisco.

Although women's banks are in business for profits just like any other bank and use the same standards for making loans, their leaders think that they are more objective about judging the ability of women to pay back and about spotting profitable businesses because they are not blinded by the filter of prejudice that sometimes makes a loan to a woman appear more risky. They also see part of their role as educating their customers to the money system, recognizing that many women have been locked out of this knowledge. According to Grover: "We are really no different than any other bank. It's just that if a woman gets turned down for a loan in our bank, she knows that it is for legitimate business reasons, and not subtle prejudice."

Hurdling the Obstacles

Undoubtedly you will run up against people in the business environment who still think that a woman's place is in the home, not behind her own cash register. However, the key to overcoming these obstacles is not to get bitter about this, as that can only hurt you in the entrepreneurial game. Remember that an entrepreneur, by definition, is someone who can get over the obstacles that exist to starting a business. The ability to cope with frustrations and anger and to turn the forces of prejudice to your advantage, appears to be a key ingredient to a woman's business success, according to both the American Management Associations study for the Task Force and the women interviewed for this book. Indeed, many of the people who have worked closely with both male and female entrepreneurs think that the fact that women have been able to conquer the additional barriers placed before them may make them stronger and more successful business owners in the end.

Dr. Henry Bender, who directed the American Management Associations study of successful women business owners, felt that the women he talked to showed major differences from the typical male entrepreneurs in that they did not go into business as naively as did men. "These women seemed to know up front that they had to be equal to, or better than, men. They were a little more in tune with reality, and with the hardships of trying to accomplish things; even though they were not necessarily familiar with the business world to the same extent." Dr. Bender notes that most of the women interviewed were making profits within the first or second year, which is unusual. He felt that it was those women who felt that they were second-class citizens who were the ones who would wash out early, whereas women who knew their worth and were realistic about their business odds were as able, if not better able, than men to create strong, growing companies. "Typically, a male entrepreneur's ego, status, and power needs are tied to money. They are unwilling to make the sacrifices necessary in the first couple of years and defer income and will tend to close up shop early if the business does not reach their profit expectations quickly."

Perhaps minority women have learned earlier than others the ability to figure ways around obstacles because they have faced racial as well as sexual prejudice. Carrie L. Fair—who is both an attorney and the majority owner of Kendrick and Company, a Washington, D.C., communications firm—learned to use prejudice to her advantage. "If I were to meet someone who was blocking somewhere I wanted to go, I would just figure out how to get around that person. And being a minority, I have always had to think in terms of how to do things in more than one way. I think lots of times men do give out helpful advice. They assume you need help because you are a woman. If they are telling me things I know, I just listen. I know it means I can get more and more information about things I don't know."

This ability to turn problems into opportunities and move on from hardships seems to be a key trait of successful entrepreneurs, especially women. The American Management Associations study found that despite the frequent tough deals the women interviewed might have been handed, few of the women appeared to have any hostility toward the world. Said this study: "One of the key character traits that these women had found useful and necessary for getting along in what is commonly assumed to be a man's world of business is the ability to use hostility, impediments, prejudice, stereotypes, etc., very much as a judo expert uses his/her opponent's weight to his/her own advantage. . . . They themselves had found within themselves the ability to cope without anger with prevailing attitudes."[3]

Successful women business owners have discovered that women must often play a win-win game, even if the rest of the world is playing a win-lose game. Denise Cavanaugh, the proprietor of Cook/Cavanaugh Associates, includes this philosophy in a course in management for women she teaches at Georgetown University in Washington, D.C. Cavanaugh points out what the only people who can win in the win-lose game are those with power, which for the most part women do not have. "When I talk about strategy for women or anyone who has less power in a situation, I tell them you have to play a win-win game. That means that you are going to win your objective and the other person is going to win theirs, too. That requires adaptation and compromise— and that, I believe, is how women are going to have to function until we get to the point where we have actually equalized the power situation. One of the ways we can humanize the work force is to spread the use of these collaborative strategies."

Although you will face obstacles and anger and frustration will often be daily experiences, remember that you can get over these obstacles. The initial obstacles will be the highest, and the succeeding ones will get smaller. The nice thing about the business game is that it is a game of strategy and stamina, not strength. It is also a game where the measure or score—money—is sexless. If you own a business, it is the bottom line, your profits, not your personality, that people use to judge you by. The only problem in the beginning is that you will not have a track record to prove that you can be profitable. However, you can get over this handicap if you take the time to learn what bankers and investors look for in backing a venture, what you should look for in a bank or investors, and how to convince them that your business will be profitable.

GETTING THE MONEY

Where the Money Usually Comes From

Most small businesses in America are intitially capitalized by equity capital, generally by money from the owner's personal savings or *angel* money, which is from family, friends, or investors. Businesses owned by women are no exception. The Task Force found that the majority (67 percent) of the women responding to its survey were initially capitalized in this way; 22 percent obtained capital from commercial banks or venture-capital firms, and only 11 percent from government programs. The American Management Associations study also showed that the majority of the women responding started their firms through private equity financing, particularly through personal savings. However, once the business was in operation, bank financing became a key money source.

Brian Haslett, who works for Venture Founders, believes that most new entrepreneurs overlook the major sources of start-up capital and waste a lot of time and energy seeking funding through commercial sources where the probability of getting loans or investors is slim. Haslett points out that the key sources of money for business start-ups tend to be the entrepreneurs themselves, who may have property they can mortgage or securities they can cash in; the immediate family and friends of the owner; and professional people, such as doctors and dentists, who have money to invest and can take risks because they need tax deductions. Additional sources of start-up capital are "deal makers," townspeople who like to invest their money in small deals. Suppliers and customers can also be a source.

Suppliers sometimes finance start-ups in order to create a customer. One dairy farmer started her business years ago when it was virtually impossible for a single woman to obtain bank financing. The only way she was able to buy her farm was because the people who would supply her milking machines lent her the capital.

A steady customer may also become a major investor. Sharon Egan Belson—owner of Belson/St. Louis, Inc., a wholesale lighting and furniture company—took this route in starting her second business, a hair salon. "I knew that my hair was important in how I felt and looked and was spending a lot of money on it. I also knew my hairdresser had talent, so I backed him financially for 50 percent of the business." Belson is now opening her third venture, a tearoom and fabric shop in the rapidly developing riverside business district of St. Louis. The idea for the tearoom came about because of her location. "We are near warehouses and the river, and in the past the only places to eat were real macho places. Now that the area is developing and more office buildings are going up, I think an alternative type of eating establishment will be a success." She has come a long way from the time, as a new divorcee, when she had to lie about the fact that she had children so that she could get a job as a receptionist.

Shopping for Money

You are now ready to approach the money markets to try to finance your business. You are prepared and know how much money you will need, what it will be used for, what kind of sales it will generate, and what you can offer bankers in terms of payback potential and investors in terms of profits.

The best way to start a successful business is to start out right—that is, with enough financial backing to keep you running long enough for you to get off the ground. Remember that if raising capital for any business venture is difficult, it is a lot easier when your bright new business idea is not tarnished by unpaid bills, a cash crisis, and perilous projections for the future. Investors and commercial institutions back a business only because they think it can make a return on their investment. Only loved ones will sink good money after bad, and they probably only do that because they love you, not because they love your business. You should therefore overestimate, rather than underestimate, your capital needs.

Also remember that when you are financing a company, you are not asking for an "allowance." You are offering someone a deal that will make them money. The attitude you should take is to ask, "How much money will they lend?" and not "Will they lend it?" If you can show an interested party that your business can grow to a point where it will bring them a larger return on their investment than will other options in the money market—such as real estate, stocks, bonds, and savings accounts—you should be able to capitalize your firm.

Although you may need money, you should be in the driver's seat when it comes to choosing the bankers or partners you want to deal with. You should shop for a bank that is sincerely interested in your business and will provide you with the services you need, and you should look for a banker with whom you feel you can develop a good ongoing relationship. Of course, it is a lot easier to shop around if you are like the woman who started the high-technology firm and had a nice wad of money from backers and a business idea with high-growth potential. However, even if you are planning to start a small retail shop, keep in mind the value of your business to the community and what its future deposits could mean for the bank. Remember that a banker's career, in terms of salary and promotion, depends on the amount of new and lucrative business she or he develops for the bank.

However, you should also be realistic about just how much your banker can do for you. Although discrimination can be very real, it is not the only reason you may not get a loan. The realities of the money market are also a factor. Jean Reid, who once counseled women at the American Women's Economic Development Corporation, believes women should realize that there just isn't much money out there to be had. "However, if she is resourceful enough and scratches hard enough, she can find it."

The reason for this difficulty in raising capital is threefold. First, we are in a time of tight money, when it is difficult for any business, much less a new business, to get money at an affordable interest rate. Second, banks are among the most conservative of the money sources, and they tend to perceive new ventures as a high risk for their depositors' money. Finally, banks just don't like to make loans for the small amount of money most new ventures need because they don't make much money on them.

The Task Force found that the banks they surveyed in eight major cities estimated that only about 5 percent of their loans were made to small businesses. Although money may be easier to get in smaller communities, where the banking officials know their customers better and have a greater interest in local affairs, it is difficult nevertheless to obtain bank financing for a new venture. It's just a cold, hard fact of business life that any bank would rather handle a $2-million loan with General Motors than a $20,000 loan with your business. The bank will make more interest money on the General Motors loan for the same amount of work and will have the benefits of larger deposits to lend out. It is therefore not surprising that many small businesses are financed through personal savings and private investors, as the big corporation obviously has an edge over you. For this reason, the Small Business Administration (SBA) was set up to help capitalize the small business sector of the economy.

THE BASIC SOURCES OF MONEY

The two major types of money you can find to finance your business are equity capital and debt financing. Some people confuse borrowing with equity capital, yet there is a big difference.

Equity capital is also often called *risk* or *venture* capital. It is investment capital that you put into your business from your savings or that is raised by selling people a share in your company. The investor bears the risk that your business will succeed and make money for her or him. In the event of failure, there is no obligation to repay this money, and there are no interim repayment terms. In raising equity capital, you take people into your company who are willing to risk their money in it, hoping for a share in its profits if the business is successful. These investors are interested in the long-term potential income from your company, rather than an immediate return.

There are two major sources of equity capital: private sources, such as family, friends, or individuals who may want to invest in your business; and institutional sources. By and large, the majority of new business start-ups rely on private, rather than institutional sources, of equity capital.

Debt capital is money you borrow; it is capital that must be paid back on a monthly or quarterly basis. Even if you have no revenues coming in you are obligated to *service* your loan over a period of time. Debt financing is therefore a less attractive option for start-up capital, unless you have sufficient cash revenues through equity financing to carry you during your start-up phase.

Sources of Private Equity Capital

A small business can have a private offering of shares of stock without registering the offering with the SEC if no more than twenty-five people are approached to invest. Thus, you can bring private investors into your business by offering them shares of stock in your company in return for their money. These investors can be brought in as partners, limited partners, or share-holders. Such stock offerings are one of the most frequently used methods of generating start-up capital. It is also a particularly good method for women who may not have the kind of credit references or collateral necessary to borrow from a commercial bank.

However, a private offering is also one of the methods most overlooked by entrepreneurs. There is a tendency among people starting their own business to be both greedy and myopic. They want to hold onto 100 percent of their firm. What they fail to realize is that half of a lot is better than all of nothing. Therefore, if you have a business idea that you think can gross you a million dollars but need $100,000 to start it, it is far better to raise that $100,000 by selling off 50 percent of the company than not to start it at all. If you don't start it at all, you will end up with 100 percent of zero, or zero. If you do start it, but only have 50 percent of the million-dollar business, you will still be $500,000 ahead of where you would have been without your investors' money. Also, you may be able to buy back the stock of the other members at a later date if there is a disagreement or if you want total control. This is a common occurrence in stock-financed start-ups.

As a new owner you may be able to use private equity sources to capitalize your entire company. Potential sources of private equity are all around you: family; private investors who can afford risks and need tax write-offs, such as doctors and lawyers; or former friends or business acquaintances who respect your competence and integrity. It is not unusual to raise all the money this way. In that case, the owners' contribution being *sweat equity*, you will contribute your energy and sweat to starting and running the venture, which will eventually make profits for you all.

You should seek an attorney's assistance in drawing up any kind of equity agreement. They can advise you on both the rules and regulations and ways to structure your deal, so that it is most advantageous to you. For example, many people who use the sweat equity route forget to write into their agreements that the profits will be split only at the point where the working partner's salary has been paid out of the revenues generated. Be sure that the attorney you hire is "deal" sophisticated. What you are looking for is an attorney who can help you structure a deal, not kill it. A lawyer inexperienced in business deals may be overly conservative for your needs.

Anne Pallie, a real estate broker in Washington, D.C., started her business with the help of two friends. Pallie had been an administrator for a large firm and had worked for Robert Kennedy's presidential campaign before he was assassinated, but she found that despite her experience she could only get work as a secretary. She therefore decided to start a summer camp that would mix rural and urban children in West Virginia. Although this venture did not get off the ground, it led her to her current business as a real estate broker in residential, commercial, and country property. "Because I was out in West Virginia, friends started asking me to look for country property for them. I enjoyed it so much I decided to become a broker."

Pallie's story is a good example of angel money. She had investors who not only backed her, but they also allowed her to buy back total control when the firm was a success. Initially, two very good friends who had a lot of faith in her invested $40,000 for 50 percent of the company and provided her with office space. However, since she had never had to use more than $5,000 of this equity, they decided that it was not fair to take half the company. The two friends let Pallie repay them and become a sole proprietor.

You may not be able to find backers as nice as Pallie's, but you should be able to find people who might want to get a larger return on their investment than a savings account and who think that your probability of success is a better bet than the stock market. If you are thinking of starting a business, it is a good idea to start bouncing your idea off people early to pinpoint those who appear receptive. But when turning to friends as potential investors, be sure that they understand the risk involved; that is, they will lose if the business is not a success. If you don't do this, you may find that you may lose your friends as well as your business.

Institutional Sources of Equity Capital

For some businesses, institutional equity capital may be a good source of financing. The institutional sources of equity capital are venture-capital firms, small business investment companies (SBIC), and minority-enterprise small business investment companies (MESBIC). Venture-capital firms provide capital for new ventures in return for a share of the ownership interest in the firms. They are often more active participants in your business than individual investors because they have a greater vested interest in its success. SBICs and MESBICs differ from other venture-capital firms in that they are licensed, regulated, and sometimes partly financed by the SBA. The federal government created SBICs and MESBICs to provide more equity capital and long-term loans for the nation's small businesses. An excellent listing of private venture-capital firms can be found at your library, and for information on how to contact a SBIC or a MESBIC, you can write to the Small Business Administration, Washington, D.C. 20416.

The Task Force found that few women knew about the venture-capital market. Less than 20 percent of the twenty-five venture-capital firms surveyed had been approached by a woman business owner seeking funds, and less than 0.5 percent of the women responding to the Task Force survey had been capitalized by this source. These low rates may partly be because women are outside the business network where they would learn about venture-capital firms. In addition, the deals a venture-capital firm is looking for are usually not the retail and service businesses that women traditionally start. What every venture capitalist is looking for is a prospective Xerox or Polaroid: a company that will experience rapid growth, high sales, and an eventual public stock offering allowing shares in the company to be sold at a substantial profit. Venture capitalists are willing to take high risks in return for the potential of high returns.

Furthermore, economies of scale make investments of at least $150,000 the minimum acceptable to most private venture-capital firms, a figure well above the normal amount of capital women seek. The Task Force found that only 7 percent of respondents to its survey had businesses which were initially capitalized at over $100,000, and the majority (82 percent) were capitalized at under $50,000. Finally, venture-capital firms have tended to be sources for expansion rather than start-up capital because a track record gives them a better estimate of the company's growth potential. However, venture-capital firms do fund some start-ups, even if the product is not a high-technology product. For example, one of the biggest recent successes in the venture-capital business was not a computer, but a company making herbal teas.

The major role of SBICs is to make venture, or risk, investments by supplying equity capital and extending unsecured loans and loans not fully collateralized to small enterprises which meet their investment criteria. SBICs are privately capitalized in participation with the government and are intended to be profit-making corporations. Most SBICs do not make very small investments. SBICs finance small firms in two general ways: by straight loans and by equity-type investments that give the SBIC actual or potential ownership of a portion of the equity securities. Some SBICs provide management assistance to the companies they finance.

The major difference between a SBIC and a MESBIC is that the latter was created to assist disadvantaged small businesses. Small businesses are considered disadvantaged if they are at least 50 percent owned and managed by individuals from groups that are underrepresented in the free enterprise system. Therefore, women are technically eligible for MESBIC financing, even if they are not from an ethnic or minority group. However, in practice, the Task Force found that there was substantial confusion among the managers of MESBICs as to whether women were eligible for funding, since the program had originally been targeted for racial groups.

Sources of Debt Financing

The major sources of debt financing are commercial banks or commercial credit institutions. There are three kinds of money you can borrow from a bank: short-term, intermediate-term, and long-term loans. Short-term loans are given for less than one year. This type of loan is most frequently used to finance inventories or to assist when you have cash problems because customers are not paying their bills on time. Lenders usually expect short-term loans to be repaid after their purpose has been served, such as when inventory has been converted into salable merchandise. Intermediate-term loans are given for between one and five years. Long-term loans are made for more than five years and are generally given to finance capital acquisitions or expansion. They are paid back in periodic installments from earnings.

Although it is often difficult for a new business to get a line of credit or a revolving credit account, these are some of the best arrangements to work toward with your banker. Under a line of credit arrangement, you may borrow money up to a certain amount throughout a year's time. You sign a note as you borrow and pay interest for as long as it takes to repay, but you do not have to reapply for the loan so long as you do not exceed the ceiling. A revolving credit arrangement is similar to overdraft protection on your personal checking account. You are usually given a book of special checks once your revolving credit account is approved. When you make one out, you are in effect activating the loan for that amount. Each month you are billed for a portion of principle plus interest on the amount you borrow. Both arrangements are helpful if you have seasonal business peaks. They also help solve the cash-flow problems created by customers who do not always pay their bills on time.

The type of money you will want to borrow will depend on what you want to use it for. For example, if you need cash to buy inventories that will be sold in three months, you will probably want a short-term note. However, if you are making a major acquisition of equipment or machinery you will need a long-term note.

The Small Business Administration

The Small Business Administration is often referred to as the "banker of last resort." This federal agency has a wide range of loans available to assist small businesses that are unable to get the funds from existing commercial sources. However, you must be turned down by two banks if you live in a city of over 200,000 people or by one bank in smaller cities, before you will be considered eligible for an SBA loan.

The two major types of loans furnished by the SBA are direct loans and guaranteed loans. Almost 80 percent of SBA loans are accounted for by guaranteed loans, primarily because they enable the maximum use of its loan funds by stimulating private lending institutions to make loans to small businesses with their own money. Under the guaranteed-loan arrangement, your regular bank handles your loan, but SBA promises to pay up to 90 percent of the loan if you should default, thereby increasing the attractiveness of banks to take a risk on small ventures.

Nevertheless, it is often difficult to find banks that will give guaranteed loans. The Task Force found that only 695 of some 14,500 banks in the United States financed more than twenty-five guaranteed loans. Bankers apparently feel that the turnaround time on an SBA loan is too long and that these loans tie up money for too long, at too low a profit; they also complain of the paperwork burden the government places on them.

If your bank refuses to lend you money even on the SBA's guarantee, you may be able to get a loan directly from the SBA. However, the amount of money the agency has available for this type of loan is extremely limited.

In the past, the SBA has been a thorn in the side of many women who often found uninterested loan officers who did not seem to take very seriously the idea of women seeking to start businesses. But under the leadership of Patricia Cloherty, the first woman deputy administrator and a former venture capitalist, there has recently been a sincere effort on the part of the agency to improve its track record with women. In 1977, the SBA began a women's campaign aimed at targeting more loan funds to women and informing them of the services of SBA through a special regional series of prebusiness workshops. In 1978, the agency targeted over $1 million per quarter in guaranteed loan funds to be placed with women and will continue the effort. The SBA has also provided funds to the American Women's Economic Development Corporation to be used for entrepreneurial training to women. Each regional SBA office has a "Woman in Business" position, and the Washington, D.C., headquarters has a "Women's Business Advocate," whose responsibility is to ensure that women are mainstreamed into each and every program that the SBA offers.

Other Sources of Business Financing

Getting money to launch your business is only your first problem. You will experience a continuing need for capital, as growth must be financed. Your business will eat up money faster than it produces it, and you must seek operating capital to keep your business going and growing. Some major sources for operating capital, aside from the previously mentioned ones, are your suppliers, finance companies, and factoring companies.

Having good relationships with your suppliers can be a big plus in terms of providing you with "vendor capital." They can give you special credit terms so that you do not have to pay for inventory or supplies immediately. Many business owners forget that thirty-day terms enable them to use their suppliers' money for thirty days. Suppliers can also help you out in times of cash crisis.

Mary Vinton, owner of Georgetown Leather Design, believes that supplier credit was the only thing that saved her business from going under when they expanded too fast without any capital planning and suddenly found themselves faced with $390,000 worth of debts they could not pay off. Vinton's business survived as a result of working out arrangements with creditors, but many don't. "In a situation like that, having a lot of candor with your creditor is very valuable. You say, 'Listen, we screwed up. This is the situation.'" Vinton points out that they couldn't go back to a bank for long-term financing once they were in a bind. It is a lot easier to make such arrangements if you have a good relationship and track record with the supplier, but most suppliers would rather take slower payments than face the chance of no payment at all if you go bankrupt. Finance and factoring companies may be a source of financing once your business is established. Although these companies have traditionally had a reputation as institutions of last resort and may sometimes be perceived as charging exorbitant fees, they offer many services that should be considered in assessing the finance costs. These sources of money are often used in short-term financing when the business cannot expand rapidly enough to meet demand or when there are lagging sales. Most finance companies lend on the knockdown value of fixed assets—the money they could raise if they were forced to sell the assets off. They usually lend only 75 percent of the market value of the assets and generally not for amounts less than $50,000. Factoring companies will purchase your accounts receivable for cash at a reduced price. Like finance companies, they usually like to do business with large firms that have a business volume of at least $1 million with a net worth in excess of $150,000. Thus, both of these sources of financing are of marginal use to an extremely small enterprise with few fixed assets.

PICKING THE BEST SOURCE OF CAPITAL

To determine the best source for your particular needs and how you can convince financiers to back your enterprise you should look at five factors: the growth potential of your business venture, how risky your business venture is perceived, how long you need the capital, what kind of money you need, and what you are willing to pay in terms of debt servicing (interest rates) or a certain loss of control over your business. It helps to look at the spectrum of the sources of capital in terms of their willingness to take risks. At the top of the list in terms of those sources willing to back new businesses are venture-capital firms; at the bottom of the list are commercial banking institutions. Although banks do finance some business start-ups, they are usually better sources for getting operating capital. You will probably find that initially all you can get is a personal loan, given against the character and credit worthiness of the individual and secured by personal collateral. Once the business is operating, you will probably be able to get financing through commercial loans that are secured through the business.

You should also look carefully at your ability to repay a loan. Your loan payment will be due each month, regardless of whether you have a customer, whereas investors wait for profits, not repayment. Although it is a smart move not to pour all your own money into a firm but to use it as collateral to borrow money, you should beware of leveraging your business too high or taking on too much debt, as you might find that your repayment schedule can sink your business when sales are slim. Every business needs an adequate cushion of paid-in capital—either by the owner or investors—to take it through the stormy times and to make sure that its bills and loans can be paid. This factor is something that a banker will be looking for in making a decision to fund your business.

What Banks Look for in Making Loans

In making loans, bankers consider the four c's of credit worthiness: collateral, capability, character, and credit. Unfortunately, most women tend to get low marks on these four factors with creditors—be they bankers, venture capitalists, or suppliers—even if no prejudice is evident. Our position in society and the work force has impacted our ability to amass savings. Moreover, we usually mingle our assets and credit history with our husbands, so that we have only a paltry or no independent financial track record—which is your passport to getting into the money game.

It is a sad reality of life that most banks will not grant a loan without the borrower putting up *collateral*—something of value that can be used to secure your loan. Collateral is the lender's security against being left holding the bag in the event that you default. It also represents an assurance that the business is not just a lark, that you have a vested interest in its success. Collateral may be in the form of marketable securities, such as stocks and bonds; savings; or personal or business property, such as your home or the firm's equipment or machinery. But for women who have never worked and for those who have made wages too low to amass savings, providing a bank with collateral can prove a problem. For many women, the financial power of their family is tied up in their husbands' names and is not theirs to invest in a business venture.

The second factor bankers and financiers judge a loan applicant by is *capability*—the capability both to make the business venture a success and to repay the loan in the event that the business does not succeed. Here too, the position of women in the work force has had a negative impact. Neither a homemaker who has never worked nor a secretary is going to have the management track record that will make a lender feel secure or the same potential earning power in the event of business failure as a person who has been a corporate executive.

If the first two factors—collateral and capability—measure a borrower's ability to pay back the loan, the third and fourth factors—character and credit—interact to measure a borrower's willingness to pay back the loan. *Character* usually relates to one's financial integrity and standing in the community, whereas *credit* refers to a person's credit rating, which for many women, is a particularly thorny problem.

A Credit Rating: Your Money Passport

Credit is perhaps the most important of the four c's of credit worthiness and the one most often overlooked by women. Today, there are still many women who do not have a credit rating, or have a poor one. Many women do not have credit cards in their own names. They do not realize that a credit rating is their passport to economic independence in our society. Unless you have some record of your individual ability to repay debts, no one is going to hand over large sums of money to you. Without a credit rating you will also find that you can't get a telephone or even buy supplies on time.

In 1974, the Equal Credit Opportunity Act was passed, prohibiting discrimination against any credit applicant on the basis of sex, marital status, race, color, religion, national origin, age, and other factors. Although the act does not give anyone an automatic right to credit, it does require that the same standard of credit worthiness be applied to all applicants. Key provisions of the law include the following:

- You can't be refused credit just because you're a woman.
- You can't be refused credit just because you're single, married, separated, divorced, or widowed.
- You can't be refused credit because a creditor decides you're of childbearing age and, as a consequence, won't count your income.
- You can't be refused credit because a creditor won't count the income you receive regularly from alimony or child support.
- You can have credit in your own name if you're credit worthy.
- When you apply for your own credit and rely on your own income, information about your spouse or his cosignature can be required only under certain circumstances.
- You can keep your own accounts and your own credit history if your marital status changes.
- You can build up your own credit record because new accounts must be carried in the names of husband and wife if both use the account or are liable on it.
- If you are denied credit, you can find out why.

The Federal Reserve Board, which is one of the agencies responsible for regulating this law, puts out an excellent pamphlet, *The Equal Credit Opportunity Act for Women,* which can be obtained by writing to the Board of Governors of the Federal Reserve System, Washington, D.C. 20551. It outlines what creditors may and may not ask of potential borrowers. It also lists the agencies that enforce the act and explains the penalties levied for violations. The FTC also puts out several pamphlets explaining how to get a credit record, pointing out that four out of five women will become single again in their lifetime either through divorce or the death of a spouse.

Judith Barnett can attest to the importance of treating your credit wisely. Barnett, who has written numerous articles on the subject, suddenly found that she was an "invisible woman" when she divorced her husband. No one recognized or trusted her financially, even though she had handled all the household books and had paid thousands and thousands of dollars in bills while she was married. She could not even rent a house, a problem she solved by having a friend cosign with her. Barnett indicates that it was a slow process to build back her financial status and one most women can avoid today if they take the time to take advantage of the new laws. "Every woman should, and every woman can, build up a separate credit record even if she is married and has no income. You may not be able to open a credit account, but you can ask the credit manager at a store to keep a file of your records in your own name."

Barnett worked for over a year and a half to build up a credit history. Her first step was having a friend cosign her house rental on the provision that after six months if she paid all bills promptly, the cosigner's name would be dropped and the record would be in her name. She then went to the credit manager of a store where she had traded and convinced him to let her purchase a sofa on a loan. She paid it off promptly and then opened a regular credit account. She thereafter periodically took out a new account, realizing that it was better to build her record slowly, since flooding credit managers with applications might look suspicious. After a while she applied for and received an American Express card. She suggested as another route taking out a small bank loan and paying it off promptly. Like many divorced or separated women, Barnett got a job at the time she left her husband. She was therefore slowly building up both her income record, or ability to repay, and her credit history.

But just getting a credit rating isn't enough; you also need to maintain it. You should not only take out credit cards in your own name but also pay them off promptly. Many women do not realize that late payment on bills can be almost as serious a black mark on your credit rating as nonpayment. If you can't pay a bill promptly, you should call or write to the credit manager and explain the situation, assuring them that you will make full payment the next month. Don't assume that they will understand.

You can check your credit record by calling your local credit bureau and asking them to send you a copy of your report. They will do this for a nominal charge, unless you have been turned down for credit. Then they must give you your record free of charge. Checking this record will give you a good idea of how you are viewed by lenders. It will also allow you to take advantage of the opportunity to correct your credit image, to the extent possible. You are allowed to tell your side of the story in the credit record on why one account has you listed as a poor risk. There may be a simple explanation, which will give creditors as better view of your financial stability.

If you are a married woman who works, you should also try to establish your own financial statement, separate from your husband's. This means not only having a bank and savings account in your own name and individual charge accounts but also building a list of assets, such as stocks and bonds or real estate that are owned in your own name, rather than jointly with your husband. Eve Grover, president of the First Women's Bank of Maryland, points out that married women are often amazed when they find that they cannot get loans without their husbands' cosignature because all of the assets have been amassed jointly.

Your goal should be to create a situation where you are economically independent and will have your own business and credit track record. With divorce so prevalent in our society, it is the wise woman who takes these precautions.

What You Should Look for in a Bank

If the first golden rule of business is that "He who has the gold makes the rules," the second golden rule is to "Know your banker." Emily Wolmach, president of the Women's National Bank in Washington, D.C., feels that finding a banker you can deal with is often more important in the long run than better conditions of short-term financing. A banker who is sincerely interested in your business and appears willing to go to bat for you can be your best business ally; she or he can be worth her or his weight in gold.

Once your banker makes a loan to you, she or he has a vested interest in your business success. If you prosper, the bank prospers. If you fail, the loan they approved is not going to be paid. To build up a good relationship, you will need to be open and honest with your bankers and keep them fully informed of your business progress. It helps if you periodically furnish them with progress reports on your business in the form of financial statements and projections, even when you are not seeking additional financing.

Kathleen Ross, an assistant vice president for credit at California Canadian Bank in San Francisco, advised in an article for *Enterprising Women*, that not only should you tell a prospective banker what benefit your business brings to the bank in terms of average balances in checking accounts, savings accounts, and present and future financial needs, but you should also ask them questions to see if you think they are the right people to handle your account. Key questions to ask bankers, according to Ross, include the following: Do they have an industry specialty related to yours? What is the average size of their borrowers? What are their professional backgrounds, especially in terms of whether they are commercial or consumer lenders? How long have they been in these positions? Do they have any latent negative feelings about women as business owners?[4]

Whether you patronize a large commercial bank or a small community bank will depend on your needs. Major banks tend to offer a wider range of services and locations, which may be important if you run a cash-and-carry business that requires nightly deposits. Community banks, on the other hand, are smaller, meaning that the banker you deal with daily may be able to make your financing decision personally or get it through the bank's hierarchy quicker. To a large bank your banking business might look minuscule compared with that of some of their other clients, whereas a small community bank may look at it as a business with growth potential and positive implications for the community.

What to Do When No One Will Lend You Money

There may be times when knowing the money markets and preparation, presentation, pluck, and persistence just don't seem to work. But the key to overcoming this financial obstacle is not to get bitter, but to get resourceful. Remember that there are more ways to skin a cat than one. If you have a viable business idea you should be able to find funding. Diane Pingree—who launched a new regional magazine, *Texas Woman*, in 1979—is an example of how one woman's ingenuity and persistence paid off. Pingree took a year and a half to get prepared with a first-class business plan and mock-up of her magazine, before she began looking for capital. After striking out with both venture-capital firms and banks, she happened to read an article about a Canadian publication that was entering the United States market. Pingree called the company and sent it the mock-up of her magazine. The Canadian publication agreed to bankroll her venture, thereby proving that if the business idea is good enough and appears to be a money-maker, you should be able to find investors.

But there are other ways you can find money even if investors are not to be found. Eileen Weinberg and Christi Finch were batting zero with both the banks and the SBA, as well as with their friends, on seeking funds to start Word of Mouth Caterers in New York City. They were finally able to finance their start-up by offering acquaintances higher interest rates than they could get at banks. "When we opened up we had exactly $50 left in the bank, and the bills were pouring in. Luckily our business was so good we were able to pay our rent and the bills and keep operating." Although neither Weinberg nor Finch would advise anyone to open so close to the edge of the cliff, it does show that anything can be done if you really want to do it badly enough.

One woman raised the capital to start her Washington, D.C., firm by opening checking accounts at a number of banks simultaneously and applying for the personal line of credit that they give customers. Since she was opening the accounts simultaneously, she could indicate to each bank that she had no other debt obligations. She was able to get three such lines based on her salary as an attorney with a major Washington, D.C., firm. This gave her enough capital to start out in subleased space in an existing law firm. A year and a half later, that initial seed money had blossomed into a fast-growing firm that now has a suite of offices.

Banks usually have a rule of thumb about how much they will allow you to have on a line of credit based on your salary level. The woman just mentioned advises women to find out this level and take advantage of establishing such credit arrangements prior to leaving a well-paid position. "I think working women, particularly if they are holding fairly responsible professional jobs, underestimate their financial flexibility in the marketplace. If you prepare yourself—before you take the leap to ownership—you may find you can get more credit than you think. Once you have a line of credit, a bank won't take it away from you as long as you pay it off and are a good customer."

Carole Hyatt is an entrepreneur par excellence. She has owned several businesses including her current business, Child Research Services in New York City, which does marketing research. Her first was a children's theater, which she launched by bringing in the man who owned the theater she needed for a percentage of her business. She has always seemed to find money for her ideas. "I'll just say 'here's an idea, who needs that idea?' I'll go out and find someone. If I have to go to two hundred people, I'll go to two hundred people until someone wants the idea or I modify the idea. At some point, if you speak to enough people, there just has to be a match." Thus, resourcefulness, not necessarily riches, can also put you in business.

CHAPTER 6

Developing Your Marketing Strategy

There is an old saying that if you build a better mousetrap the world will beat a path to your door. The first thing to remember in owning a business is that this statement is dead wrong. If you think that your product, your service, or your reputation is so good that the customers will flock to you the minute you hang out your shingle, think again. You are both being naive and making a serious mistake.

Developing an effective marketing strategy is one of the most important things you will have to do as a business owner. It's a basic reality of business that if you haven't got a customer, you haven't got a business. Anyone contemplating starting a company or opening a store should remember some of the basic business truisms.

- There are a lot of businesses out there that are just as good as, if not better than, yours.
- When you start a business you not only become a new competitor, but you will also generate new competition for yourself.
- The customer is basically lazy.
- If you don't sell yourself, no one else will.

The latter factor appears to be a hard pill for women to swallow.

125

WOMEN AND MARKETING

Carole Hyatt, owner of Child Research Service, believes that too many women just start their business hoping the world will come to them. They don't realize that you have got to get out there and hustle and convince people to buy your product, or you just aren't going to make it. Hyatt teaches a course for women at the New School for Social Research in New York City and has recently written a book, *The Selling Game: How to Sell Yourself and Anything Else*. The goal of both the course and the book is to get women over the psychological obstacles Hyatt thinks inhibit them in marketing their products and to teach them specific selling skills. While teaching a course on how to start your own business, Hyatt found that although most of her students had marketable ideas and some even had found funding, almost three fourths of them didn't know how to sell their products. "Most of them had a dream that they were going to get an outside partner, or someone, to take care of the selling. However, they were having difficulty finding this person who would make it 'whole' for them, since their businesses were such that there wasn't enough money in it for this type of person. What they wanted was a growing business, but what they had was a "ma-and-pa" shop, with the dream that the outside person would bring growth."

Hyatt found that the women had difficulty accepting the fact that they could do their own selling. "For some reason, the whole thing seemed dirty and they didn't want to be a part of it, or they were afraid of it." Hyatt thinks that part of this comes from the fact that women have never learned to ask for things directly because that was never our role. As she expresses it:

Women have never learned how to ask for things directly, which is necessary in selling a product. We have wonderful skills—like the skill of listening. The skill we are missing is the action skill. We rely on our passivity, rather than our actions, and we don't know how to ask directly. We have internalized an indirect approach—the power behind the throne kind of thing—and we are afraid to be direct because it might be thought unfeminine.

Hyatt points out that transferring the manipulative skills you learned as a wife or daughter may make you end up selling your person and your sex, rather than your product. Although it may work initially for some women, you might not want to deal with what you have unknowingly promised silently, and you often feel guilty because subconsciously you know that you are selling the wrong thing.

Hyatt also thinks that the distaste for selling is compounded by a fear of rejection. Since we have never been conditioned to ask directly, we are also not used to getting no for an answer. She feels that if you ask most women what word is the worst—yes, maybe, or no—most women will tell you no, when really maybe is worst. If someone tells you no, you can move on to another opportunity to get a yes; but if someone tells you maybe, you are caught in 'maybe-land,' waiting for a yes that may never come. Although Hyatt thinks that men don't want the nos any more than women, she feels they have been socialized to the fact that they are expected to perform so that they don't get as involved in the emotions of the no as do women; they learn how to take the no and move on. The expectations for women, on the other hand, are different. Women tend to get stuck in maybe-land.

What Hyatt tries to do in her course is to make women understand that no is not rejection, rather, it is just one of those statistics that you have to gather to get a yes. She feels that one has to understand that there are statistics to winning on a sales call, just like in everything else. These statistics will differ with each person and business. She explains that everybody has a set of statistics for winning. "If you go out on a sales call, and are realistic, then you know that for every one contract you land, you will probably have to do ten interviews. But, as you get more expertise and better credentials, then you will probably be closing one out of every two or three calls. Being realistic means that you have to realize that you have to make a greater number of sales calls and collect a few nos in order to get a yes."

Jean Reid, who formerly trained women for the American Women's Economic Development Corporation, affirms that learning how to collect nos without feeling rejected can be a hard thing for women. "Some of the women that we see tend to take their businesses much too personally. It becomes an extension of themselves. This makes them take a no on a sales call as a personal, rather than a business, rejection. They want to go home to bed and pull the covers over their heads, rather than to continue to sell; while a man will just keep trying different angles until he convinces the customer and gets a yes."

Yet, even women who do not face these psychological obstacles in marketing their products often face a second set of obstacles outside their control: subtle prejudice toward women business owners. The Task Force found that many women felt they faced a market credibility problem because of their sex, particularly if they were in a male-dominated field. Mary Zulalian, who once owned Holden and Company, says that a woman is still a rarity in the brokerage business, and that she has had difficulty getting accepted by "the boys on the Street." Although her business grew steadily, she still had few institutional clients. It took her three tries to get a seat on the stock exchange, something she feels would have been easier had she been a male owner. Zulalian, like many women in nontraditional fields, signed her letters with her first initial, rather than her given name, unless she knew the person. "I was in a field where it was hard being a woman and I didn't believe in taking any unnecessary risks in case someone might be prejudiced."

Prejudice is not limited to the private marketplace. The Task Force found that only 11 percent of the women responding to its survey had acted as prime contractors, and only 7 percent as subcontractors, to the federal government—

primarily for extremely small contracts of under $10,000. The Task Force noted that little had changed since the United States Commission on Civil Rights made its 1975 report, "Minorities and Women as Government Contractors." This report found that women participated in the government market even less than minorities and that they were hampered in the procurement (buying) process by both an unavailability of information and biases built into the system.

The Task Force concluded that women were getting a minuscule piece of the federal procurement dollar, primarily because it was a game in which the deck was often stacked against them. Discrimination, though difficult to prove, was mentioned time and time again as a real barrier to women being able to compete equally in the government selling game. Women writing to the Task Force reported being insulted by insinuations that their businesses were not serious endeavors or that they got business in exchange for sexual favors. Others pointed out that the old myth of women not being able to balance their checkbooks or manage their financial affairs continued to hamper them in areas where subjective decisions about a firm's capability played a major role.

THE MARKETING GAME

Although women undoubtedly face more obstacles than the average man in trying to run a business and market a product, these obstacles are not insurmountable. It is the product's characteristics, not your personal characteristics, that eventually make you a winner in the marketing game. And indeed, women may have a few advantages in this aspect of the business game. What lies behind a successful marketing strategy is the ability to be innovative and creative—something women have not had bred out of them as much as men have by the "must do's" of the business world. Obviously, painting ribbons on your delivery truck is not a marketing strategy many men would use, but it worked for Marie Tarvin of Sun City Delivery Service in El Paso, Texas.

Once you understand that what works is what counts in the marketing game, you will realize that marketing is actually a lot simpler than you think. Although marketing experts like to throw around a lot of technical mumbo-jumbo, like "tapping latent demand" or "positioning the product," creating an effective marketing strategy for your business is basically common sense, like everything else in business. The basic objective of any marketing strategy is to get your product to the customer in a fashion that will induce her or him to buy it in a quantity and at a price that will meet your profit goals. It takes into account the entire range of what it takes to merchandise your product, including your product development plans, pricing policies, and advertising plans.

That is why I like the concept of developing a marketing strategy. A strategy takes into account the dynamics of the business environment in which you will be playing. In the marketing game, the opponents, or competitors, change frequently, and the spectators, or customers, come and go. If you aren't alert, you may easily find yourself still playing in left field, when everyone else has gone home. As the whole nature of the business environment is based on change, there is no such thing as "cornering a market," at least not for long. There is no patent on ideas; and chances are that if you have truly stumbled across something good, someone will follow you into the marketplace and become your competitor. The truly skillful small business player is one who can take her or his firm over the growth hump and into the realm of big business when the sweet smell of success begins to make others interested in your game.

Jim Molloy—owner of TRAMCO, a management consulting firm for troubled enterprises in Cambridge, Massachusetts—points out that often the best thing that a small business person with a truly innovative idea can hope for is acquisition by another firm. "If you aren't acquired and your product catches on, chances are that you'll be pushed out of the marketplace by a big business." He explains that the larger company will be able to produce your item faster and cheaper and reach more people because of its existing distribution system. Although imitation may be the best form of flattery in some walks of life, in business it hits where it hurts—in the cash register. Isabel Mitchell—owner of Ambience Accessories, a New York City firm that manufactures and wholesales lighting fixtures and decorator accessories—believes that one should be *aware* of the competition, but not be *ruled* by it. "The important thing is to keep doing what you are doing better than anyone else."

You must be both alert to competition and ready to deal with it. Sandy and Mel Schifter, a husband and wife team who started Le Sportsac, are prime examples of people who believe firmly in staying one step ahead of competition. Their original business concept had been to design and produce a series of bags for carrying tennis and other sports equipment. However, they quickly found that the bags were easy to copy and that they were being followed into the marketplace by many competitors who were selling cheaper versions. The strategy they adopted was to switch to a fabric no one else had—parachute material—and they came up with their current line of merchandise, which includes carrying bags and luggage. Although the Schifters feel relatively secure in their market because they are buying as much of the raw material as is currently produced, they still make sure that they continually change their line of merchandise. They are now expanding from bags and luggage into ponchos, jackets, and other products made out of the same material.

Therefore, one of the first things you should do in business is face up to the realities of the game. Recognize that just when you think that the field is clear for an easy win, some other players are bound to show up and require you to change your playing strategy. However, competition is not always all bad. It can broaden as well as narrow your market. For example clothing stores cluster to shopping malls, and fast-food franchises tend to be situated on restaurant strips in the suburbs. These businesses are located where they know the customers are coming, and they plan to use the special qualities of their stores or product lines to get the customers to choose them over the others. You should not be afraid of competition but should keep your eyes on the game and develop a marketing strategy that is flexible enough to keep you winning against your opponents. Effective marketing strategy involves three operations:

- Understanding your market environment, in terms of what customers want and what competitors are supplying
- Defining your market niche, or that part of the total customer market you will try to satisfy with your product
- Developing a marketing formula that will convince the customers to buy your product rather than your competitor's

UNDERSTANDING YOUR MARKET

Recognizing Market Dislocations

Understanding your market environment is the first step you have to take in developing your marketing strategy. Most new businesses are started because there is a dislocation in the marketplace that allows a new firm to break through, just as an opening in the opponent's line of defense in a football game can give the opposition a chance to score. Joel Pitlor of Venture Founders points out that the most successful entrepreneurs his organization has helped launch have not been those who started highly innovative businesses that created new markets but have instead been primarily the result of a market dislocation. These firms found a market niche which was not currently being met by big business. For example, one of the entrepreneurs aided by Venture Founders has ridden the crest of the outdoor market with a tent factory; another started a sanitary napkin firm at a time when the industry, by coming out with diversified products under new names, was destroying the extreme brand loyalty that had traditionally closed this market to newcomers.

Therefore, the important thing in marketing your product is to keep your eye on the market environment and recognize when a dislocation occurs. You can then develop a strategy that will match this dislocation. There are basically four types of market-dislocation syndromes to watch out for: supply and demand, corporate umbrella, the better mousetrap, and the sleepy industry.

THE SUPPLY AND DEMAND SYNDROME.   The supply and demand syndrome is probably the one with which you are most familiar. It occurs when there is an excess of demand for a product or service that is not currently being met and is undoubtedly the most frequently used strategy for getting into the business game. When this syndrome occurs, you see a lot of "me too" companies joining an existing business parade.

THE CORPORATE UMBRELLA SYNDROME.   The corporate umbrella syndrome occurs when an existing corporation's policy prohibits it from providing some services that are needed, thereby enabling a newcomer to enter the marketplace to fill the demand. Control Data was born out of such a situation when an employee decided to fill some of the market demand that a large company was not meeting because it did not want to diversify too rapidly.

THE BETTER MOUSETRAP SYNDROME.   The better mousetrap syndrome involves a product innovation strategy. A new company fills the market gap by introducing a new product that creates new demand or a changed product that captures share in the existing market. Xerox is a good example of the former, whereas Tampax is a good example of the latter.

THE SLEEPY INDUSTRY SYNDROME.   When the sleepy industry syndrome occurs, a new company gets its start because the existing industry is complacent and is offering either poor-quality products or low service. An example of this market dislocation is Federal Express, the business that went into guaranteeing fast delivery service because the mail service was so bad. The company's motto is "absolutely overnight service."

Any one of these market-dislocation syndromes may be operating at any time. To win at the entrepreneurial game, you need to both recognize the dislocation and develop a strategy to deal with it. You also must be prepared to change strategies if new dislocations occur. Too many people make the mistake of letting personal preferences, rather than true market demand, dictate the type of business they decide to start. The key ingredient to marketing success is whether there is a need for the product in a sufficient quantity to provide both you and your competitors with a market, and this demand must also be at a price that is high enough to earn you a profit.

Finding Out About Your Market Environment

Finding out about your market environment—which consists of your customers and competitors—is what is meant by market research. You do not have to spend a lot of money, or hire a fancy research house to uncover this information, as the important thing is not how fancy or complicated your research is, but how current and accurate. All you need to do is know what to look for and where to look. Any information that can help you make marketing decisions is good information. You can conduct your own research or hire someone to do it for you. An inexpensive and often overlooked way to get a good market study done is to hire a graduate business student to do it for you. She or he will probably relish the opportunity to work on a real-life business problem and will provide you with excellent market intelligence.

Most of what you will be looking for will revolve around answering the basic who, what, when, where, and how questions of marketing. Regarding competitors, you will want to know who is producing or selling a similar product; what they are selling in what quantities and at what price; when they are selling it; where they are selling it; and how they are selling it. And for customers, you will want to know who your potential customers are, in terms of age, location, occupation, and earning power; what types of products they need in what quantities and at what price; when they buy, in terms of the time of day or season; where they buy, in terms of both the places of purchase and current competitors; and how they buy, in terms of paying cash or using credit cards and open accounts.

You will find that much of this competitive side of the coin will have already been researched for you. The marketing departments of trade associations periodically conduct such market research for their members and make it available to the public. Trade publications and industry directories are also sources of information about competitors, and the United States Department of Commerce publishes some general market indices.

You can easily identify the trade associations you might want to contact by using the *Encyclopedia of Associations*, which is available at most public libraries. Dun & Bradstreet and Robert Morris Associates also put out a variety of publications that can tell you a great deal about what you can expect from your firm and how well your business is stacking up against industry standards. These publications are often available in public libraries.

Another source of market information is the United States Bureau of the Census, which provides information on retail, wholesale, and selected service industries in its *Census of Business*, which is taken every five years and published in the years ending in two and seven (for example, 1967 and 1972). These reports present data for various businesses on the numbers of retail establishments in an area, paid employees, payroll size, and sales data. The information is broken down not only by county and city but also by central business district in large urban centers. Two other useful sources of information from the Census Bureau are the *Statistical Abstract of the United States* and the *County and City Data Book*. These two publications include many consumer market statistics—such as income, employment, housing, and population characteristics—by state, county, and city.

Census data is available for every city, town, or village in the United States. For cities of 50,000 or more inhabitants, the data are broken down into smaller units called census tracts, with populations of 4,000 to 5,000. Summary information is available for the entire metropolitan area in which a city is located, as well as for the individual blocks within the city. This information is available at most libraries, and a catalog of Census Bureau publications can be obtained from the United States Department of Commerce.

Census data can tell you a great deal about the economic strengths and weaknesses and market potential of your trading area. Such information can help you not only answer many of your key marketing questions but also decide where to locate your store or how to advertise.

FINDING YOUR MARKET NICHE

Once you have a fix on the competitive market, your next step is to find your market niche—that position in the marketplace which you think your firm can fill better than others. It is your "unique selling proposition," to use the marketing term, that makes you different. Your market niche is your starting point for developing marketing strategy. To find your market niche, you need to know what business you are in and how you differ from your competition.

Defining Your Business

Not truly understanding what business you are in is one of the classic marketing mistakes, and it is made by owners of both large and small businesses. The tendency for big firms to define their businesses too narrowly is one version of what Theodore Levitt calls "marketing myopia."[1] For example, Levitt contends that the railroads declined because they defined their business narrowly as rail travel, rather than broadly as transportation. They failed to move into alternative forms of transportation and were edged out of the passenger market by airlines. Likewise, the movie industry was seriously hurt by television because they failed to see that they were really in the entertainment business, rather than in the film business. Small businesses, on the other hand, tend to want to be all things to all people. They do not define their business narrowly enough so that they can target their sales efforts and stick to their market niche. According to Jim Molloy of TRAMCO: "They don't figure out where they are going or where they want to go. They are content with the trees and can't see the forest."

Trying to be all things to all people can prove to be a particular problem for service businesses, the field that many women choose because its capital requirements are low. Barbara Patinkin—who ten years ago started Visual Concepts, an advertising and marketing firm in New York City—attests that it took her five years to finally be able to express concisely what she does and how it benefits customers. She advises women to start with knowing the benefits of your product or service to help customers understand your expertise and to avoid misleading them. Doing that reduces the chance that you will waste valuable marketing dollars with a message that doesn't sell to an audience that doesn't want to buy. Patinkin counsels people to be specific. "Don't say you offer the 'best service'; say it precisely. Does that mean you offer care and thoroughness, a low price, or speedy service?"

Luke Bandle—owner of Luketon Ltd., a Washington, D.C., public relations firm that specializes in the arts and entertainment fields—also stresses the importance of knowing your selling message. "It is certain that if you don't know who you are, no one else will. It isn't enough just to say you do consulting or advertising. You have to tell them more—make them specifically want your services over other people's."

Patinkin feels that the mistake she made, and one that a lot of women have made, was to be so afraid of losing a sale that there was no focus to her marketing. "You can't view everyone as a potential customer and the world as your market. In order to use your marketing dollars most effectively, you need to focus on those who can best benefit from your product." Thus, it is crucial that you first know your market niche and what makes your product unique before targeting your market.

Your business will be defined to fill that gap between what competitors offer and what you think you can offer best. Bill McCrea of the Entrepreneurship Institute—a nonprofit organization in Worthington, Ohio, that provides weekend seminar training for would-be and existing entrepreneurs—points out that entrepreneurs are basically the innovators in our business environment. "They start businesses to fill vacuums that exist in the system. Something they can do better than large businesses, because they are smaller, more flexible, and probably have lower labor costs."

It is therefore important that you figure out if there is a gap in the marketplace you can fill better than someone else. You should not only find something you can offer that has unique advantages over what is currently available, but you should also gauge the consumer demand for this product or service. This is why it is important to understand both your market and your competitors. Unless you know both the market gaps and consumer demand, you may wake up to find that no one else was in the market because there were no customers. Your idea just wasn't a viable business idea.

Once you know the market potential of your product you are ready to take the last step in developing your marketing strategy—figuring out the best way to reach and convince your customer to buy the product or service you offer. It is at this point that you will get into the more technical and creative aspects of building a marketing formula that will work for you.

DEVELOPING YOUR MARKETING FORMULA

There are five basic ingredients—the five p's—that make up the formula for a successful marketing strategy: product, price, packaging, place, and promotion. All these factors interact to determine the level of sales your business will generate, and although your formula will involve some aspect of all five, it will probably be pegged on one. For example, Freddie Laker's Sky Train air service anchors its marketing appeal on price. He offers inexpensive, no-frills air transportation. Some products, such as fast-food stores or shopping malls, focus their marketing appeal on convenience of the place in terms of location. Others, such as cosmetic industries, rely heavily on promotion to build an image, rather than stressing the inherent benefits of the product. Products that promise to clean faster and brighter are relying on their product characteristics. What works best for you will depend on your industry, your competitive environment, and your customer.

Product Strategies

Your product strategy—the central core of your marketing formula—will correspond to what you have decided is your market niche. It will depend upon what you have identified as being needed by the customer and what is not being offered currently.

Look at any business and you can begin to see their product strategy. Corrine Travis, owner of Rose Lash International Ltd. in New York City, uses product strategy to her advantage. Her marketing strategy is pegged on selling clothes that meet the needs of today's career woman. This strategy recently led her to take out a full page ad in *Vogue* in order to prime the market for her franchising plans. The ad was designed to project the image of the product Travis offers, which is a line of beautifully tailored and functional clothes that can be dressed down for work or up for evening.

Travis, a former dress designer, feels that her experience in the fashion industry helped her identify a successful market niche in the very volatile retail industry. Travis designs some of her line and has it manufactured in the United States and Europe. Her idea was to develop a small, select, European-style boutique that caters to women who want the atmosphere and service you usually find in Europe but with clothes to fit the everyday needs of working women. "We cater to the woman who wants quality, not quantity, and try to help by acting almost as a personal shopper and making suggestions. When we get a new item, let's say a blouse that might go with a suit that they bought in the spring, we call them up and tell them what we have."

Travis is also a firm believer that knowing the industry you are in is a key to success. Since she has some of her items manufactured in Europe, she has to decide on her line of merchandise prior to seeing what is predicted as being good sellers in the trade press. So far she has been on target every year, a factor she attributes to the years she has spent in the fashion industry.

Sandy Hancock, owner of Sandy Hancock Enterprises in Dallas, Texas, is another woman who uses product strategy to her advantage. Hancock started her business a year and a half ago after consciously trying to search for a business idea that would work. The market dislocation that Hancock found was that department store mannequins, which cost several hundred dollars, must frequently be replaced because of damage. She then started a business that would repair the damaged mannequins. To make her business even more popular, she is now offering a new service to clients—creative makeup for the mannequins to match their costumes or the window display. "If a store is doing a window in pink stripes and polka dots, we can create an exotic look to the mannequin that will catch the eye of the customer." Hancock feels that most of her business satisfaction comes from the learning process of a fast-growing business. She already has her eye on the Canadian and Mexican markets and may start manufacturing her own mannequin wigs.

Pricing Strategies

Price can also be a variable in your marketing formula that you can use to get customers to buy your product. For example, retail chains such as K Mart and Korvette's use discount prices to try to develop customers, whereas Neiman-Marcus uses a pricing policy to appeal to the luxury segment of the market. Many new and small businesses use pricing strategy to enter the marketplace because their lower overhead enables them to offer lower prices than more established businesses. Corrine Travis, owner of Rose Lash International, points out that offering quality, well-tailored clothes at a price lower than you would usually expect to pay is a key ingredient in her marketing formula. Such a strategy also helped boost sales in Mary Vinton's first retail store, and Georgetown Leather Design now operates out of six locations in Washington, D.C.

The pricing policy of your firm will depend on the market niche you have set for your firm in terms of price. There are many pricing strategies, but there is only one best price—the one that yields the most dollars after costs are subtracted. The best price should either offer the highest mark-up on each unit or generate maximum sales because of volume.

You should take care in developing a pricing strategy, as a pricing strategy that successfully attracts customers may at the same time force you out of business if your prices are too low to cover costs.

Unless you know the break-even point of your business, you run the risk of being fooled by the ring of the cash register, rather than the amount of the sale. *Break-even analysis* is an important management tool that can help you avoid this problem, as well as help you make some of the business decisions that arise out of the relationship of volume, costs, and revenues. It uses a mathematical formula consisting of two components: fixed costs and variable costs.

Break-Even Formula: fixed + variable costs = sales at break even

Fixed costs are those costs that you have irrespective of whether you make one sale or a hundred. They usually involve overhead costs, such as rent, electricity, and executive salaries. *Variable* costs vary with the number of sales you make. They change in direct proportion to your change in volume of sales or production, such as direct materials, direct labor, or commissions. Break-even is the point where your sales equal the sum of your fixed and variable costs.

The break-even formula can be used to calculate the total dollars in sales, the number of units you need to sell if you are a manufacturer, or the percentage of production capacity you should aim for to cover costs. It provides you with a valuable tool for setting prices and judging the profit impact of other management decisions. Knowing your break-even point and your own profit objective will enable you to set a price floor for the lowest price you can charge. The price ceiling will be set by the competitive market.

Your accountant can help you learn how to calculate your break-even point, or you can learn from two pamphlets published by the SBA: *Guides for Profit Planning* (SBMS No. 25) and *Attacking Business Decision Problems with Break-Even Analysis* (Management Aid No. 234). The SBA also publishes three other pamphlets that will be helpful to you in learning how to price your products: *What is the Best Selling Price?* (Management Aid No. 193), *Pricing for Small Manufacturers* (Management Aid No. 226), and *A Pricing Checklist for Small Retailers* (Small Marketers Aid No. 158).

Packaging Strategies

How you package your product can be an important variable in the marketing formula. Examples abound of businesses that have used packaging and distribution strategies to their advantage. The Pet Rock was a business idea that relied heavily on creative packaging to sell the product. L'Eggs hosiery developed a winning marketing strategy by using both creative packaging and product placement. That company switched its product distribution strategy to supermarkets and drugstores, rather than sticking with the traditional hosiery channels of clothing and department stores.

Many service businesses make the mistake of thinking that the packaging ingredient in the marketing formula does not apply to their businesses. Although service products are less tangible than manufactured products— which can be picked up, felt, compared, and even returned to a store if disliked—packaging your product is just as important in a service industry. You should develop packaging for both yourself and your business in a way that will project the firm's image and help you sell the service. People sometimes tend to forget that professional image is as much a part of your marketing strategy as your advertisements or brochures.

Luke Bandle, whose business is public relations, feels that women do themselves a great disservice by not recognizing the importance of putting forth a professional image in everything they do. "You're starting off with one strike against you anyway as a woman, and it's not going to help if you use cutesy, feminine-looking stationery or your home typewriter. The first thing I did when I started my firm was to get two IBM Selectrics. You don't have to buy them; you can rent them. It doesn't matter if you are doing the typing yourself, you just have to have letters that look like you aren't." Bandle notes that the number of people you will have a chance to tell personally about your business will be small compared with the number of people who will come in contact with your stationery, calling cards, brochures, or other promotional pieces. She went through three designs before she settled on the crisp, uncluttered, but imaginative logo she thinks projects her firm's image.

Peg Shaffer—owner of Paradigm, Inc., a marketing research and consulting firm in Potomac, Maryland—is another woman who believes strongly in packaging both yourself and your business to project a professional image. Shaffer, like many women business owners, is careful about the image her clothes project. She has also given a great deal of thought about the way to effectively package her business. Her whole marketing strategy begins with the idea that busy people do not like to read much and that you only have a few minutes to register an impression about your business. "We have devised a very short brochure, which fits into a standard number 10 envelope, a man's suit pocket, or a woman's handbag. It is designed to be the first introduction of Paradigm, and can be read in less than two minutes. . . . Once people are interested, they ask for more information." Shaffer has also found that adding a personal, but professional, touch can pay off. She decided to use letterhead notepaper the same size as the brochure, on which she could write handwritten notes. The response to her efforts was very high, as the personal touch seems to be appreciated in such an automated age.

Place Strategies

If you operate a retail store, the fourth p in the marketing formula is critical. Owners who locate in shopping malls are relying on place—that is, location— as a key factor in their marketing strategy. They recognize that the convenience of the mall and the added drawing power of many stores will increase sales.

Many business owners forget a truism of business: The customer is basically lazy. Only your Aunt Tillie will walk that extra mile because she loves you and wants to support your business endeavor. Most customers will go to the place that offers the best buy at the greatest convenience. For many people convenience is even more important than price. The location of your business is therefore just as important as the price or quality of your product.

For Isabell Mitchell, owner of Ambience Accessories in New York City, the location of her business in New York City's prestigious Decorators and Designers Building is a key part of her strategy. "I was offered space at a lower price in another building, but turned it down. I knew it was important to be in this building, because this is the major showroom for my industry." Mitchell designs, produces, and wholesales lighting fixtures—many of which have won design awards—and sells home accessories, primarily to interior decorators or the design divisions of department stores. Her strategy is to fill an existing market gap for a decorators' showroom that sells the finishing touches to rooms—everything from ashtrays to African art—in one place.

Anyone who is opening a business should take into account the proximity of their customers and their competitors and the potential impact this will have on business. If you are in retailing or offering services that rely on walk-in traffic, you should also look at specific things such as street location, parking facilities, traffic flow, and the availability of transportation. You'd be surprised how much difference even a little factor like being located on the sunny side of the street can make in sales volume. The SBA publishes two pamphlets that will help you learn how to locate your business: *Using a Traffic Study to Select a Retail Store* (Small Marketers Aids No. 152) and *Locating or Relocating Your Business* (Management Aid No. 201).

Virginia Mapel—whose store, Gazebo, is located on the corner of Madison Avenue and 66th Street in New York City—says that she never realized what a difference having the corner location for display purposes would have on business. She had been looking for a cozier environment, but her husband convinced her that the items she was displaying (silk flowers, wickers, quilts, and other handicrafts) would create the atmosphere and that the windows on two streets would give her a better opportunity to catch the attention of more people. Mapel also tells a horror story that illustrates the importance of being sure you hammer out all of the items in your lease carefully, preferably with your attorney. She had signed with her landlord to take the space "as is" and later found that "as is" to the landlord meant with no electricity and no ceilings. "I had given up my other space and the movers were scheduled to come and move me. I was finally able to convince the landlord I was serious about demanding lights and a ceiling when I threatened to operate by candlelight and have my grandchildren picket the building."

If you are in a professional service business, such as public relations or consulting, and are thinking of working out of your home, you should weigh carefully whether both you and your customers will take your business seriously in that location. Suzanne Ives, owner of Ives and Associates, now owns her own office building after working out of her home for a while. She had worried about the effect not only on her clients but also on herself. A friend advised her to go downstairs every day, step outside, close the door, and then enter as if she were arriving at work. She never actually followed her friend's advice, but thinking about it helped her to make the psychological transition from home to office. Ives feels that having to get up and get dressed, put on makeup, and go to the office represents a kind of commitment that impacts how serious you think you are and how serious you are perceived as being.

Eve Grover, president of the First Woman's Bank of Maryland, also attests to the importance of perceptions. Grover was working out of her home during part of the initial organization phase of the women's bank. She decided to incur a larger overhead by moving to office space after an incident with a reporter who had interviewed her at home. "The article that appeared did not help the bank's cause or my credibility. It described me as having financial papers spread out on the kitchen table and a pot of spaghetti cooking on the stove." This description was hardly the image of a banker, despite her impeccable banking credentials.

Beverly Jackson, of Jackson/Summers Associates, is still ambivalent about working at home. She sometimes thinks her business can become overwhelming, as she never gets away from it. She has to leave town to get a day off.

However, some women find working at home a boon. Peg Shaffer, owner of Paradigm, Inc., chose her second home because it would allow her to have the kind of expanded office space she wanted. She finds working at home no different than working in an office and much more convenient. Her formula for making it work is to treat the home office just as you would any other office—which means getting dressed for work and letting your kids know that they are not to disturb you while you are working.

Promotion Strategies

The final and perhaps most important ingredient in any marketing formula, is promotion. Many people make the mistake of thinking of promotion in a narrow sense as advertising, or they myopically view it as something they can't afford when they start out. Promotion is anything that presents and sells your product. For some businesses, such as cosmetics and travel industries, promotion is the major component in their marketing formula. These companies may spend millions annually on ads that rarely tell you about the inherent characteristics of the product. What their ads try to sell is hope, not the product.

Business owners tend to forget that they must tell, convince, and move people to buy their particular product or there will be no revenue and certainly no profit. There is a tendency to be so in love with your product that you think the world will be also. You may have just invented the most fantastic device in the world, but if you can't get your message out to your consumers that it exists, it isn't going to sell. You must also think about how you can reach people and get them interested in buying the product.

Your promotional strategy can be as varied as your products. For some firms, it may involve developing existing contacts by personal calling, announcements, letter writing, or direct mail advertising. For others, it might involve special promotional events, such as gala openings, or paid advertising. The type and quantity of promotion you need will depend on the business you are in, the level of your competition, and the size and characteristics of the market. Obviously, if you have just stumbled across the cure for cancer, you are going to get a lot of free publicity that will make your promotional efforts easier than if you are starting a retail firm. The key to developing a good marketing strategy is to develop an integrated and consistent strategy that can grow with your business.

Once you know your market niche, the attributes that make your product unique, and the audience you want to reach, the rest is simple. Developing a promotional campaign revolves around your ability to answer three key questions:

- What is the message you want to promote?
- What is the best medium for reaching the people you want to sell to?
- How much money do you want to spend on this effort?

What I mean by message is not just your advertising message, but the total message your firm is trying to convey in the marketplace. The business image of your firm is grounded in your concept of what the business is; it starts with your stationery and calling cards, and ends with your paid advertisement. Getting your message across does not always have to involve great expense or paid advertising. Although promotional media is usually referred to in terms of advertising media—print, radio, or television—brochures or a mail campaign can also be used to get your message across.

Luke Bandle has spent most of her career working with cultural organizations that have had small sums of money and have known little about marketing. Prior to starting her own public relations and planning firm, Luketon Ltd., she was the director of communications and marketing for the Wolf Trap Foundation for the Performing Arts and for the Opera Society of Washington. Bandle is currently working on a manual to help similar organizations and small businesses realize that they can set up their own promotional campaigns without a lot of money. She believes that all a woman starting out on a shoestring needs to promote her business is a good logo, a good brochure, a car, and a lot of energy and that the best thing to do is to be visible in her new community, where her customers are. "Join trade associations; make speeches; do anything you can do to increase your visibility. If you are artistic, you may even be able to get away with designing your own sales materials. The important thing is to develop something that looks professional and gets your message across."

A woman should not wait until she has the money to hire a public relations or advertising firm to develop her marketing strategy. Plenty of people can help you initially. The ad salesmen at newspapers will advise you on how to get the types of ads you need cheaply, since a good salesman is looking for a steady, not a one-shot, customer and will tend to be very helpful. If you do decide to invest in a public relations or advertising firm, you should look for one that can develop a marketing plan for you, not just ads. The firm should be able to survey your market and tell you what kinds of clients you weren't getting that you should be able to get; it should also be capable of developing a look, a logo, and a whole plan of promotion over a certain period of time. If the firm says it is just going to put an ad in a newspaper, you can do that yourself.

The very least you need starting a business is a crisp, professional logo, stationery, calling cards, and a brochure. This brochure will probably be your major sales piece initially, and it should concisely and clearly state what you can do for a client, who you have done it for before, and why you can help them. The goal of any sales piece is to build confidence in your firm's credibility and its ability to produce for a client. Most brochures always list past and present clients to give the potential customer the nice feeling that she or he is not alone.

However, although letting the client know that you have done the work before and that they aren't being your first guinea pigs helps make them feel comfortable, that alone is not going to sell your service. You must also tell your client why they should want to buy the service. Carole Hyatt of Child Research Service feels that the best way to make a sale is to hit the customer where it counts—in the pocketbook. "Nothing helps you more than telling a potential client that you performed a service for another client that saved them $50,000 or brought in 200 customers." Denise Cavanaugh, co-owner of Cook/Cavanaugh Associates, would agree with Hyatt. "One of the things I discovered early, when we were learning how to market our services, was that we had to talk about our organizational values and talk about them in a way that counted in terms of the bottom line and profits."

If you decide to go the route of advertising your firm, you may need the help of an advertising agency, unless you plan a simple ad campaign. The SBA publishes a number of pamphlets that can be helpful to you: *Plan Your Advertising Budget* (Small Marketers Aid No. 164), *Measuring the Results of Advertising* (Small Marketers Aid No. 121), *Advertising Guidelines for Small Retail Firms* (Small Marketers Aid No. 160), *Advertising—Retail Store* (Small Business Bibliography No. 20), and *Selecting Advertising Media—A Guide for Small Business* (SBMS No. 34).

The key principle to remember in establishing an advertising campaign is to develop one that is consistent and has continuity. The goal of advertising is to develop a group of customers, not just to generate a single sale. Your basic ad decisions will be based on the message, the target (who to say it to), the copy (how to say it), and the media (where to say it). The basic rule of thumb in establishing an ad campaign is that it usually takes 80 percent of your budget to carry the ads and 20 percent to develop them.

For the best return on your money, you should conduct an advertising "campaign" rather than a one-shot advertisement. This will require an advertising budget. There are three ways businesses use to arrive at this budget: (1) figuring ad expenses as a percentage of past, current, or future sales or some combination of these factors; (2) establishing the amount you will spend on each unit of sales; or (3) setting your market objective to increase sales by a certain amount. The first method is the one most frequently used by new and small businesses. Your budgeted dollars should then be spread over the types of media or calendar periods that you will use in your campaign, the results of which are usually measured by the cost per sales generated. You should beware of creating a campaign that is inflexible, spread too thin, sporadic, based on personal preferences, or of a poor quality. As Mary Vinton of Georgetown Leather Design points out, no ad at all is better than a poor one.

THE GOVERNMENT AS A REGULATOR AND CUSTOMER

Meeting Your Obligation to Trade Fairly

The backbone of the American free enterprise system is competition. The theory behind this philosophy is that rivalry among sellers of goods and services will, on the whole, yield better products at lower prices than would be obtained if there was no competition. As a business owner you should know about several federal acts that have been passed to assure such free and ethical competition. Your attorney should know how these acts affect your particular business. However, it helps to be aware of what regulations and laws exist that impact on your business. A wise investment in time and money would also be to become familiar with the Uniform Commercial Code. This code is the body of law that governs modern business, and it deals with everything from negotiable instruments to sales, bills of lading, and your contractual obligations to clients and customers. Most colleges offer a one-semester course in commercial law. Although you shouldn't try to be your own lawyer, having an overview of your legal rights and responsibilities as a business owner can be extremely valuable.

THE SHERMAN ANTI-TRUST ACT.   The Sherman Anti-Trust Act was the first federal legislation passed to discourage monopolistic trade practices. This act makes unlawful any contracts, combinations, and conspiracies that would restrain trade. It was passed in 1890 and was followed in 1914 by two more-specific laws, the Clayton Act and the Federal Trade Commission Act.

THE CLAYTON ACT.   The Clayton Act defines and enumerates unlawful trade practices and specifically deals with illegal price discrimination. This act makes it unlawful for a seller to discriminate in price between different buyers, unless the differences are based on variations in the grade, quantity, or quality of the product or in promotion and transportation costs. It was amended to define price discrimination more sharply in 1936, as independent retailers had become alarmed over the growth of chain stores, which were getting price concessions from suppliers.

THE MILLER-TYDINGS ACT.   The Miller-Tydings Act modified the restrictions on product pricing to allow suppliers of trademarked products to enter into arrangements with sellers about the level of the price of their resale items.

THE FEDERAL TRADE COMMISSION ACT.   The Federal Trade Commission Act created the FTC and gave it authority to regulate unfair trade practices and prosecute offenders. Whereas the Sherman Act deals with combinations in restraint of trade; and the Clayton Act makes illegal certain specific practices leading to a monopoly; the Federal Trade Commission Act attempts to stop any practices considered unfair. It deals not only with monopolistic practices but also with deceptive acts or practices, misrepresentation, commercial bribery, boycotts, fair packaging, and false advertising.

THE LANHAM TRADEMARK ACT. The Lanham Trademark Act allows a producer to trademark a word, name, or identifying symbol so that it cannot be used by another person.

THE CONSUMER PRODUCT SAFETY ACT. The Consumer Product Safety Act requires that manufacturers produce products that are not hazardous to consumers and that consumers be advised of dangers attached to using products. This act is administered by the Consumer Product Safety Commission, which has the power to enforce uniform safety standards, recall product deliveries, and halt production. If you are a manufacturer, you should write to this commission for information on what you need to do to comply with the Consumer Product Safety Act.

The Government as a Customer

Although the federal government may at times seem like a huge gray octopus whose tentacles are prying into every aspect of your business life, remember that this octopus has to be fed with everything from paper to penicillin in order to stay alive. Therefore, the federal government, along with your state government, is a valuable potential market that you should not overlook. Chances are that the government will become an even better market now that a national policy on Women's Business Enterprise has been established by the federal government. This policy is an outgrowth of the Task Force on Women Business Owners work, and mandates federal agencies to implement special programs and targets for women.

The federal government is the largest single buyer of goods and services in the United States, purchasing over $72 billion—or about 7.5 percent of all the goods and services bought in 1977. However, the Task Force found that few women participated in this market, primarily because they don't know about it and because they have been discriminated against. But some federal agencies are taking positive steps to find and contract with women-owned firms. The Department of Transportation has defined women as being included in all their minority business enterprise programs and has contracted with the National Association of Women Business Owners to develop a directory of women-owned businesses to alert women to possible procurement opportunities under the Railroad Revitalization Act. The Department of Interior has made some positive efforts to attract women to share in the contracts for the construction of the Alaska Pipeline. The General Services Administration (GSA) is now sponsoring procurement seminars and conferences to teach women and minorities how to find out about and bid on federal contracts. In addition, the GSA is requiring its thirteen regional business service centers to make periodic reports on the number of women they have counseled and is also trying to get the membership of women and minorities up to 15 percent on its public advisory panels in architecture and engineering. The SBA has made an effort to assist women in getting a greater share of the federal procurement dollar by establishing a computerized Procurement Automated Purchasing System, which will provide a directory of small businesses, including women, to all federal agencies.

Understanding the Federal Selling Game

Competing in the federal market can be tedious, time-consuming, and expensive. But it can be lucrative if you win. If you decide that you want to play in this game, you must find out about contracting opportunities. There are two ways to do this.

The first is to locate the federal agencies you think might be interested in your product and get on their bidders list. To get on a bidders list, you need to advise a particular agency that you are interested in receiving advance notice of any future contracts for your particular product or service. Sometimes you will be asked to supply information, such as an annual report, that can substantiate your ability to fulfill the contracts prior to being put on the list. The regional offices of both the SBA and the GSA can help you identify the agencies that might be interested in purchasing the products and services your firm produces, and they can also be a good source of counseling and information about how to break into the federal market. A list of these offices is in the back of this book. Data on the purchases of all the federal agencies will soon be compiled and computerized on the Federal Procurement Data System. This system should provide valuable market information for any business interested in selling to the government, since it will track where federal procurement dollars go in terms of both the products bought and the agencies making purchases. The only current comprehensive guide to both civilian and military purchasing is the *U.S. Government Purchasing and Sales Directory*, published by the SBA and available in its regional offices. Once you are on an agency's list, you will automatically receive information about any upcoming contracts.

The second way to find out about contracting opportunities is to subscribe to the *Commerce Business Daily*. A subscription to this publication costs $75 a year, plus $66.90 for airmail services, and is available through the United States Government Printing Office, Washington, D.C. 20402. It advertises daily all new contracts the federal government is seeking to let and announces who was awarded previously advertised contracts. If you see a contract in which you are interested, you can request a copy of the contract specifications from the particular agency and decide if you want to bid on the contract. These specifications are called "requests for proposals" (RFPs) or "requests for bids" (RFBs) in Washington's business jargon.

The federal government buys the goods and services it uses by two means: formal advertising and negotiated procurement. Formal advertising is a highly disciplined process of competition that awards a contract to the lowest bidder who can demonstrate the financial stability, technical expertise, and production capacity necessary to produce the product or service desired. Negotiated procurement, on the other hand, allows for some discussion and bargaining to occur in order to reach agreement on the contract terms and prices. Usually the requests for solicitations for negotiated procurements are stated in more general terms, and businesses compete on their proposed method of doing the work. There are a number of variations in negotiated procurements, ranging from RFPs published in the *Commerce Business Daily* to sole-source or personal-service contracts. Sole-source contracts are allowed if a firm can show that the contractor has the capability for performing the service that could not be found elsewhere or if they do not have time to go through a formal bidding process. In general, the regulations allow agencies to make small purchases, not to exceed $10,000, without going through a formal solicitation and without receiving a proposal from a contractor. These types of procurements are a bone of contention for many women who believe that the "old boy" network that exists in the procurement system works against them getting these types of contracts.

Another type of purchases made regularly by the government are made from the Federal Supply Schedules. These schedules contain more than 4.2 million items and are somewhat like a mail order catalogue for the day-to-day needs of federal agencies. The schedules are put out by the GSA, whose regional offices can tell you how you can get on them.

To win a federal contract you must make sure that your bid or proposal conforms to all the requirements of the RFP. Your proposal will be judged in terms of both the price and the ability of your firm to do the work. Usually there is a list of the judging criteria enclosed in the RFP, which will give you an idea of how the factors on which a proposal is judged will be weighed. Since the competition for government work is fierce and the task of preparing a government proposal can be a costly and time-consuming effort, it is a good idea to look at these criteria carefully and assess whether you have a high probability of winning before you waste valuable time bidding. Often the two or three firms who are chosen as finalists are asked to come in for further negotiations before a final decision is made.

In addition to the regular contracting procedures, the federal government has an established policy of selling to groups that are disadvantaged in the marketplace so that they can get a "leg up" in the competitive marketplace. Such groups include the handicapped, the blind, Vietnam veterans, firms located in labor surplus areas, prison industries, small businesses, and minorities. Under such preferential methods of contracting, a portion of the federal procurement dollar is directed to specific groups, based on the premise that limiting competition to only those groups and allowing them to compete only among themselves would be more equitable. Currently, women are not designated as one of these listed groups, although the Task Force has recommended that special programs be developed for women.

Currently, the only preferential programs in which nonminority women can participate are the small business set-aside programs. However, women who are of a racial minority are eligible for the minority business enterprise programs, including the technical assistance programs operated by the Minority Business Enterprise Office of the Department of Commerce and other special minority programs of other agencies. This office of Minority Business Enterprise is the best source of information about these programs, and the agency may establish a special program for minority women in the near future in accordance with a Task Force recommendation.

Since most women who would be competing in the government market own small businesses, the two federal programs that offer the most potential for spearheading their entry into the federal market are the small business set-aside program and the federal subcontracting program. Under this set-aside program, the federal government sets targets for federal agencies to spend a portion of their purchasing dollar with small businesses; that is, some contracts are set aside for small businesses, and competition by large businesses for these contracts is excluded.

The goal of the subcontracting program is to get large businesses to funnel a portion of the dollars they receive from the government as prime contractors to small businesses as subcontractors. Under this program, the government requires prime contractors with contracts of over $500,000 to establish specific subcontracting programs aimed at three groups: minority business, small business, and firms located in labor surplus areas. However, contracts for less than $500,000 require only the "best efforts" of contractors with no quotas, incentives, or specific reporting requirements. In addition to these formal obligations, procurement representatives in the SBA's regional offices keep tabs on local prime contractors in order to recommend small firms to them which might be potential subcontractors. Therefore, it is a good move to get in touch with the procurement specialist in the SBA office nearest you to express your interest in subcontracting.

If you decide that you do want to enter the federal market, you should also consider some little-known facts often overlooked by firms not sophisticated in the bidders' game. As all proposals submitted to the government are in the public domain, you can obtain copies of previously won bids and gain a good idea of what type of proposals a particular agency likes. In addition, all agencies are required to give explanations of why you lost the bid. This "post-bid" interview can be valuable to the beginning contractor because it can help you find out what you did wrong and how you can improve your batting average. Finally, it is possible to arrange some prepayment on the contract, although some experts feel that asking for this financial arrangement may jeopardize your chances of getting the contract because the contractor may fear that you do not have adequate financial stability. If you are turned down on the grounds that your firm does not have the necessary financial and productive capacity to perform a specific government contract, you can ask the SBA to determine if it believes you can meet the contract requirements. If the agency feels you are competent to perform the contract, the federal agency must accept the SBA's findings as conclusive. The SBA puts out two pamphlets that will help you understand more about selling to the government and their programs: *Selling to the U.S. Government* and *SBA's Procurement and Technical Assistance Programs*.

You should read all the contract specifications with care, refuse to bid on unreliable descriptions or specifications, and avoid excessive optimism in assessing the job in terms of risks and your in-house capabilities. You should also avoid bidding for tasks that are beyond the state of the art or accepting impossible project time frames. Making a careful cost estimate for the job is critical, a problem especially for novices in the federal market. Many a firm has been burned because they do not realize that if the contract is for a fixed price, it cannot be modified to reimburse you for miscalculations. A common mistake is that some business owners may be so eager for government work that they underestimate their costs and end up having to perform on a contract that is actually losing them money. If you are a large business, you might be able to absorb this cost overrun; but if you are small, you could be knocked out of business by the mistake.

CHAPTER 7

Staffing Your Organization

Your staff is an important part of your entrepreneurial team. Studies have consistently shown that it is the lack of prompt, courteous service from employees that is the major cause for customers ceasing to do business with a firm. Although more difficult to quantify, your employees are as much an asset as the more tangible assets, such as inventory or equipment, that appear on your balance sheet. They are also infinitely more fragile than your other assets. Unlike inventories or materials, they cannot be purchased in mass, stored, or easily replaced once lost. Therefore, the management of this asset is one of the most difficult and most critical aspects of owning a business, second only to the management of your cash resources in determining your success.

Good employees can make a marginal business idea succeed, whereas poor employees can destroy the best business. Kandra Driggs—owner of Wing Conferences, a San Francisco management consulting firm—stresses the importance of having a courteous and competent staff. She has been told by many of her clients that the reason they have contracted with her is because of the initial impression made by her staff over the telephone. She uses the same criteria in doing business with others. If someone cannot adequately explain their service or product over the telephone she assumes that the management has been slipshod about training their staff and will be slipshod in other areas as well.

Too many businesses make the mistake of considering their employees only as a business expense, rather than as an asset. Your salary expense is often one of the biggest costs of doing business, particularly for service industries. As you keep your eye on that barometer of the health of your business—your profit and loss statement—it is easy to mistakenly view salary expenses only as a cash drain, rather than linking this cost of doing business to sales and the revenues coming in.

149

How well you utilize your employee asset will depend on many things, among them your recruitment and staffing polices, your pay and benefits practices, and your management of these resources. Remember that the time you spend recruiting replacements is valuable lost time, which could mean money for your firm. Like a machine that has downtime when shifts change, your firm will experience its downtime when time and energy must be invested in replacing a valuable employee. This loss can be especially painful if the employee leaves at a critical time. You can avoid this problem by building your staff slowly and thoughtfully.

DEVELOPING AN EFFECTIVE STAFF

Planning Your Staff Needs

Like everything else in business, developing an effective staff requires planning. The small business person who hastily opens an office and hires staff without any concept of her or his immediate, short-range, and long-range needs is asking for trouble. You may soon wake up to find yourself faced with all kinds of personnel problems that could have been avoided. You may find that you don't have enough business coming in to warrant the position, or pay the salary, because you neglected to estimate sales properly. You may find that you've hired the wrong person for the job because you did not analyze the type of skills you need for the task. To avoid such problems you need to sit down and think about your personnel requirements and policies and plan your staff needs carefully.

Developing a sound recruitment practice and organization requires an assessment of your present operations and your foreseeable work requirements while figuring in your probable turnover. This operation may sound a little like asking you to look into a crystal ball, particularly when you are just starting out in business. However, it should be conducted periodically to ensure that your organization is meeting the demands of your customers and growing steadily without strapping your organization. Any long-range recruitment and personnel policy should be flexible enough to meet the demands of their particular business environment. Such thought and preplanning will allow you to avoid contributing to the bad reputation small businesses have for job instability. The last thing you want to do is hire staff and then be forced to let them go because you underestimated your business volume and cannot carry the expense of their salary. Such a move can be a sure sign that you are on shaky financial ground, and can hurt the image you would like to project to suppliers and customers as a solid, reliable business.

The first step in planning your staff needs should be to take a careful look at both your immediate and future needs in terms of the types of skills you require, the amount of time you need them for, and the amount of money and other compensation you can afford to offer for these skills. For example, you may think that what you need now is a full-time secretary or clerk, when what you really need is a part-time secretary and a part-time research assistant—which you could switch to full-time positions as your business grows. Or if you are starting an advertising firm and feel that a key to your success will be finding a good graphic artist, you undoubtedly will want to offer this person different growth options in your firm than the person you are hiring as a receptionist or secretary. By hiring for growth, rather than for immediate needs, you may be able to lower employee turnover where desirable.

The Staffing Problem

In looking for a staff for your business, you are looking for more than just workers; you need people with the kind of talent that can help you play out your business strategy. For a small business, the problem is not finding employees, but finding *good* employees. In trying to build your business team you may often feel that you are low on the totem pole when it comes to choosing members. As a new and struggling business owner you will find that you can offer neither the wages nor the fringe benefits of the larger firms in your area.

Nevertheless, your business does have its benefits. Although you may be small, you are also growing. You can offer opportunity to talented people, an asset often overlooked in hiring. Your new and struggling business may not realistically be able to offer a prospective employee job stability and an impressive list of fringe benefits, but it can offer job flexibility, a less-structured organization, a more informal work environment, accelerated work experience, increased business contacts, and, most important, growth potential if your business succeeds. For many talented people, these benefits are greater bonuses than the paid fringes offered by many larger organizations.

The key to attracting good employees is to know your own work habits, your work philosophy, and your personnel policies. You should form an idea of the work environment you intend to create. For example, if you are a person who has a low need to control and who likes to have people around who will take the initiative and work with little supervision, you will be making a mistake if you hire someone with a strong need to be directed, controlled, and supervised.

Deciding If You Really Need a New Employee

In planning your recruitment and personnel policy it is important not only to assess your real needs but also to assign costs to the time and effort you spend in hiring. Before adding a new staff member, you must realize that this person will become a daily responsibility—in terms of meeting your payroll every Friday, managing this resource, and making a commitment to the person's future.

Remember that it is always easier to hire, than to fire someone, and it is done a great deal faster. An unsatisfactory employee is rarely fired immediately. They are given several warnings during which time your resources can be severely drained. Therefore, before you add new employees haphazardly, you should ask yourself some hard questions. First, you should assess whether you are utilizing your current employees to their full capacity. You might be able to realign the tasks in your business so that you will not only utilize the talents of your existing staff more effectively but also cut down on the need for new employees.

Second, you should analyze your work flow. If having so much overtime is causing you to think that you may need an extra pair of hands, you should first assess what is causing this overtime. Is it an actual shortage of staff, or are you not managing your work flow effectively and planning for work crunches? You might find you can save yourself a lot of money in terms of staff time by developing a system to plan your work flow better.

Finally, you should analyze the staffing options available to you. If what you are dealing with is extreme peaks and valleys in your work flow, it might be more economical to use overtime or temporary help, rather than hire a full-time employee. If your problem lies in a low sales volume and you think adding a salesperson will help, you might weigh the options of paying a low salary plus commission or even just straight commission, rather than a guaranteed salary.

Whatever your staffing problem, it will vary with your business and organization. In considering the options available, it is important to add in all the costs attributable to the employee. For full-time employees, these will include both your recruitment and training costs, as well as salary and fringe benefits. For temporary employees, your costs will include the service charges to personnel agencies, as well as the hourly rate of the employees. In addition, the quality of the work of temporary employees may not be up to your firm's standards, you might be paying more per task than if you had an in-house employee who understood your work methods. The basic rule of thumb is to watch the size of payroll relative to your sales—the payroll-sales ratio—and to hire someone only when you judge that the job is really necessary and that the new employee will increase your firm's profitability.

Staffing Alternatives

A lot of people don't realize that you don't have to run right out and hire a big staff the moment you open your business. There are many alternatives to full-time help. Many employers, particularly those who are in businesses with widely varying business volumes, often use temporary, part-time, or contract employees. A *part-time* employee is an employee of your firm. You are thereby bound by all the federal and state employee regulations, which require owners to deduct taxes, social security, and unemployment compensation from the wages of these employees. A *contract* employee, on the other hand, has offered her or his services to you and is therefore responsible for her or his own federal and state payments. A *temporary* worker is an employee of the temporary agency, which files all the necessary federal and state paperwork. You merely pay an hourly rate, much as you would do if you rented a typewriter or desk. The positive side of these options is that you do not have to pay full-time salaries when business is slow, but the negative side is that you may not be able to get the type of talent you need when you need it.

Peg Shaffer, owner of Paradigm, Inc., a consulting firm in Potomac, Maryland, has learned the benefits of using available talent as contract workers, rather than building a large internal staff. Shaffer says: "The advantage of being able to find good, high quality labor just for the duration of a contract allows you to deliver a very high quality product at a reasonable price, which is much lower than if you had to carry these experts on your payroll year-round." She adds that she rarely misses having a full-time staff except between projects. "The one thing that you miss is not having someone on the same side of the fence as you are to brainstorm with when you are developing ideas or when you are trying to evaluate something that has happened."

Shaffer's business is in the Washington, D.C., area, where there is a large pool of professional labor, and she has never had a problem finding qualified people in the ten years she has been in business. However, she points out that the rules covering contract labor are very definite. For example, you cannot dictate when, where, or in what manner these employees carry out their work since they have contracted only to provide you with a finished product.

Finding Employees

As mentioned, finding people to work for you as a small business owner will probably not be a problem, but finding good people at a price you can afford will be. People are easy to find, often without having to go to the expense of advertising or hiring a commercial agency. Some possible sources are friends, who may know of able employees; former employees; your own employees; trade associations, which may have job banks; customers and suppliers; universities; and state employment agencies.

Two important pools of highly educated and currently underutilized talent that you should not overlook are other women and retired people. The flexible staff needs of small, new businesses will be attractive to both groups. The chances you offer for career advancement may be attractive to women who may wish to work part-time because of family commitments or who may be reentering the work force and want the chance to gain the maximum amount of work experience quickly. Retired workers may be looking for flexible hours and some supplemental income and, therefore, may not mind the lower wages or minimum fringe benefits of your business. Retired workers offer the added advantage of providing you with years of business experience, which can be extremely helpful to a new owner.

Like many professionals who become business owners, Marjorie O'Connell Amey—a Washington, D.C., attorney who started a law firm, specializing in tax law—soon found that most of her time was being eaten up by administrative chores. She had little time to do the kind of "lawyering" that was her talent and the reason for establishing her own firm, which specializes in tax law. After several bouts with ineffective office managers, she found a retired military officer who not only had years of organizational and administrative experience but was a CPA to boot. He now works half-time for the firm and has taken over the financial and general office management, leaving Amey free to use her legal talent to build her firm and to do the things a boss is supposed to do—set policy, make key decisions, and monitor the business. O'Connell Amey and Associates now has three associates, a full-time support staff of four, as well as part-time helpers.

Nora Cunane also knows the benefits of using available pools of labor. Although her business, Guardian Construction, now concentrates primarily in the general construction field, she started out three years ago in the lawn maintenance and landscaping business. Having little knowledge of this industry and a limited budget, Cunane was able to overcome both of these obstacles by hiring experienced retired workers and inexpensive college students who needed summer work. She was thereby able to meet her needs for experienced labor in a cyclical business while staying within a tight budget.

As a small and new business, you may want to concentrate on using the free sources of employment leads. But as your business grows or if you have a business with extremely cyclical and frequent employment needs, you might want to develop a relationship with a commercial employment agency. You will find that the fee paid is often offset by the time you save by having them do the initial screening function of employees for you. It is a good idea to shop around for a temporary agency willing to understand your firm's operations and needs, rather than one that just supplies "bodies."

Advertising for your employees in newspapers through classified or display ads is, of course, the quickest way to generate a large number of responses. Display ads are usually used for highly specialized jobs, whereas classified "help wanted" advertising can be used for all types of employees. Although it may cost you a few more advertising pennies to be specific about your firm and your needs, it will save you the time of having to weed through applicants who do not meet your qualifications. Many employers prefer to use "blind" advertisements with box numbers, rather than "open" advertisements in order to both maintain confidentiality among employees and to screen applicants without having to acknowledge each application.

Predetermining the type of people you feel might be attracted to the type of business or firm you are developing will also help you in recruiting and keeping good employees. For example, your inability to provide job security or substantial fringe benefits may make little difference to a twenty-two-year-old college graduate, whereas it would mean a lot to a forty-five-year-old person with a family to support.

Job Descriptions—Organizational Building Blocks

No matter what kind of business you are in, or its size, having a thorough understanding of the characteristics of the particular job that you need filled is the basic starting point for recruiting or hiring people, figuring out how much to pay them, establishing performance measures, and controlling and managing your employees. The tool that will help do this is a *job description*. I am sure you have heard jokes about people refusing to do work because they say a task is not in their job description, but this interpretation is a negative, rather than a positive, one of what a job description can do for an organization. The idea behind a job description is not to create rigidity in an organization but to create a better understanding among workers and managers about who is doing what tasks.

Small business owners commonly make the mistake of thinking that physical proximity to employees automatically means that communication exists. A job description—which is an everyday tool in large corporations—can be useful in even the smallest organization because it is a written record which allows both the manager and the employee to have a common understanding of the job. It is a method for clarifying authority, responsibilities, and performance. In addition, it is a valuable tool in hiring because it outlines the skills needed for the owner and helps prospective employees decide if they want the particular job. It can cut down on the duplication of efforts and can increase productivity by telling how specified jobs relate to other jobs in the organization. It is the basic building block of your organization.

A job description is basically a written summary of the duties, responsibilities, and requirements of a particular job. It tells the duties involved in the job, how these duties are to be performed, the skills needed to do the work, why the job is necessary to your organization, and how it ties in with the other jobs in your business. It is concerned with detailing the facts about the content of the job that are necessary to the performance of your business, independent of the person who may currently be in the job, and the way it is being performed. A job description is not a tool for measuring performance, but only a tool for specifically defining the parameters of the job so that performance measures of that job can then be established.

Developing a job description can help alleviate one of the biggest problems in personnel management—giving employees a clear answer to the question, What is my job? If management has never sat down and clearly identified exactly the duties and responsibilities of specific employees, they may erroneously find fault with an employee and destroy morale when a job is poorly performed. In actuality, the basic problem may have been that the worker did not know what she or he was supposed to be doing and was therefore doing something different than the job for which she or he was being judged.

In the long run, the little amount of time it will take to do this kind of detailed thinking about the job you have to be filled will save you money. A job description will both allow you to be more specific about your needs in ads or with employment agencies, and thereby freeing time that might be spent screening and interviewing. In addition, it can help lower your employee turnover rate by avoiding any misconceptions about the job when employees are hired.

Job descriptions are easy to write. They can be as simple or complex as the job and the organization. The SBA puts out a free brochure, *How to Write a Job Description* (Management Aid No. 171), which includes sample forms which an owner can use and modify for her or his situation. A sample job description is reproduced on pages 157–161. The key facts in any job description include the following:

1. Identification of facts—job title, location of job, number of employees on the job, salary, and working hours
2. Skill requirements—educational requirements, job experience, relation to other jobs, job duties, and job knowledge
3. Facts about responsibilities—information as what aspects they can make decisions on without checking with a superior, who they report to, and how the job interrelates with other jobs

Other facts that are often provided on job descriptions concern physical effort required, such as lifting, or personal characteristics desired, such as being well-groomed, showing initiative, and working rapidly. Some job descriptions also include facts about working conditions, including the physical characteristics of work space, the number of other people, if any, the employee will be working with, and the amount of pressure.

Interviewing Prospective Staff

You should always interview two or three candidates for the job before making your final selection. In a larger organization two people should interview the person to get the benefit of another person's viewpoint. You should also check all references, keeping in mind that the candidate puts down those people they think will give favorable references. Therefore, it is important to question the person about the specific skills needed and to listen for what the person *doesn't* say versus what they *do* say. Few people give negative references, but they do hedge on providing a great deal of information if they do not think highly of the person.

It is important to try to maintain your objectivity for each candidate. Also, remember that the equal opportunity laws apply in the interviewing process. These laws prohibit job discrimination on the basis of sex, race, or age and preclude you from asking questions related to marriage or child-rearing. You can write to your state's Equal Employment Opportunity Commission for a free pamphlet on what *not* to say to a prospective employee in this regard, or you can write to the Federal Equal Employment Opportunity Commission in Washington, D.C.

SAMPLE JOB DESCRIPTION

Identification Facts

Form 1

Job Title ___________________________ Location ___________________________

Other titles used ___________________________ Number employed: M ___________ F ___________

Brief summary of nature or function of job* ___________________________
____

Code number** ___________

Salary range: Minimum ___________________________ Maximum ___________________________
   Average bonus or incentive payment ___________________________
Working hours: Shift: ___________ From: ___________ To ___________
   Overtime: ___________   never ___________ seldom ___________ frequent; average hours per week: ___________

Misc. ___________

*A 1-sentence definition, to give a general idea of job.
**Job definition (from the *Dictionary of Occupational Titles;* your local State Employment Service Office can be helpful.)

Skill Requirements

Form 2

Educational Requirements: (general education—grade or years)
   Grammar   High   Business
   School ___________ School ___________ School ___________ College ___________
Specific education for job ___________________________

Job Experience:
Previous experience required: None _______
    Acceptable type and length _______________________________________
Average length of time with organization _______________________________
Previous jobs normally held ____
Next job in line of promotion ____
Relation to Other Jobs: Contacts regularly as part of job:
Within the Company _____________________________ Outside the Company _____________________________
______________________________________   ______________________________

Exercises Supervision Over:
    Position of individual: ____
    Subject of supervision: ____
Is Supervised by: *Position of Individual*   *Subject of Supervision*
Immediate supervisor ___________________   _____________________________
Others ___________________________   _____________________________
Job Duties:
Regular:
    Before open for business ____
    During business hours ____
    After business hours ____
Periodic (weekly or monthly):
    Performed on regular time ____
    Performed after hours ____
Occasional: Performed on regular time ___________________________________
            Performed after hours _______________________________________

Job Knowledge:
General

Policies and Regulations

Special and Departmental

Procedures and Methods

Technical Information

Related Information

Use of Equipment: Types of equipment: _______
Special operations _______

Responsibilities

Form 3

Direction & Group Leadership:
None _______   Occasional _______   Frequent _______   Continual _______
Nature of responsibility _______
Business Operation:
None _______   Occasional _______   Frequent _______   Continual _______
Nature of responsibility _______
Care of Equipment:
None _______   Occasional _______   Frequent _______   Continual _______
Nature of responsibility _______
Safety and Health of Others:
None _______   Occasional _______   Frequent _______   Continual _______
Nature of responsibility _______
Contact with Public: None _______   Occasional _______   Frequent _______   Continual _______

Effort Demand

Physical Activities

——— Standing
——— Walking
——— Balancing
——— Climbing

——— Turning
——— Running
——— Stooping
——— Sitting

——— Reaching
——— Throwing
——— Lifting
——— Carrying

——— Pushing
——— Pulling
——— Fingering
——— Feeling

——— Smelling
——— Tasting
——— Hearing
——— Seeing

Worker Characteristics

——— Planning
——— Directing others
——— Writing
——— Showing enthusiasm
——— Being well groomed
——— Controlling emotions
——— Using arithmetic
——— Working accurately
——— Discriminating colors

——— Talking
——— Showing initiative
——— Getting along with people
——— Working at various tempos
——— Concentrating amid distractions
——— Remembering names and faces
——— Remembering details
——— Examining and observing details
——— Attending to many items

——— Making decisions
——— Working rapidly

Working Conditions

____ Inside	____ Hot	____ Dirty	____ Inadequate light
____ Outside	____ Cold	____ Dusty	____ Inadequate ventilation
____ Humid	____ Dry	____ Odors	____ Working with others
____ Hazards	____ Wet	____ Noisy	____ Working around others
____ High places			____ Working alone
____ Change of temperature			____ Working under pressure

Details of Working Conditions (summary based on working conditions) ________________

Details of Hazards ________________

Permissible Handicaps: ________ Limb ________ Hearing ________ Sight ________

SOURCE: *How to Write a Job Description*. Management Aid No. 171. Washington, D.C.: Small Business Administration.

A last word of caution: Beware of friends. Being the boss is a different role from that of a friend. The decision to hire a friend should be well thought out and talked about. You should realize that the working relationship may ruin the friendship and that you may have to fire the friend. And you should be as objective about their qualifications as you are about those of others.

COMPENSATING YOUR STAFF

You will find that one of your biggest problems as a small business owner will be trying to figure out how to meet your payroll every pay period. Salary expenses cannot be deferred. Because salaries are one of the major costs of doing business, particularly for service businesses in which women are heavily concentrated, it is important to get the most for your money in terms of both hiring and utilizing people. Too often new businesses err by thinking it is best to hire cheaply in order to save money. However, it sometimes might be wiser to pay more and hire experienced workers who can aid you in your initial stages of growth.

But small business owners may not be able to afford as attractive salaries as competitors. It is therefore important to remember that employee compensation can involve more than just making sure you have enough money in the bank to meet your payroll. The wages and salaries you pay are only one part of your total compensation *package*. Once, the term *employee compensation* was almost synonymous with wages and salaries. But today employees usually decide to take jobs based on the *total* compensation which includes not only direct wages and salary but also extras such as pay incentives, bonuses, and fringe benefits such as health and life insurance, profit-sharing plans, and retirement benefits.

Thus, you should consider both monetary and nonmonetary incentives when you begin to tackle the problem of what to pay an employee. You will find that your wage and salary system will be not only the cornerstone of your compensation system but also your key to effectively managing your operation. Although job satisfaction is an important ingredient in keeping an organization healthy, and more will be said in chapter 9, "The Final Move: Playing the Game," about how to motivate employees and be the boss, don't forget that money is still the prime motivator for most employees.

The hierarchy of needs outlined by Abraham Maslow in his book *Motivation and Personality* will probably hold true in your shop. Maslow, an organizational psychologist, maintained that every person possesses a four-level hierarchy of needs: basic survival needs, such as food and shelter; social needs, such as social acceptance; ego-gratification needs; and self-actualization needs. It is difficult for a person to rise to the next highest need level, unless the preceding level of needs has first been fulfilled.[1] The sixteen hours a day we may put in as business owners may help us meet our ego-gratification and self-actualization needs but such long work does not fulfill these needs for employees. For owners, long hours lead to deferred income that will come if profits increase. For employees, it merely means hard work unless they are adequately compensated for it either by pay or other options, such as compensatory time off or bonuses.

Remember that no employee will love your firm as much as you do, unless she or he has a vested interest in its growth—a factor women seem especially prone to forget. Kandra Driggs of Wing Conferences has found that many women business owners tend to treat their business as their baby, making it difficult for them to see why friends and family don't understand and why employees don't view their firm as something deserving of similar dedication.

Developing a Compensation System

To develop an effective salary system, you should make sure that your system has both external and internal fairness. External salary fairness means paying fair market rates for the qualifications, such as academic level or years of experience, that you are demanding for positions. You can find out about competitive salaries from many sources. Trade associations are one of the best sources of this type of information. Other good sources are informal business contacts and newspaper advertisements. Once you are aware of the competitive salary practices in your area, you may be able to get away with paying lower salaries if you can offer opportunities other than salary, such as profit-sharing, stock options, greater promotional opportunities, and on-the-job training or better fringe benefits, such as bonuses, longer vacations, and more sick leave.

Internal salary fairness means looking at whether you are paying fairly in terms of the responsibility and expertise that each job within your business requires. Your job descriptions will be the basis for determining the internal fairness of your pay system because they will afford you an objective way to rank jobs in a hierarchical order. You will find that internal fairness will be the key to effectively managing your organization, which will be discussed further in chapter 9.

Structuring Your Wage and Salary System

Wage is the term used to refer to the amount of money paid per hour or per piece of work. *Salary* is the term used to refer to the amount of money paid for a job, irrespective of the hours put in or performance produced. Wage earners are usually those employees covered by the minimum wage laws of the Fair Labor Standards Act. The goal of this act is to provide a common livable base for employees by setting wages for work done in a specific time span and paying a premium rate for overtime work. Your local state employment office can provide you with information about the requirements of the Fair Labor Standards Act and any local employee salary requirements that may apply. Four classifications of positions are exempt from the act: executive, professional, administrative, and outside sales positions. These employees are generally paid salaries.

The job description is the basis for most salary structures in large corporations. These descriptions allow you to rank the positions in your business according to the responsibility and importance they have to your overall goals. You can then develop a hierarchical range of salaries. Many firms establish a salary structure that utilizes a salary range, rather than a flat salary, for a particular job. In this way they can provide a low salary figure to begin with, while having an intermediate pay level for advancement in the position, and a top figure beyond which they cannot go for the particular job. Usually top-management jobs have a wider percentage spread between the low and high salary figures than lower management because the possibility for upward mobility is more limited at the higher level; thus advancement in higher positions must rely on salary raises, rather than promotions. Normally the midpoint in the salary range for any position is set at the competitive level for the salary in your area.

There are benefits to establishing such a salary system. It allows employees from the outset to understand that your salaries are both consistent and fair within the organization. It also gives them some insight into the possibility for career advancement within your business.

Be sure to include your own salary in this compensation system and structure, although you may, at times, have to forgo drawing all of this salary because of cash crises. It is important to budget your salary as a business expense in your records in order to have an adequate picture of the health of your firm. Your salary should be valued at the level you would have to pay should some unforeseen crisis make your replacement necessary. Knowing your own pay rate will have the added advantage of helping you delegate work and hire additional employees to take over some of the tasks that you are doing. Remember that your time, as the owner, is best spent at those things you do best and not at handling jobs that someone else can do for half the price.

Types of Pay Systems

There are two basic methods of paying wages and salaries: time spent at the job and number of units produced by the worker. This latter method, which is sometimes referred to as an "incentive wage," is normally used when the units of output are measurable and there is a clear relationship between output and the worker's effort. Such a pay system is more prevalent in manufacturing operations than in service or retail industries. Most small businesses tend to establish their pay system based on time, since this method is easier to compute.

Any standard textbook on personnel management will give you descriptions of many varieties of pay systems. For example, many retail stores pay clerks base salaries plus a commission on sales as an incentive. Some sales people work on a small basic salary but draw large commissions, whereas others draw a fairly substantial salary and have a smaller commission. The important thing is to develop a compensation system that you can afford and that matches the characteristics of your firm and business. Obviously, the compensation structure of a firm that has a stable sales growth and offers little potential for upward mobility will differ from that of a firm with fluctuating sales but tremendous growth opportunities.

Paying for Performance

The key to the effectiveness of your salary system is that increases in pay be linked to performance. Too often, companies tend to pay for *input*, or the hours put in, rather than for *output*, or the work done. Yet the success of any business depends on output because the latter will produce your profits. The key to a successful compensation system is to reward those who truly produce. By doing that, you can avoid such problems as paying employees too much in fat times and having them expect raises in lean times. Paying for performance will also enable you to quantify performance and minimize employee dissatisfaction that may occur if employees feel some people are being paid more because they are friendly with the boss.

Peter Drucker, the dean of management philosophers, often points out that focusing on contribution to the business is the key to effectiveness in one's work and in one's relations with superiors, associates, and subordinates. Paying for performance relies on three factors: setting performance goals, measuring this performance, and communicating satisfaction or dissatisfaction. For example, if your goal for a given year is to increase sales by 20 percent, you can then reward your salespeople according to how well they meet these targets. But if you merely say that the goal is to increase sales you have no yardstick against which to measure performance. The problem with many organizations is that they use extremely fuzzy factors in measuring performance, making it difficult for the owner to decide if a person deserves a raise and hard for a person to understand why she or he did not receive it. The resulting employee dissatisfaction that can be avoided if you learn to measure performance by quantifiable output and communicate to the employee how they are being judged.

Fringe Benefits

The fringe benefits you offer will be an important part of your total compensation package and are now part and parcel of the total wage picture in the minds of most employers and employees. There is a wide range of fringe benefits you can consider offering your employees. Some of these include profit-sharing plans, bonuses, pension plans, stock options, and deferred compensation plans, along with the more traditional fringe benefits of insurance plans, sick leave, holiday and vacation pay. Profit-sharing plans, bonuses, stock options, and deferred compensation plans are all incentives designed to reward employees for higher levels of performance. They differ as to their timing and the basis for the extra compensation which they provide. The cost of fringe benefits can sometimes be lessened by tax deductions allowed by the IRS. For example, bonuses may be deducted as a business expense for tax purposes in some instances when it can be proved that they are "reasonable." Payments to both profit-sharing plans and pension plans also can be deducted as a business expense, if you take the precaution of following the IRS rules on such deductions.

PROFIT-SHARING PLANS. Profit-sharing usually provides for an annuity to all employees who have been with a company for a specified time and is based, as the name implies, on profits earned.

BONUS PAYMENTS. These are not necessarily made annually, though they may be, and are usually determined by the performance of a group. In some instances, individual performance is rewarded by such payments. These bonuses, which may be paid quarterly, semiannually, or annually, can be an excellent tool both to motivate individual performance and to encourage team spirit. For example, in some manufacturing plants, production quotas are set for each department. A percentage of extra earnings from what is produced over the quota is then divided among the workers.

Companies that pay bonuses may pay less in salaries than comparable non-bonus-paying companies. Most bonus plans are tied to company profits and are established by a formula. Participation is limited to those people whose performance has had a significant effect on profits, with payments based on this performance.

You should consider two questions before establishing a bonus plan: First, if an employee's total income varies greatly from year to year, will that work as an incentive or detraction? Second, do you want to have the task of deciding the relative performance of employees in order to establish bonuses each year? This latter problem makes it particularly important that bonuses be linked only to performance that is quantifiable. A consistently given bonus that is not tied to performance will not act as a motivator.

STOCK OPTIONS AND DEFERRED COMPENSATION PLANS. Instead of cash bonuses, stock options and deferred compensation plans are often offered as performance incentives to employees in higher tax brackets. Under stock option plans, employees are given the option to buy a predetermined number of shares at a price that is usually somewhat lower than market price. Deferred compensation systems provide for continued pay—usually in reduced amounts—after retirement, thereby spreading a high salary over a longer period and reducing taxes.

PENSION PLANS. Pension plans differ from deferred compensation plans in that they are devised to take care of long-term employees, regardless of the company's earnings or the level of an employee's performance. They act as incentives to retain employees, rather than to boost performance. The Self-Employed Retirement Act of 1962 has greatly helped small businesses in setting up retirement plans. This act enables the owner of a small business and her or his employees to set aside a certain amount of their earnings for retirement, which is currently tax-free if set up according to legal requirements. Your insurance agent, bank, or attorney can help you provide this benefit for yourself and your employees under the Keogh Act or Employee Retirement Insurance Security Act. The IRS puts out a brochure, *Retirement Plans for Self-Employed Individuals* (Document No. 5592), that will be of assistance to you and is available from your local IRS office.

Most pension plans require employees to make a cost contribution to the plan, a factor that may add to the employee's incentive to remain with the firm. This contribution is usually limited to a stated percentage of annual earnings, with 5 percent being a common figure. Your trade association may be a source of information concerning pensions in your industry. It is possible, though costly, to use an insurance company as your pension program administrator, or you can set up a self-administered pension trust according to Treasury Department requirements.

INSURANCE PLANS.   Insurance plans are probably one of the most sought-after fringe benefits. You may find that you can provide coverage to your employees under a group plan for relatively little more than it would cost to insure yourself individually.

REGULATIONS DEALING WITH EMPLOYEES

Many regulations have been promulgated to protect employees, making sure that workers have a safe and healthful place to work, that they are paid fairly, and that they are employed equally. Although your trade association can be helpful in keeping you abreast of new legislation, any employer hiring staff should check with the following five federal agencies regarding labor rules and regulations and the forms that must be filed with the government: the National Labor Relations Board, the United States Department of Labor's Wage and Hour Division, the Occupational Safety and Health Administration, the Equal Employment Opportunity Commission, and the IRS.

The National Labor Relations Board deals with management-union relations and was created under the National Labor Relations Act. The board puts out two books, *A Layman's Guide to Basic Law Under the National Labor Relations Act*, and *Jurisdictional Guide*—both of which will be of assistance to business owners and are available from the Superintendent of Documents, United States Government Printing Office, Washington, D.C. 20402.

The Department of Labor puts out a book, *A Handy Reference Guide to the Fair Labor Standards Act*, that explains the minimum wage laws and other requirements. It is also available from the Superintendent of Documents. The Department of Labor also administers the Employee Retirement Insurance Security Act (ERISA), which regulates the use of pension funds of firms.

The Occupational Safety and Health Administration is charged with ensuring that the work environment of employees is adequate for safety and health. You can find out about the standards that apply to your business in a book entitled *General Industry Digest,* which can be obtained by writing to OSHA Publications, United States Department of Labor, 20 Constitution Avenue, NW, Washington, D.C. 20210.

The Equal Employment Opportunity Commission regulates fair employment practices. In setting up your compensation system, you should keep in mind that you must be able to justify pay differentials paid to men and women, or between races, in light of the law that calls for "equal pay for *substantially* equal work."

The Internal Revenue Service will provide you with information on federal tax requirements. Consult your state revenue service for state tax requirements.

Laws You Should Know About

Although your attorney is the best person to keep you advised of any legal requirements, the following is a brief rundown of some pertinent laws governing employees. Equal employment opportunity is guaranteed by Title VII of the 1964 Civil Rights Act, which prohibits discrimination on the basis of race, creed, color, sex, or national origin. This act has been further expanded by the Equal Employment Opportunity Act. Two other laws also relate to your hiring practices: the Equal Pay Act and the Age Discrimination Act. The Equal Pay Act requires that pay be determined only on the basis of skill and that the same wages be paid to persons performing substantially similar jobs. The Age Discrimination Act, which was passed to protect those workers between the ages of forty and sixty-five, forbids job discrimination on the basis of age. Regarding the minimum wages you can pay employees and the number of hours they can work without having to be paid overtime, you should be aware of the Federal Fair Labor Standards Act and applicable state laws. For example, these laws may specify such things as the fact that all employees must have at least twenty-four consecutive hours off in a calendar week and an hour per day for lunch. Be sure to find out if your state has additional requirements over and above the federal regulations. For example, New York State stipulates that employees must be paid in cash, unless permission to pay wages by check is obtained from the Industrial Commissioner. As an employer, you must keep records of the hours worked by each employee covered by the minimum wage rate, the wages paid to all employees, and any other information required. Your state's department of commerce and Wage and Hour Division of the United States Department of Labor are good sources for information about the laws you will have to observe in paying employees.

You will be required to carry workmen's compensation insurance if you have one or more workers. Whether the nature of the employment is hazardous is no longer a determining factor for whether you need this type of insurance. However, the rates for workmen's compensation insurance vary according to the nature of the employment and hazards involved. The Workmen's Compensation Law was enacted to make sure that employees who sustained injuries during the course of their work or who died as a result of those injuries were adequately compensated. Employers must post a notice in a conspicuous spot in the place of business stating that they have complied with all the rules and regulations governing workmen's compensation.

The Disability Benefits Law provides additional protection for a worker who may become disabled from a nonoccupational injury or sickness. Employees are sometimes asked to contribute to this insurance premium. Most insurance agents experienced in providing business insurance can give you more information about these requirements.

There are laws to adequately protect employees who are laid off. Unemployed workers are covered by the Federal Unemployment Tax Act, which requires employers to help bear the cost of state and federal payments to unemployed workers. Under this law, each employer is liable for contributions to the Unemployment Fund for each employee covered. The unemployment insurance tax system operates on a cooperative state-federal basis, with contributions collected from the employer only and paid to employees when they become unemployed. The unemployment insurance division of your state's department of commerce is the best source for additional information on how the law applies to your business. They can give you a handbook that explains the employer's responsibility and rights under your state unemployment insurance laws and will also furnish you with information on the kind of payroll records you must keep and the reports you must submit.

Retired and older workers are protected under the Federal Social Security Act. The Social Security Act was passed to provide income for retired workers and, in the event of their deaths, their surviving dependents. Any employer who employs one or more persons is liable for social security tax and must file for an identification number when his or her business is started. This number can be obtained through your district IRS director, who will also handle your other federal income taxes. Under the Social Security Act, the employer currently pays a tax on the wages of each employee up to a certain level, and the employee matches that amount. The employee's share is deducted by the employer at the close of each pay period. Even if you are self-employed, you will have to pay this tax. With few exceptions, anyone having her or his own trade or business and earning $400 or more in annual net income as sole owner or as a partner is subject to social security tax. Two publications available from your district IRS director will help you understand your requirements under this law: *Employer's Tax Guide* (Circular E) and *Special Information for Self-Employed People*.

The 1974 Employee Retirement Income Security Act (ERISA) was promulgated to protect the money that employees contribute to retirement and welfare plans—such as life, health, and disability insurance—from any abuse by the employer. The act requires employers both to provide information about the plans and how they are vested to employees and to file reports with the government. Although the purpose behind the act is a good one, it can increase the paperwork burden on a small company. Therefore, many small companies have found that it is better to use one of the external pension plans—IRA and Keogh—allowed under the Self-Employed Retirement Act of 1962 as a mechanism for providing payments after retirement to employees, rather than creating an internal pension fund subject to ERISA provisions.

The Occupational Safety and Health Administration's job is to see that employers meet their obligation to furnish employees with a safe place to work, free from recognized hazards that could cause serious injury or death. The Agency has promulgated hundreds of regulations and sends out inspectors to make sure that industries are observing the regulations. If you have even just one employee you are expected to comply with these regulations and must display a poster setting forth the responsibilities of the employer. If you have more than eight employees, you are required to keep records of occupational injuries and illnesses.

Under the Labor Management Relations Act, rules have been established to prevent unfair labor practices and to determine collective bargaining and arbitration procedures. These regulations, which are administered by the National Labor Relations Board also protect employees from such unfair labor practices as blacklisting workers who are active in unions, requiring workers to refrain from organizing a union as a condition of employment, and refusing to discuss grievances. Many states have state labor relations boards that can provide you with a list of labor practices currently considered unfair. However, these lists are not conclusive, and you should check with your attorney and your local officials.

CHAPTER 8

Controlling Your Company

Winning at the entrepreneurial game takes not only having a viable business idea but also learning how to manage the three mainstays of business: money, manpower, and market resources. Of all these, managing your money resources will prove the most critical to your business survival. The entrepreneurial game is one in which money is the measure for keeping score and in which all the plays have to do with the inflows and outflows of cash.

Cash is to business, what blood is to your body—the basic ingredient that keeps you alive. Finding cash to start your business is only half your battle. The other half is the daily struggle to keep cash flowing smoothly through the veins of your organization. It is not enough just to *make* money in business; you also must be able to manage your finances so that it flows in and out of your business in a predictable, scheduled way.

Financial management simply means the effective management of your money resources to enable you to undertake the growth and expansion of your business in the way you desire. Just as doctors have tools like stethoscopes and electrocardiograms to monitor the health of the human body, there are tools, such as your business records and your profit and loss and cash-flow statements, that will enable you to monitor the health of your business. Becoming a good financial manager involves three steps: (1) understanding the language of business, so that you can understand these tools and communicate with your financial advisers; (2) keeping good business records, so that you will have the information you need to develop your financial scorecards, such as your balance sheet and your profit and loss statement; and (3) interpreting your financial statements, so that you can recognize any danger signs that may be occurring in your business. This chapter will help you learn these basic principles of financial management; experience and your accountant will teach you the rest.

THE LANGUAGE OF BUSINESS

Every profession has its own jargon—a special language that enables people in that profession to communicate in a verbal shorthand, which often confuses and mystifies the outsider. As a newcomer to the business environment, you will soon learn a strange language that revolves around your daily business, including terms such as acid test, liquidity ratio, gross margin, and net worth. Bankers and accountants use this language most often, sometimes with a fluency that makes it appear to be their native tongue. Although you do not need to gain their fluency in this language, you do need to learn the basics. Trying to play the entrepreneurial game without having some understanding of the jargon, is a little like trying to play football without understanding the signals: you are bound to lose. It sounds better to tell a banker that you have a cash-flow problem than to say you have just run out of money, even though both statements mean the same.

It doesn't matter if you are in Des Moines or Dallas, or whether you are selling dresses or drugs. The dollar is the basic yardstick by which you measure not only your business success, but also all the actions that you take in your business. This means that although you may say that your reason for starting a business is to be your own boss or to use a talent or skill, rather than make money, it all boils down to the same thing—money. This is because money is the name of the game in business. Profits are the ingredient that will keep your business afloat, whether you are running a women's collective bakery, or are a budding capitalist who dreams of building an empire.

Women and the Language of Business

The first step in learning this jargon, is to realize that its basic root is the dollar. Business essentially boils down to cold, hard dollars and cents—a reality many women find difficult to accept. This is because our heritage has led us to believe that "money-grubbing" is bad, that "mothering" is good, and that handing finances is "a man's job." As a result many women make the mistake of handing over the financial management of their businesses to male partners, employees, or accountants. In effect, they have entrusted the life of their business to a stranger who should be acting as an adviser, not as manager, of this critical resource in their business. An owner who is unable to take the pulse of her or his business, or monitor its vital signs through financial statements, is in deep trouble. She or he is operating in the dark without any knowledge of how her managerial decisions impact on that basic substance of business—profits.

One of the reasons women seem reluctant to learn the plays and the language of business is that the language of business is also a numerical language. It is the rare woman who has not felt "math anxiety"—that panicky feeling that makes your mind go blank when you are asked to figure out what time two speeding trains leaving from points A and B will meet. Sheila Tobias concludes in her book, *Overcoming Math Anxiety,* that sex differences "seem to be lodged in *acquired skills;* not in computation, visualization, and reasoning *per se,* but in ability to take a math problem apart, in willingness to tolerate certain kinds of ambiguity, and in careful attention to mathematical detail."[1]

Beatrice Fitzpatrick, director of the American Women's Economic Development Corporation, has found that uncomfortableness with money and math is a frequent, if irrational, problem among women. Women don't seem to realize that the numbers side of business is simple. It is basically one plus one is two. You don't have to be an Einstein to learn how to do it and business math is not difficult, women probably just think that it is. It is basically the type of arithmetic that you help your child with, not algebra or calculus. All you have to do to start being a good financial manager is to bury your fear of math, arm yourself with enough business jargon to ask questions, and then learn how your business records work, and how to interpret your financial statements.

THE IMPORTANCE OF BUSINESS RECORDS

Keeping and understanding your business records is the first step to good financial management. These are the tracking system of your business and can help you learn from your past, understand your present, and plan for your future. Yet too many people insist on conducting business "out of their hip pocket" until it is too late and the company is so unhealthy that they find it impossible to raise the funds that they need to keep it afloat. These people play a defensive rather than an offensive, business game—which is a little like trying to play the entrepreneurial game blindfolded when your opponents are not.

One Seattle woman knows what it feels like to not use financial records adequately. She made policy changes and business expansions without considering what these actions would do to the financial stability of her business. After inheriting the business, she had taken on a new partner and had decided to expand. But as sales grew, she could no longer see what was happening with the cash. "It was just pouring in and pouring out. I was writing $5,000 checks without knowing if I had the money and without being able to see the forest for the trees." This woman suddenly woke up to find that she was left with $70,000 worth of bills at the beginning of her slow season. Luckily, she had a good relationship with her bankers and was able to get loans to pay off these debts. If she hadn't, she would have been out of business— killed by that well-known business disease called a *cash crisis.*

A cash crisis when you do not have enough ready cash to meet your payroll and pay your creditors is a little like a heart attack. It is a strangulation of your lifeblood. As such, it can both kill your business or damage its business health. Although small businesses are especially prone to this illness, big businesses are not immune to it. It was basically a cash crisis that caused the collapse of W. T. Grant, the multi-million-dollar retail business. It's just a sad reality of business that listening to the cash register ring is a lot more fun than listening to the death knells your financial statements may be orchestrating. Thus, wise business owners will realize that unless they manage their money resources, they will not be in business long enough to manage the other two resources: markets and manpower.

Cash crises kill or injure thousands of businesses yearly. For some, death comes quickly; for others, it is a lingering illness that eventually drains the business's strength to the point where it dies. Yet you can minimize or avoid a cash crisis by having a good recordkeeping system. While most business owners greet the thought of keeping accurate records with a groan and tend to see them as something their banker and the IRS require, good records can warn you when the strength of your business is being strained, tell you when to slow down your growth rate, and advise you when you will need a cash infusion to keep operating. They can also let you gauge how well you are performing in comparison with your competition or with industry standards. They are the only way you have of periodically taking the pulse of your company and testing its vital signs. Even if you are starting off small, or on a part-time basis, you should start off right. You may not need a formal set of books, but you do need records of what you spent and what you took in.

Patty Bissell, owner of a CPA firm in Rockville, Maryland, points out that your records are like your report card. "Records are an indication to bankers and others of how you run your business. Poor records create a bad impression. They can also make you lose money and contracts. If you don't keep and use good records, you can pay people that you don't owe, or wait forever to get your money back. You will also not know if you are making or losing money and will be operating completely in the dark."

Developing Your System

The key to having a good tracking system of your company's health is to develop it early, keep it simple, and keep it up-to-date. It is a lot easier to record daily transactions in a systematic fashion than it is to unravel and organize a shoebox full of receipts six months or a year later. Patty Bissell always shudders when someone comes in with a suitcase full of receipts and slips of paper and wants us to do their taxes. "I know it is going to take days to piece them all together and cost them a lot of money when it would have been so easy for them to keep a simple recordkeeping system in the first place."

The particular business you are in will affect the type of books or records that you will need. The goal is to design your system in a way that will give you the depth of information that you need for gauging management decisions without unnecessary detail. You will also want a bookkeeping system that will be able to grow with your business.

It really doesn't matter *what* recordkeeping system you use. You just want one that is simple enough that you *will* use it. The objective of any recordkeeping system is to provide reliable, accurate, and consistent information on a timely basis. It should be simple to use and easy to understand. The fanciest system in the world doesn't do you a bit of good if you don't keep it up-to-date and don't know how to interpret it. And your CPA can help you learn how to analyze your business records.

Patty Bissell believes that the owner should be able to do everything in the business. "That doesn't mean that they *have* to do it, but they should know everything about their books so that no one can ever fool them. Also, if someone is ever sick, you can handle the job." She also feels that the owner should look at the records at least once a month to feel the pulse of her or his business.

The easiest way to get a recordkeeping system that will meet the needs of your particular business is to hire an accountant to set up your bookkeeping system and teach you how to use it. Another way is to choose one of the copyrighted systems available in most office supply stores. These systems provide simplified records and instructions for how to use them. In addition, two excellent booklets can help you understand your bookkeeping better: *Financial Recordkeeping for Small Stores*, which is published by the SBA (SBMS No. 32); and *Businessman's Information Guide*, which is put out by the American Society of Certified Public Accountants. The latter can be purchased for $3.00 from the American Society of Certified Public Accountants, Inc., 666 Fifth Avenue, New York, New York 10019.

Understanding Your System

The basic purpose of your records is to keep a running account of your daily transactions in a way that will allow you to evaluate how well you are doing in the entrepreneurial game. In this sense, your records are your scorecard, and your bookkeeper is your scorekeeper. To understand your recordkeeping system you need to know the relationship between the basic components: the receipts you write and receive each day, your journal, your ledger, and your financial statements.

It helps to think of your records as the building blocks of your financial management system. Rather than keep these various bits and pieces of paper in a haphazard fashion, these transactions are consolidated in one place—a journal. There is usually a journal to record cash inflows—sales and cash receipts—and one to record cash outflows—cash disbursements, purchases, and expenses. The logic behind this is that any business transaction is basically an exchange of one thing for another. For example, if you purchase new inventory, you will generate a decrease in your cash account but an increase in your inventory account.

Journals—sometimes called books of original entry—are simply a record of the daily transactions of the business. Each journal entry shows the date of transaction, a brief description of it, the amount of money involved, and the type of income or expense affected by the transaction. To make the information recorded in the journal more usable for management decisions, each item is later posted in the general ledger. The general ledger consists of separate accounts (called T-accounts because of the way they are posted) for each asset, liability, capital, income, and expense of the business.

The general ledger enables the business owner to keep track of what the business owns that has cash value (assets) and owes (liabilities) and the amount of money that really belongs to the owner (equity or capital)—the three basic components of any business. It also provides a way to double-check all entries, since, each transaction is recorded twice in double-entry bookkeeping systems.

Using Your System

Even if you hire an accountant to design your recordkeeping system, you will still have to tell her or him what items of information you want in the system to help you make business decisions. For example, if you own a restaurant, you might want to be able to track the differences in day and night sales. If you own a drug store, you might want to know your annual profit on perfume, or you might only want to know it for your entire cosmetics line.

Your system should include the following records:

- Cash receipts
- Cash disbursements (the firm's expenditures)
- Sales
- Purchases
- Payroll (the wages of employees and their deductions)
- Equipment (the firm's capital assets, such as equipment, office furniture, and motor vehicles)
- Inventory (the firm's investment in stock, which is needed to arrive at your net income on financial statements and for income tax purposes)
- Accounts receivable (what the customers owe the firm)
- Accounts payable (what the firm owes its creditors and suppliers)

These records can be kept on either a cash or accrual basis. Under a cash basis, transactions are recorded only when the cash is actually received or paid out. On an accrual basis, the transaction is recorded at the time of the sale or purchase, rather than at the time of payment. Your accountant can help you decide which method is best for your business and what types of records you will need. Once your recordkeeping system is set up, you can do the daily recording of transactions, but you may want to have a bookkeeper come in for an hour or two once a month to post your daily transactions in your general ledger and prepare your financial statements. The cost of the bookkeeper is usually minimal compared with what you save in terms of time, headaches, and errors.

Joyce Huber, owner of Georgetown Employment Service, believes that one of her biggest mistakes was to not have an accountant or bookkeeper monitor her books in the beginning. Had she done so, she thinks that she would have saved a lot of money. "A lot of things were spent in the wrong way and money was not used effectively. We didn't build for the future like we should have. If I had it to do all over again, I would definitely have an accountant set up the books and a bookkeeper watching it each month, even if it's just an hour a month."

To simplify the recordkeeping, you should establish a separate business bank account no matter how small your business is. It will not only establish you with your banker as a businesswoman but will also provide a complete and clean record of what went in and what came out of your business for tax purposes and you won't have to mess and try to figure what expenses were business and what were personal. You should also carry about a book for notations from each day—such as how many miles you drove, and how much you paid for parking—so that you have back-up data for the IRS should you be audited.

FINANCIAL STATEMENTS

There are two kinds of financial statements: position statements, which show the position of the firm at any point in time, and flow statements, which show what happens between periods of time in terms of the inflows and outflows of cash, inventory, or whatever they are measuring. The three basic financial statements that you should understand are your balance sheet, your profit and loss statement (also called an income statement), and your cash-flow statement. The first two of statements are position statements, and the last is a flow statement. Although all three statements track the dollar measures of your company, the balance sheet and income statement track retained earnings and net worth or profits, whereas the cash-flow statement tracks the actual cash you have in your coffers to pay existing bills.

All three of these financial statements are critical to the effective management of your company. They not only tell you where you stand and what your score is at any point in time, but they also provide you with a tool enabling to start playing an offensive, rather than a defensive, business game. They give you a means to try out business strategies on paper and estimate their cash impact before you implement them.

John Welsh—who directs the Caruth Institute for Owner-Managed Business at Southern Methodist University in Dallas, Texas, and who also conducts a nationwide seminar in cash management—points out that you can't control the past or even the present; but you can have some control over the future by using your financial statements wisely, both to track the financial health of your business and to budget the limited resources in your business. Such projections and budgets will help you identify potential red flags in your business and develop strategies to avoid them. They will also serve as your business scorecards by providing a way to compare your actual results against your projections and chart how well you think you are playing your own game.

A simplified description of the major indicators used in financial analysis is included in appendix 2.

Your Net Worth Scorecard

The basic scorecard to measure your net worth is your balance sheet, which is drawn up using the totals from the individual accounts kept in the general ledger. A sample balance sheet can be found on page 179. The balance sheet shows how your business is doing in terms of assets, liabilities, and capital. It shows your score in terms of net worth, or what you have left when you pay all creditors.

The reason it is called a balance sheet is because of the formula that accountants use to develop your net worth score: Assets less liabilities equals capital (net worth). If you take your total assets, or things owned by the company, and subtract the total liabilities, or things owed by the company, you will come up with what is left over for the owners. This is the *net worth* of the business and is the bottom line you are trying to increase in the entrepreneurial game. The balance sheet is constructed so that the assets and liabilities sections must balance—hence the name balance sheet.

Assets are anything that the business owns. They can be *current* assets, such as cash or inventory that can be converted within a year to cash, or *fixed* assets, such as land and equipment. You sometimes also hear the term *quick* assets, which refers to items that can be quickly converted to cash, such as cash in banks or accounts receivables. *Liabilities* are anything that the business owes. These can also be current, such as amounts owed to suppliers or long-term, such as notes owed to the bank. *Capital* is the owner's rights in the business and is sometimes called equity, proprietorship, or net worth. On a balance sheet, capital can include three types: owners' capital (paid-in capital), investors capital (common stock), and new capital generated from business operations (retained earnings).

You can tell how well you are doing in terms of increasing your net worth by examining the capital section of your balance sheet over time. Your balance sheet can tell you if your business is growing or stagnant, and it can disclose the soundness of your financial position in terms of the assets held or the level of your liabilities. It can alert you to whether you should add more cash to your business or if you have too much cash lying idle, which could be better used to pay off outstanding loans or to finance expansion.

Your balance sheet is also a valuable gauge of your *liquidity position*, or the amount of ready cash you have to operate with. The liquidity position of a business is a measure which can help you avoid the danger of a cash crisis. A firm with poor liquidity is one which does not have sufficient current assets to pay current liabilities as they come due. A cash crisis is caused by inadequate working capital and shows up operationally when you have to scurry about to obtain funds in order to meet your normal business bills or are unable to take cash discounts offered from suppliers. Such actions can be avoided if you watch your financial records.

XYZ COMPANY

BALANCE SHEET AS OF DECEMBER 31, 1979

Assets

Current

Cash	$ 9,460
Accounts receivable	412,000
Inventory	115,000
Prepaid insurance	6,000
Total current assets	$542,460

Fixed

Capital equipment	$380,400
Less: accumulated depreciation	39,880
Total fixed assets	$340,520

Total Assets $882,980

Liabilities

Current

Accounts payable	
Direct materials	$110,000
Other general and administrative	14,100
Advertising	27,600
Accrued taxes	32,340
Total current liabilities	$184,040

Capital (shareholders' equity)

Common stock	$388,000
Retained earnings	310,940
Total capital	$698,940

Total liabilities and capital $882,980

The balance sheet is a snapshot of the business at a particular point in time. It can be produced quarterly, semiannually, or at the end of the calendar year. It can be compared with previous snapshots, but does not give you any indication of how daily transactions have affected the company during the year or quarter. For such a moving picture, you must examine your profit and loss (or income) statement.

Your Profit Scorecard

The profit and loss statement shows the interaction between the managerial actions you take and the impact of these actions on your profits. It is a detailed month-by-month tally of the sales revenues the firm receives and the expenses it incurs to generate these sales. For example, decisions to increase your advertising, let some of your employees go, and buy new equipment or move to larger office space—all show up on your profit and loss statement as numbers. A drop in sales will also be registered there, as will changes in the cost of supplies. Sample profit and loss statement appears on page 181.

Your profit and loss statement not only enables you to track the impact of managerial decisions on your net profit, but it also provides a tool to actually try them out on paper before actually going ahead. For instance, if you currently contract to have your products produced, rather than producing them in-house, you can figure out if making the switch actually increases your net profit or just creates an added overhead burden. All you need is pencil, paper, and a pocket calculator.

A profit and loss statement normally includes four kinds of information: sales, direct expenses, indirect expenses, and income. The sales information normally lists the numbers of units sold and the total revenues generated by these sales. Direct expenses—the cost of goods sold—includes the cost of direct materials, direct labor, and manufacturing overhead but does not include normal overhead. Indirect expenses are costs incurred in the business even if the products are not produced and sales are not made. Normally referred to as general and administrative expenses or normal overhead, they include such things as salaries, rent, utilities, insurance, depreciation, office supplies, taxes, and travel and entertainment.

The last category of information found on the profit and loss statement—and the one your banker, investors, and tax collector are most interested in—is income. Income is normally shown as both pretax and after-tax, or net, income. The IRS is interested in your pretax figure, whereas your banker and investors are concerned with your after-tax figure. After-tax income is the amount of money you have left over to pay off debts, distribute as dividends, or plow back into the company. It is the "bottom line" in your business or is an indication of your success.

As a manager, you will want to look at more than just your bottom line. The other lines of the profit and loss statement are the ones that can give you some indication of whether you are managing effectively. They contain information that you can use to compute such things as your inventory turnover, your gross margin, or measure the productivity of employees. Most of these indicators are computed as a percentage of sales, since sales are the mainstay of all businesses. For example, if you total your overhead expenses, such as rent, light, and heat, and take them as a percentage of your sales, you will gain some idea of the extent to which these continuous expenses are eating into your potential profits. You can then decide if you should try to make cost savings in this area. Your total marketing expenses as a percentage of sales can help you judge if increases in advertising expenses are actually having a cost-beneficial impact on sales. You can get a general gauge of employee productivity by dividing your sales figure by the number of employees you have.

Your profit and loss statement allows you to both track your profits and losses and look at individual costs to pinpoint managerial actions that might

XYZ COMPANY
PROFIT AND LOSS STATEMENT, 1978

			Month				
Revenues	1	2	3	4	5	6	7
Units Sold	80,000	84,000	88,000	94,000	100,000	106,000	110,000
Sales	$160,000	$168,000	$176,000	$188,000	$200,000	$212,000	$220,000
Expenses							
Cost of goods sold							
Direct labor	$ 8,000	$ 8,400	$ 8,800	$ 9,400	$ 10,000	$ 10,600	$ 11,000
Direct materials	80,000	84,000	88,000	94,000	100,000	106,000	110,000
Manufacturing overhead	5,400	5,400	5,400	5,400	5,400	5,400	5,400
Total direct expenses	$ 93,400	$ 97,800	$102,200	$108,800	$115,400	$122,000	$126,400
Gross profit	$ 66,600	$ 70,200	$ 73,800	$ 79,200	$ 84,600	$ 90,000	$ 93,600
General and Administrative							
Rent	$ 4,000	$ 4,000	$ 4,000	$ 4,000	$ 4,000	$ 4,000	$ 18,000
Salaries	13,800	14,900	15,000	16,700	16,700	18,000	4,000
Depreciation	340	340	340	340	340	340	1,000
Insurance	1,000	1,000	1,000	1,000	1,000	1,000	
Other	6,000	8,200	9,100	11,000	13,200	14,100	15,700
Marketing							
Advertising	22,100	22,200	23,000	24,600	25,800	27,600	28,600
Brochures	900	900	900	900	900	900	900
Total indirect expenses	48,140	51,540	53,340	58,540	61,940	65,940	68,200
Total expenses	$141,540	$149,340	$155,540	$167,340	$177,340	$187,940	$194,940
Pretax income	$ 18,460	$ 18,660	$ 20,460	$ 20,660	$ 22,660	$ 24,060	$ 25,400
Income taxes	4,062	4,106	6,472	9,916	10,876	11,548	12,028
Net profit	$ 14,398	$ 14,554	$ 13,988	$ 10,744	$ 11,784	$ 12,512	$ 13,372

help cut these costs. It also provides you with the information you will need to compare your business program with that of others in your field. Comparative data is available in the various publications put out by Robert Morris Associates, Dun & Bradstreet, and trade associations. Further analysis of profit and loss statements is given in appendix 2. However, remember that these scores provide only gross gauges since they take industry averages, and your company may be much smaller.

You will find that much of the jargon you hear in business comes from financial statements and the business indicators that they provide. The words you will hear most often are questions about your gross and net profits and gross and net margins. Your profit figures are expressed in dollars and your margin figures are in percentages. Gross profit is that amount of money left over from sales revenues after subtracting the cost of producing the goods. The gross margin is gross profit as a percentage of sales. The gross margin does not include the general and administrative costs, or normal overhead, that you incur irrespective of whether you produce the product or make a sale. Net profit is the amount left over after all operating expenses and taxes have been subtracted. The net margin is net profit as a percentage of sales. Gross and net profit margins are indications of how much the firm retains on its sales.

Although your balance sheet and your profit and loss statement are the two scorecards that indicate how well you are doing in the entrepreneurial game, they do so in terms of net worth and profits, not cash. And cash is what can keep you in, or knock you out, of the entrepreneurial game.

Your Cash Scorecard

As a business owner, it is important to realize that there is a difference between profit and cash. Profit is the amount of money you *expect* to make if all customers paid on time and if your expenses were strung out over a 12-month period. However, it is not your day-to-day reality. Business, unfortunately, does not run in nicely measured increments, as shown on a profit and loss statement. Cash is what you need to keep the doors of your business open while you are trying to make this profit. You can't spend profit; you can only spend cash. Profit will not pay your payroll on Friday, or buy the groceries; only cash does that. Profit may be what your banker and investors are interested in, but cash is what your employees and suppliers want; and if you don't have cash, you can't make your profit.

Business owners must not only keep track and project what they think their profit will be but must also keep track and project what they think their cash needs will be in order to make this profit. The tool you use for this is a cash-flow statement. Just as the profit and loss statement is a moving picture of your firm, the cash-flow statement is a moving picture of your checkbook. The cash-flow statement takes the items in the profit and loss statement and recasts them into a schedule of expected cash inflows and outflows.

The difference between a cash-flow statement and a profit and loss statement is that a profit and loss statement spreads the costs of items across a year period, when, in fact, they may have to all be paid for in one month. Also, the income statement registers sales when made, rather than as customers actually pay you. Although your profit and loss statement lists interest payments, it does not list any outstanding loans whose principal may be due. All these factors mean that while you may show the business earning a good profit at year-end, according to your profit and loss statement, the firm may actually be in dire straits trying to meet its payments as they come due. The reality is that customers do not pay promptly in thirty days, and creditors will not let you spread out payments to them over a year's time.

An example of how a company can show strong profits but still be in a cash-flow bind can be seen by looking at the profit and loss statement on page 182 and the cash-flow statement on page 184 for the XYZ Company. These two statements show the profit and the cash position of this company, and although the profit picture is positive, showing a net profit of $13,032, the cash picture is negative, with an overdraft at the bank of $7,580.

You often hear a business owner say that "business was never better than in the month we went out of business." Although this statement may sound contradictory, what this owner is really saying is that although the business was making record sales, there was not enough cash on hand to keep operations going until credit customers finally paid. However, such headaches can be avoided if an owner follows the basic principles of cash management.

Cash management means knowing when, where, and how your cash needs will occur; what the best sources are for meeting additional cash needs; and keeping good banking relations so that you can get this cash when you need it. The goal in effective cash management is to receive and pay out cash in an orderly way that benefits your company. Cash in itself is not productive. Cash earns nothing unless it is invested, either in producing more products or in earning interest. A dollar idle means money lost. Large corporations therefore use electronic funds transfers, rather than the mail, to speed their dollars to the bank so that they can start earning interest as soon as possible.

For large corporations, cash management usually revolves around managing money so that money-making opportunities are not lost. If you are General Motors, and transferring hundreds of thousands of dollars daily, any interest lost can amount to thousands of dollars. Cash management in the small business, on the other hand, involves trying to make sure that you have enough cash on hand to meet your monthly obligations. For many companies, this problem can be critical. For some reason, cash inflows into the business always seem to be more noticeable than its cash outflows. It is easy to count the coins in your cash register and think that the business is doing fine while forgetting that the payment on the new delivery truck is coming due that month.

You will find that watching your cash inflows and outflows will become one of your major management tasks if you are to have a healthy company. The outflow of cash is those checks you will write every month to pay salaries, suppliers, and creditors. The inflows come from three major sources. The first source is the cash generated from sales of the product or service of your

XYZ COMPANY
CASH-FLOW STATEMENT, 1978

			Month				
Receipts	1	2	3	4	5	6	7
Common stock		$350,000					
Sales receipts	$148,000*	$154,000	$160,000	$168,000	$176,000	$188,000	$200,000
Total received	$148,000	$504,000	$160,000	$168,000	$176,000	$188,000	$200,000
Disbursements							
Direct materials	$ 80,000*	$ 80,000	$ 90,000	$ 90,000	$100,000	$110,000	$110,000
Direct labor	8,000	8,400	8,800	9,400	10,000	10,600	11,000
Manufacturing overhead							
Salaries	13,800	14,900	15,000	16,700	16,700	18,000	18,000
Rent	4,000	4,000	4,000	4,000	4,000	4,000	4,000
Insurance	12,000						
Capital equipment		366,000					
Other	5,600*	6,000	8,200	9,100	11,000	13,200	14,100
Advertising	21,800*	22,100	22,200	23,000	24,600	25,800	27,600
Brochaures		5,400					
Taxes	40,600*			14,640			32,340
Total disbursed	$185,800	$506,800	$148,200	$166,840	$166,300	$181,600	$217,040
Total cash flow	$(37,800)	$ (2,800)	$ 11,800	$ 1,160	$ 9,700	$ 6,400	$17,040
Beginning balance	$ 21,000	$(16,800)	$(19,600)	$ (7,800)	$ (6,640)	$ 3,060	$ 9,460
Ending balance	$(16,800)	(19,600)	(7,800)	(6,640)	3,060	9,460	(7,580)

*From operations during prior periods.

business. This source of cash, retained earnings, is the major source of working capital for businesses. The second source is the cash generated from borrowing money from commercial institutions, or debt financing. It is normally used primarily to finance short-term expansion, such as new inventory. The third source is the cash generated by selling stock in your company. This source of cash is called equity financing and is used most often to finance long-term expansion or acquisitions, such as the purchase of equipment or building new buildings.

Of these basic sources of cash, retained earnings are the real lifeblood of your business. They are the cash that is internal to your organization and, therefore, under your control. They also do not cost you anything. Earnings retained from sales enable you to purchase new materials or hire new people to produce the products or services that will generate increased sales and more retained earnings. The other two sources, debt financing and equity financing, are often used for cash infusions into the company, just as blood transfusions provide new sources of blood.

The name of the game in business is making sure that the inflows of cash are always adequate to cover the outflows. However, you will soon find that this sounds easier than it is. There is nothing static and certain in business. The business game is a dynamic interplay of customers, competitors, and creditors—all of which can change daily. While you must pay your bills promptly in order to stay in the entrepreneurial game, there may be times when you have not received payment from your customers, and you will be in a cash bind.

The starting point for avoiding a cash crisis is to develop a cash-flow statement or projection—a schedule of the monthly inflows and outflows of cash into the business. It is the basic tool you will need to help you manage your cash situation. It can help you plan in advance to have additional cash on hand to meet a cash crisis. It is a lot easier to go to a bank in advance and explain your need for money than to run to them in a panic. Banks frown on throwing good money after bad and do not like to bail out companies that could have avoided troubles by exercising better management control over their finances.

An example of a cash-flow statement is provided on page 184. You will note that it lists the total cash available to the firm for the month—coming from both accounts receivable collections, bank loans, and stock sales—and the total cash disbursements—including payroll, overhead expenses, taxes, suppliers' bills, and payments due on bank loans. By subtracting the total receipts from total disbursements, you can determine whether your cash flow for the month is positive or negative. A negative cash flow means that you have more money flowing out of the firm than coming in, whereas a positive cash flow means that you have more money coming into the bank than going out.

The only items you need to know to construct a cash-flow statement is the sum and average age of your accounts receivable and the sum and when the payments fall due on each of your expense items. For example, you must pay your employees promptly every two weeks, but your income taxes will only be paid quarterly. Figuring out the average age of your accounts receivable means figuring out what proportion of these bills are paid in 30 days, 60 days, 90 days, or longer. You will then estimate your receipts from accounts receivable in line with this trend. For example, if 50 percent are paid in 30 days, 45 percent in 60 days, and 5 percent in 90 days, you will apportion your monthly receipts in this fashion across the three months. The age of your accounts receivable is at the bottom of any cash-flow problem.

Remember that the name of the game in managing your profit picture is to try to increase sales while you decrease expenses, whereas the goal of effective cash management is to decrease the length of time it takes your customers to pay their bills so that you will increase your monthly supply of cash on hand and pay your own bills. You want to make your receipts come in sooner, and make your disbursements happen later.

THE GOVERNMENT'S IMPACT—TAXES

Paying taxes is a painful, but basic, business reality. Although any business owner would prefer to look at the rosy pretax profit shown on their profit and loss statement as an indication of the success of their business, the real bottom line is the figure after taxes. Often the tax bite can be painful. It cannot only dim your profit picture, but it can also plummet you into a cash crisis if you have neglected to take tax payments into account when you were figuring your operating cash needs. Paying taxes as a business owner involves planning in order to ensure that you pay the lowest possible taxes and that you have enough cash on hand to meet these obligations. Tax planning is an integral part of financial management.

There is nothing sinister about arranging your business affairs in a way that will keep your taxes as low as possible. Everyone does it. No one has a duty to pay more taxes than the law requires. Such tax planning is just the sign of wise financial management. A common mistake made by business owners stems from seeing taxes, like death, as both inflexible and inevitable. Although taxes may be inevitable, they are flexible. There are many legitimate ways to use allowable deductions to lower the level of the taxes you pay. For example, many of your business expenses are deductible items, such as the interest you pay on loans, incidental repairs you make to your premises, bad debts, and depreciation.

A good accountant can help you plan your managerial actions in a way that will reduce your tax burden. For example, she or he can advise you when it would be more advantageous for your tax situation to lease equipment, rather than buy, or when you should time purchases. Your accountant can also advise you on the best method for depreciating equipment and when you should switch your company from a sole proprietorship to a corporation in order to receive greater tax advantages. A common mistake is that business owners use their accountants as technicians, merely to prepare and file their tax returns, rather than using them as advisers before the fact to help them plan their actions so that their year-end tax bite is reduced. According to Patty Bissell, who frequently helps small business owners with their tax planning, people lose a lot of money because they have failed to keep adequate records of their business expenses. "I always recommend that business owners keep a diary with them at all times to record what they did and what they spent. That way you can be sure to capture everything from out-of-pocket outlays to the mileage you can claim."

Although the IRS does not prescribe any specific accounting records or systems, they do require that the owner-manager maintain permanent records, which can be used to identify the firm's income, expenses, and deductions; which can be inspected, if necessary. If you are subject to state income taxes, you will also want to make certain that your records are kept in a way that will help you document state taxes as well. Keeping your records in a neat, orderly way is essential in case you are audited by IRS.

As a business owner, you will be playing two roles in managing your taxes. In one role, you are a debtor, owing the government taxes on your earnings; and in the other, you are the government's agent, collecting various taxes and passing the funds on to the appropriate government agency. The latter role is the one you perform when you deduct social security and other payroll taxes from your employees' salaries or when you collect sales taxes. Meeting your tax obligations as an owner is much more complicated than as an individual. Both the number of taxes you will have to pay and the two roles of debtor and agent you will play make tax planning and management essential. For example, whereas your quarterly income taxes are due on the fifteenth of the last month of each quarter, social security remittances are due on the last day of the month, and federal excise taxes must be remitted monthly or semimonthly depending on the volume.

Tax planning is not only a good management idea, but it is also something that is forced on you by the IRS. The government likes business owners to pay their taxes on a pay-as-you-go basis, meaning that you will not have the luxury of hanging onto your tax money until the end of the year. You will be required to make a "Declaration of Estimated Tax" on or before April 15 of each year, and you must then make payments on this estimate each quarter. The declaration is an estimate of the income and self-employment taxes you expect to owe, based on expected income and exemptions. Adjustments to the estimate can be made at the time of each payment. If you own a corporation, the date of your quarterly payment will vary according to the fiscal year you select, since corporations can select a taxable year other than a calendar year.

A good way to plan and keep track of the payments that you must make, is to keep a schedule of which taxes you must pay and when they are due. You can estimate how much you think each payment will be from your sales and payroll projections. The worksheet on page 188 should assist you in doing this planning. It is designed to help you manage your firm's tax obligations. You may want your accountant or bookkeeper to prepare it so that it can be a

Worksheet for Meeting Tax Obligations

Kind of Tax	Due Date	Amount Due	Pay to	Date for Writing the Check
Federal Taxes				
Employee income and social security				
Excise				
Owner-manager's and/or corporation income				
Unemployment				
State Taxes				
Unemployment				
Income				
Sales				
Franchise				
Other				
Local Taxes				
Sales				
Real estate				
Personal property				
Licenses (retail, vending machine, etc.)				
Other				

Source: *"Steps in Meeting Your Tax Obligations. Small Marketers Aid No. 142. Washington, D.C."* Small Business Administration.

reminder for paying your tax obligations. Several pamphlets can help give you a clearer picture of what your tax obligations are: *Tax Guide for Small Business* (Publication 334), which is put out by the IRS every year; and *Steps in Meeting Your Tax Obligations* (Small Marketers Aid No. 142) and *Getting the Facts For Income Tax Reporting* (Small Marketers Aid No. 144), which are published by the SBA.

Income Taxes

Income taxes will be the biggest contributor to your annual tax bite. The amount of federal income taxes you will owe will depend on the amount of your company's earnings and on your type of business organization—individual proprietorship, partnership, or corporation.

If you are a proprietor, you pay your income tax just as any other individual citizen does. The only difference is that your income is from the earnings of your business, rather than from salaries or wages. You file the same form as an individual taxpayer, plus an additional schedule that identifies expense and income items for your business.

If you are a member of a partnership, the partnership must file a return to reflect the income and expense of the business. You report only your share of the profit on your individual return.

If your business is a corporation, it normally pays taxes on its profit. In addition, as owner-manager of the corporation, you pay an individual tax on the salary and dividends which your corporation pays you. A corporation may also select a taxable year different from the calendar year. An odd fiscal year can prove to be a benefit if your company experiences regular swings in sales because it enables you to plan your tax payments around your business cycles.

As an employer, you are responsible not only for making your own tax payments but also for withholding federal income tax payments from your employees' salaries and periodically passing these funds on to the government. When a new employee joins your company, she or he must sign Form W-4, "Employees Withholding Allowance Certificate," on which she or he lists the exemptions and additional withholding allowances claimed. This form gives you the authority to withhold income tax. At the end of the year, you must furnish each employee with copies of Form W-2, "Wage and Tax Statement." You must also send a copy of this form to the IRS. In states where there is a state income tax, these procedures must be followed as well.

Social Security and Unemployment Taxes

Another type of withholding tax you will have to collect from your employees' salaries are social security taxes. In 1979, social security tax rates indicated that you must deduct taxes at the rate of 6.13 percent on the first $22,900 of an employee's wages. You must match that amount for a total payment to the government of 12.26 percent. When an owner-manager uses social security for his own retirement, he must pay the tax for himself.

If you are in a type of business that involves tips, such as in a restaurant, employees receiving cash tips of $20 or more in a month must report these tips to you for income tax and social security purposes. You then deduct the employee's social security and income tax from wages due the employees, but you are required only to match deductions made on wages, not on tips.

Your business is liable for federal unemployment insurance taxes if you paid wages of $1,500 or more in any calendar quarter or you had one or more employees in each of twenty or more calendar weeks. These twenty weeks do not have to be consecutive. You will be required to deposit these funds quarterly and to file an annual return at the end of year. The basic tax rate is 3.2 percent of the first $4,200 of taxable wages received by each employee. However, you may pay much less if you are paying state unemployment taxes, since the federal government gives you credit for such payments.

Excise Taxes

Federal excise taxes are imposed on the sale or use of some items, transactions, or occupations. For example, there is an occupational tax on wholesale and retail dealers in beer and liquor. You should check with the IRS to see if your business is subject to such taxes. If you are liable for any excise taxes, you must file a quarterly return and make monthly deposits of that tax every time you owe more than $100 a month or semimonthly deposits if you are liable for more than $2,000 in excise taxes during any month of the previous quarter. If you own or operate trucks in your business, you will have to pay a federal highway use tax; and if your business is involved with gambling, firearms, narcotics, liquor, or gaming devices, you will have to pay an occupational tax.

State Taxes

The federal government will not be the only one nibbling on your profits, as your state government may also require you to pay taxes. Since these taxes vary from state to state, it is best to check with your state's department of commerce or tax service to find out what their requirements are. Most states have four major kinds of taxes: income, unemployment, personal property, and sales. In collecting sales tax, you will be acting as the agent of the state and should therefore make sure that your record systems conform with state requirements.

Some counties, towns, and cities also impose various kinds of taxes on real estate, personal property taxes, gross receipts of businesses, and unincorporated businesses. They may also require a license, which is a form of taxation.

CHAPTER 9

The Final Move: Playing the Game

You are now equipped to play the entrepreneurial game. You know how to assess whether you want to play, to find a team and backers, to target your market, and to even control your business. Now comes the hard part—playing the game. You must learn how to manage a growing business.

You will find that once you are in operation and your business begins to grow, you will have to develop new skills. Although you may start small, the time will come when the tasks involved in your business will become overwhelming. You will be forced to hire additional staff and begin to delegate work. The touch and smell of day-to-day contact with customers will fade, and you will begin to spend more and more of your time managing your growing organization.

This change can be traumatic for many business owners. Denise Cavanaugh, a management expert and owner of Cook/Cavanaugh Associates, points out that there are all kinds of pains and agonies involved in changing from an entrepreneur to a manager as your organization grows. "When you first start out, you are doing everything. You are keeping the books, hiring people, selling, delivering, etc. As the business grows, you can't have your hand in everything. You need different managerial skills." She believes that a lot of small business owners who are successful in the beginning fail later because they can't begin to let go and delegate work to others.

Doing "business as usual" in the face of growth can be a mistake. Cavanaugh, who teaches a management course, feels that a business owner needs three different sets of skills to create a successful company: entrepreneurial, technical, and managerial. These skills are needed in different proportions at different times in the life of your business. For example, when you first start a business, your entrepreneurial skills and technical skills will be needed most. These entrepreneurial skills include your ability to live with financial risk and ambiguity and to be strategic. As Cavanaugh puts it, "the ability to live on the edge and cope with it." The technical skills involve the knowledge of the trade or business you need for your specific business venture. However, once your business is launched, a third set of skills—management skills—becomes critical to your success. These skills, which involve knowing how to hire and supervise employees, how to make decisions, how to delegate, and how to control your business, will determine whether your business hovers in that twilight zone between success and stagnation or experiences a healthy growth pattern.

Unfortunately, however, you will find that many of these skills must be learned from experience. Business seems to be a game in which you take the test first and learn the lesson later. While this book will teach you the basic principles behind the game, your plays and strategies will depend upon the market and economic conditions and the opponents you face. Although this chapter will provide some basic management pointers, only playing and studying the game further will give you practice in developing the management skills and strategies you will need to win in the entrepreneurial game.

The important thing to remember is that there is nothing mysterious about management. Management is something you do every day, whether it's managing your life, your home, or your business. Management is the ability to use whatever resources you have at your disposal to achieve your objective, and in this sense, it is a skill that is developed, not taught.

William Copulsky and Herbert McNulty point out in their book, *Entrepreneurship and the Corporation*, that few graduate business schools actually teach management. What they teach is the development of problem-solving and decision-making skills, not managerial skills. Much of management comes from experience and perception, based on the use of intuitive judgments and hunches, as well as a knowledge about the business environment. An effective manager is somewhat like a Grand Master who can look at a chess board and an opponent's play and see power patterns that indicate the strength of the positions.[1]

It is the playing strategy, not the individual moves or plays themselves, that makes you a winner. But just as certain skills, such as tackling, passing, and receiving, are necessary to implement a football strategy, certain managerial skills are necessary to implement business strategies. These skills include the ability to plan, direct, and control the major resources of your business so that your business can grow.

DEVELOPING MANAGERIAL SKILLS

Although external competitive conditions will, of course, affect the level of your success, it is usually poor management that drives most businesses into the ground. Jim Molloy, of TRAMCO, points out that most owners wrongly blame their business illnesses on the lack of sufficient capital. "But, that's just the symptom, not the cause." Molloy concludes that management is the cause, as a well-run company can always raise money.

Dun & Bradstreet agrees that poor management, not competitive conditions, kills most firms. According to Dun & Bradstreet, the nine major items contributing to the high level of small business failure are as follows:

1. Lack of business experience. This includes a lack of knowledge about how to buy merchandise, how to attract customers, and how to handle finances.
2. Lack of money. This includes both not having enough money to operate for the first year and not knowing how to estimate and control your money needs.
3. Picking the wrong location. This includes not analyzing your market properly.
4. Inventory mismanagement. This includes both purchasing the wrong kinds and the wrong amounts of inventory and creating a drain on cash.
5. Putting too much capital into fixed assets. This includes neglecting to plan for needed operating or working capital.
6. Poor credit-granting practices. This includes its impact on the cash-flow situation of the firm and on needed extra debts to carry charge customers.
7. Taking too much money out of the business for yourself.
8. Not planning growth. This includes the money problems and management problems caused by unplanned expansion.
9. Having the wrong attitude toward business. This includes not having the spirit and determination that it takes to be an entrepreneur and taking the business too lightly or chiseling the public.[2]

This list shows that the major problems small businesses face are internal to the company, rather than external. The ability for an owner to learn managerial skills and leave her or his entrepreneurial skills behind as the firm grows is a key factor to business success. Unfortunately, however, many of the very personality traits critical to launching a business can become managerial problems. The extreme independence, drive, and high performance standards of the entrepreneurial personality can make it difficult for owners to be tolerant of employees, to delegate authority, or to take advice, and as a result, they may misutilize or underutilize their personnel. As a business owner, you will find that you must learn to adjust with the growth of your business and to manage your business growth, your staff, and yourself.

MANAGING YOUR GROWTH

Growth can be tricky for a small business. If it comes too fast, it can swamp and sink what was once a viable business. However, if it does not come at all, you also run the risk of going out of business. Most experienced business owners will tell you that growing is relatively easy; the hard part is learning how to handle growth. Unfortunately, the whims of the marketplace usually mean that growth does not occur in a nice, logical, incremental fashion. It comes in spurts that can tax your staff and your capital base.

The decision to grow is one that cannot be avoided. It will face you often. It happens every time you decide to take a new contract that exceeds your current capacity, hire a new employee, or invest in a larger inventory. Growth can be risky because you never know if it will continue. However, you can reduce the risk by learning to manage your growth. You can make decisions about when and how you will grow, rather than letting these decisions be made by an erratic marketplace. This process also entails learning one of the basic managerial skills—planning.

There are seasoned business players who can sniff the competitive winds and make decisions in a knee-jerk fashion. Somehow, their decisions usually seem to turn out all right. However, those people are playing a defensive, rather than an offensive, business game, and they are rarely building growing enterprises. They have their eyes on today, not on tomorrow. The only way you are going to get the tomorrow you pick is to plan your future.

Planning is the key to winning in the entrepreneurial game. It is the basis by which you set your business goals and plan your business strategies. Planning means that you must take your eye off today's problems, which may seem immense and immediate, and look into the future. This move can be hard for many small business owners to make, but it is critical to their success. Unless an owner is able to step back from her or his day-to-day operations and business crises and take a hard look at the business as an integrated whole, she or he risks always playing minor skirmishes rather than the major strategies that are needed.

The ability to control your own environment is one of the major differences between business success and failure. Yet it is a sad fact that many people who go into business so that they can control their own destinies wake up to find themselves not in control at all, but at the mercy of circumstances, creditors, customers, and competitors. The way to avoid this trap is to recognize that one of your major functions as the owner of a business is to be the person with the clearest vision about where the firm is headed. You must be the person who establishes the firm's business philosophy, as well as policy, and who does the planning necessary so that the firm can reach its objectives.

The firm's business philosophy will revolve around the goals you set for the business including your operating orientation, such as whether your business goal for the year is to increase existing sales or develop new products, as well as your sales, organizational, and financial goals. You need to know what these goals are in order to develop the strategies to attain them.

Coping with the Planning Process

Initially, you may find the planning process painful. It requires reflective thinking, self-analysis, and a hard look at the business and its resources. Mary Vinton, owner of Georgetown Leather Design, has discovered that it's hard to sit back and do that long-term planning when you are so involved in the day-to-day operation of the store.

> I think this is so typical of small businesses. I see it with friends of mine who have small businesses. When I ask if they have done any financial planning, they say "Well, I was gonna do it this month, but boy, our sales were really good and I had to get all these reorders in." We were very lucky to survive in our business, because we made this mistake, too. There are a great number of decisions that were made out of gut feelings. They were emotional decisions, which, of course, should have been hard, cold business decisions. We made the right decisions, but not for the right reasons.

Vinton feels every business should have an overall plan for at least a year if you are growing rapidly and for two or three years if your growth is stabilizing. Although most of us would not think of starting on a long trip without a road map hundreds of business owners start on their business journey without such a map. We all know that it is much easier to get somewhere if you know where you are headed and the actions that will help you get there. This is what planning does for you. The plans and projections you draw up for bankers and investors are not static documents; they are vital management tools.

How to Develop Business Plans

There is nothing mysterious or complicated involved in planning. It simply takes the ability and the discipline to step back from your day-to-day operations and look at the long-range future of your firm as an integrated whole. Planning involves setting business goals, assessing the resources you have available, establishing timetables to measure progress, and developing the business strategies that you will use to achieve the goals. Thus, your game plan ensures that all members of your entrepreneurial team are playing the same strategy.

The starting point for your planning process lies in your business records. These records provide you with historical trends to use as the basis for your business plans. The other input you will need will be information from the key people who will be responsible for implementing the strategies and goals. Although you will have the final decision in setting your organization's goals and strategies, it is important to use your staff in the planning process and let them know that their performance will be measured against these goals. Doing this makes your plan a working document, rather than a piece of paper that is ignored by employees.

Your plans can be drawn up for months, quarters, or years, based on your planning needs. Most large businesses have both short- and long-range plans, sometimes stretching out for five to ten years. However, as a small business owner, you may find your company changing so fast that such long-range planning will not be needed, unless you are preparing for a major business expansion or diversification.

Your plans should be as detailed and specific as possible. They should also be in writing. They should identify the key personnel responsible for achieving the goals and should set timetables to check on results. The goals should be clearly stated and realistic. For example, your stated goals should not be to merely increase sales but to increase sales by a certain percentage in a specific period. However, your plans should never be cast in concrete. They should be flexible enough to be adjusted to new opportunities, mistakes, or changes in the business environment. The goal of the planning process is to allow you to anticipate problems in advance and develop strategies to cope with them, not to develop a straight jacket for your business.

One added benefit of developing target goals and plans for your business is that it gives you a means of measuring the actual performance of your business against the planned performance. Mary Zulalian, who once owned Holden and Company in Boston, feels her profit and loss statement and her business plans are like report cards; they tell her how well she is performing. "I'm highly competitive. I was a downhill racing champion as a teenager and have always thrived on competition."

MANAGING YOUR ORGANIZATION

Learning to Be Boss

When you first start your business there will be times when you do not feel that you have enough hands or hours to accomplish everything that you need to do. You will hardly seem like the chief executive officer (CEO) you thought you would. Peg Shaffer, of Paradigm, Inc., describes being a business owner as feeling like the "pooh-bah" in the Gilbert and Sullivan operetta *The Mikado*. A "pooh-bah" was the First Lord of the Treasury, Commander-in-Chief, Groom of the Backstairs, Lord Chief Justice, Master of the Buckhounds, Lord Mayor, Acting and Elect, and so on. As the owner-manager of a business, you will also wear many hats.

In the beginning, most of the problems you react to as an owner are problems created by external factors, such as coping with delayed supplier deliveries or irate customers. As your organization grows, you will find that the nature of your problems will change as well. You will begin to face problems created by internal, rather than external, factors. You will start finding out that being the CEO of your own business is a difficult and delicate job. As a small business owner, your managerial problems are not that much easier than those of the CEO of a large corporation. The only difference is that in your business *you* are the organization, whereas in a large business, the organization seems to have a life of its own. Your organization is so closely tied to you and your actions that if you sneeze, the organization catches a cold.

Learning how to be the boss in such a closely knit organization is one of the most important skills you will have to develop. However, if learning how to be the boss can be difficult for anyone, it can be especially difficult for women. Unfortunately, our traditional positions in society have never prepared us for the skills that are necessary in running an organization.

Margaret Henning and Anne Jardim point out in their book, *The Managerial Woman*, that our traditional socialization has taught us to excel as individuals but has given us little experience in working with teams, a factor that impacts our management ability. The prestigious sports for girls tend to be one-on-one sports, such as tennis or swimming, whereas boys learn about team behavior through their sports.[3] Women therefore tend to be very good at the technical aspects of a job but less skilled at the important managerial aspects of setting goals and developing work teams that can help achieve these goals.

Dr. Margaret Fenn, who teaches a course in management at the University of Washington in Seattle, agrees that women tend to be experienced in only one of the three skills needed for effective management. Fenn defines those skills as diagnostic (information collection), decision making, and conflict resolution (action). According to Dr. Fenn, these skills are as different from one another as the skills of a detective, a judge, and an executioner. Women tend to excel in the first, which is a more technical skill, but to be inexperienced in the other two skills, which are critical if one is to be the boss.

The diagnostic skill involves the ability to observe, screen out, categorize, organize, and interpret relevant information in a way that will lead to the next set of skills: decision making. The decision-making skill involves a simple go/no-go mental process in which a person recognizes decision points and takes responsibility for decisions that affect others. The conflict-resolution skill is the ability to establish the goals, to formulate courses of action to accomplish the goals and gauge their expected consequences, and to choose the course that would best accomplish the goal set. According to Fenn, women have well-honed diagnostic skills, since we are used to screening the environment for clues that give us a measure of our worth. However, we have not developed decision-making or conflict-resolution skills because society has encouraged us to take dependent, passive, and supportive roles that encourage reaction, rather than pro-action.[4] Says Fenn: "Most women executives get promoted because they are the best darned 'doers' around. When they move into the realm of management, they are often shocked to find that management is another type of activity. Many of the tasks involved in the management of a firm or business are not job-specific. They are more general in nature. However, they are just as important to getting the job done."

Fenn believes that women sometimes make the mistake of thinking that being the boss merely involves giving orders. She points out that being boss should also involve the ability to listen to the input of others, represent the needs of the business to the outside world, and lead and motivate employees to accomplish the goals you set. Being the boss, doesn't mean being bossy. As a boss, you are a leader, a manager, and a motivator but not a dictator.

However, learning how to be the boss can be a difficult transition for women. The major problems we seem to face in putting on the mantle of boss stem from our upbringing. We tend to feel more comfortable exercising technical skills, rather than managerial skills; and perfection is more important for us than it is for men. In addition, we have never learned how to judge risk, a factor that impacts our decision-making ability, and we tend to have a high need for affiliation, which can get in the way of our leadership ability.

Fenn points out that an effective leader does not seek love and affection from her staff, but respect. Yet women have difficulty separating their need for love and affection from their need for respect and recognizing that people are one of the basic resources of a business that must be managed for a business to succeed. We tend to become trapped in the interpersonal aspects of management, particularly in a small firm where employees seem like a family.

Rosemary Tucker, owner of Tucker Tire Company in Covine, California, attests that learning to be the boss is not easy. When Tucker, who has been in business for twenty years, took over her business, she knew nothing about the products or the business, but she learned fast. With the help of supplier credit, she was able to turn the company around. However, she says she never felt comfortable making decisions and being boss for the first seventeen years she was in business. "I was operating out of fear, fear of failure. Having the sole responsibility of six children, I knew I couldn't fail since the only thing I had was the business. It wasn't until I took an executive seminar that I got the kind of self-affirmation I needed to feel like the boss. I now feel totally comfortable with the role, and my business has grown tremendously since that time." Tucker has seen her annual gross revenues skyrocket to $2 million from $200,000 four years ago, showing that learning how to manage well is an important part of creating a successful business.

Tucker also feels that many of the experiences that women have in making quick decisions in their homes can be translated to business. "If a pot is boiling over you don't sit down and have a conference. You do what's necessary. The same thing happens when a child is hurt." Other women have expressed the same feeling. Indeed, some management experts are beginning to agree.

Although women in corporations are consistently judged by male managerial stereotypes, a 1975 study conducted by the Johnson O'Conner Research Foundation reported that there were no significant differences between male and female respondents in 14 of 22 basic aptitudes studied.[5] In the remaining 8 aptitudes, the women excelled in 6, whereas the men were superior in only 2.[6] So, if women have certain inherent entrepreneurial traits, as we found in chapter 3, they also have certain inherent managerial traits—which only need to be developed more fully in a business sense, in order to create vibrant industries. Women have always excelled in such skills as listening, two-way communication, negotiation, and consensus building, all of which are vital to effectively manage people and businesses.

The Various Roles of the Boss

Although most management textbooks will tell you that the functions of a manager involve planning, organizing, staffing, directing, coordinating, and controlling the resources in a business, I think it helps to understand the various roles you will be playing as boss. These roles involve three levels of managerial activity: supervision, management, and administration. As the owner of a small firm, you will probably be performing all of these activities at different times in your daily operations. When you first start out you will probably be acting primarily as a supervisor; but as your organization grows, you will move more and more into the managerial and administrative roles, and you will find yourself delegating the supervisory role to others.

The first role, supervision, involves overseeing a particular function or task, whereas management involves integrating and coordinating dissimilar functions that have a common objective. Although the distinction between supervision and management is clearer than the distinction between management and administration, administration differs from the other two roles in that it involves setting long-range objectives and politics of an organization and developing strategies. Managers then translate these strategies into short-term objectives and tactics that employees can execute to reach these long-range objectives.

You will be wearing your administration hat when you develop your yearly goals for your business, review your business objectives, and act as a strategist. In this role you will guide the organization, rather than direct it. When you wear your management hat, on the other hand, you will be directing. Your role will be to tell employees what is to be accomplished and to counsel them as they work toward these objectives. As a manager, you are a tactician, rather than a strategist, and you try to integrate and coordinate the dissimilar functions of your organization to accomplish a common goal. You translate the overall objectives of the business into individual and collective objectives for your staff and develop plans for accomplishing these objectives. You put on your supervising hat when you begin to tell people how to do a specific task and directly oversee the completion of that task.[7] How well you carry out the three roles involved in being the boss will depend upon your ability to learn to communicate with your staff and to delegate authority.

Communicating Effectively

Communication is one of the areas where small businesses fare the worst, partly because the owners are so preoccupied with keeping the cash register ringing or the orders flowing that they fail to take the time to adequately train and indoctrinate their employees to either the business' overall goals or the specifics of the job that they were hired to perform. They make the mistake of thinking that the physical proximity of employees in a small organization will end the chance of communication mix-ups. However, physical proximity has nothing to do with effective communication.

Dr. Norma Loeseur, dean of the Business School at George Washington University and co-author of a book on executive leadership, feels that the major personnel problem facing small business owners stems from the lack of proper training and indoctrination to the job and communication. This factor can be especially important for the new business owner, since many of the employees you can afford will probably be relatively inexperienced. Loeseur believes that the first six months of an employee's life with a business are the most important in terms of training and communicating the overall goals and policies of the firm to the individual.

One business owner who has discovered the benefits of providing training to employees is Frances Young, a black woman who is the president and general manager of DeForest Wood Products Company in St. Louis. Young's firm manufactures wood products to customer specifications. Established more than thirty years ago, it has between twelve and eighteen employees, depending on business fluctuations. This factor complicates Young's employment problems and often make planning her staffing needs difficult. Although she has no trouble getting employees in times when she has peak work loads, it is difficult to find reliable employees who will stay with the firm. She feels the key to keeping good employees is to provide adequate employee benefits, such as health and disability insurance, and to promote from within—even if it means retraining an employee in a new skill so that she or he can move to a higher position. When her plant foreman retired recently, she decided to hire from within, rather than advertise for an experienced foreman. It meant that she had to train the person she picked for the job, but she feels that he is now both a good asset and loyal worker, who performs better than any new employee would have, no matter how experienced.

An employee handbook will help you solve many of your communication problems. A handbook gives a new employee an immediate understanding of the company's policies and rules, while taking some of the burden off of you to describe these verbally. It can also help alleviate employee turnover by giving prospective employees a clear idea of what to expect if they work for your organization so that they may enter the business with realistic expectations. Perhaps an even greater benefit of an employee manual is that it forces you, as the owner of your business, to take your eye off today's problems and to develop the long-range policies you will need. Putting these policies in writing helps everyone in the company start off from a common communication base.

The employee handbook should list all the firm's policies and rules, as well as information concerning vacations, holidays, pensions, profit-sharing plans, insurance plans, and other benefits. The SBA puts out a pamphlet, *Pointers on Preparing an Employee Handbook* (Management Aid No. 197), that can help you in this matter. A sample table of contents of an employee handbook is provided on page 201.

Other building blocks of your organizational communication system will be written descriptions of your compensation and performance evaluation system, as well as individual job descriptions. These will help the employees answer critical questions that deal with what their jobs are, whom they report to, how you expect them to perform the job, how you will judge their performance, and how this performance will affect their pay and promotions.

However, the written components of your communication system will not take the place of the face-to-face interaction. Just as a good general or coach needs to be close to the troops or team, you will need to be visible and nearby when your staff has problems.

SAMPLE CONTENTS PAGE FOR AN EMPLOYEE HANDBOOK

I.   Welcome message
II.   History of the company
III. This is our business
IV.   You and your future
V.   What you will need to know
    Working hours
    Reporting to work
    Rest periods
    Absence from work
    Reporting absences
    Employment record
    Pay period
    Shift premiums
    Safety and accident prevention
    Use of telephones
    How to air your complaints
VI.   Your benefits
    Vacations and holidays
    Group insurance, hospitalization, and surgical benefits
    Training programs
    Christmas bonus
    Savings plan
    Profit-sharing plan
    Suggestion awards
    Jury duty and military leave
    U.S. old age benefits
    Unemployment compensation
    Equal employment opportunity
VII. Special services
    Credit union
    Education plans
    Medical dispensary and company cafeteria
    Employee purchases
    Monthly magazine (or newsletter)
    Leisure activities (annual outing, baseball team, etc.)
VIII. Index

SOURCE: *Pointers on Preparing an Employee Handbook*. Management Aid No. 197. Washington, D.C.: Small Business Administration.

According to Jayne Spain, a former senior vice president of Gulf Oil Corporation as well as a member of many corporate boards, the most important asset of any business is its human resources. A good manager not only resolves problems but also listens to the thoughts, feelings, and ideas of her employees. Spain began her career in the 1950s when she took over Alvey-Ferguson, a privately held family business started in 1901.

At the time Spain took over the company, it had five hundred employees. "When I inherited the company I had little experience. I was familiar with the business, but did not know the technical side of it. I asked the employees if I should sell it or if we should run it together. They told me not to sell; they would teach me about the business." Spain ran Alvey-Ferguson for twenty years, during which time sales quadrupled, before it was finally acquired by Litton Industries.

To be an effective manager, Spain believes that you must let your employees know that they are a vital part of your business and your business team.

> You aren't the boss; you are a co-worker. What you are operating is a team, and you just happen to be playing this [boss] position. You have to sincerely believe that your employees are your major asset. It can't be rhetoric. It must be sincere. A lot of people say they believe this, but they don't implement it. I've found that if you believe in your employees and believe that they can do something, they'll break their backs and hearts for you; and you for them.

Spain feels that one of the things that helped her manage Alvey-Ferguson was that she took the time to know her employees individually and interface with them. She felt that a regular part of her managerial duty was to walk through the plant twice a day, stopping to talk with the workers, so that employees knew she was accessible and sympathetic to their problems.

Structuring the time to allow for such interfacing is an important part of management. You should plan routine staff meetings, which will enable you and your staff to engage in a formal interchange of ideas. You should let your staff know that not only is your door open to listen to their problems, but also you want to hear them. Even the best "open-door policy" does not work if you seem harried and act as if your employees are bothering you when they come to talk. As the boss, learning to listen and feel the pulse of your organization is as important as learning how to give directions and orders.

It is also extremely important to provide feedback to your employees. Motivation can be spurred by praise, as well as pay, and it is much less expensive. You need to strive to make your employees feel continually that they are a vital part of your entrepreneurial team and the future of the company. Take the time to compliment them when they do things right, and structure their participation into your decision-making processes. When you do have to criticize or reprimand an employee, be sure that you do it in private and that you criticize the task that was not performed, not the person.

One technique that Mary Ann Petery, owner of Selma Pressure Treating Company in Selma, California, uses to keep in touch with employees is to take a group out to lunch periodically and let them tell her what is going on, what their complaints are, and what they think is working or not working well in the company. The staff knows that they are going to talk about company issues and that the company will pick up the tab, and they can interact in a friendly atmosphere away from the office, telephones, and interruptions.

Petery started her company with her husband in 1961, but now owns 100 percent of it. She has built up the company—which preserves wood for such uses as construction, highway guard rails, and fences—to the point where it has forty-two employees. She feels that both interpersonal and financial skills have been helpful to her in running the business. She recently participated in the "Smaller Company Management Program" at Harvard Business School, an experience she found invaluable. According to Petery, it taught her to look at the business from a distance, rather than to get blinded by the day-to-day process of putting out fires and moving from crisis to crisis. It also taught her analytical approaches to problem solving, planning, forecasting, and budgeting. Both Harvard and Stanford have such programs, which are several weeks long and limited to firms with certain levels of sales or work force.

Petery feels that the key to motivating employees is to be friendly, but not friends. Walking that thin line between friendliness and friendship can be difficult for women, both because we have strong needs for affiliation and because many of our employees are women. Dr. Henry Bender, who conducted the research for the American Management Associations study of women business owners, found that many of the women he interviewed felt that they had more difficulty dealing with their female employees than their male employees because many women would feel they could take advantage of the boss because of "sisterhood" and would verbalize their feelings more with a woman than a man. This is something that Aline Berman also found. She started a Chinese restaurant, the Court of the Mandarins, in Washington, D.C., and has found that employees tend to come to her because they think she will be more sympathetic to their problems than will her male managers. And Edith Schubert, owner of the China Closet and Martins, also in Washington, D.C., has found that many employees have difficulty understanding why she should make so much money when she is just like they are. "What they don't realize is that they don't have to take the risks and stay up late at night worrying about the business. That's what I get paid for."

Many women business owners have difficulty dealing with the role that being the boss puts them in. Mary Vinton, of Georgetown Leather Design, has learned not to let her identity get so emotionally caught up in her business.

> I used to feel guilty that I was the one that was making all the money, while it was my employees that were doing all the work. I felt I should be paying them more. I would apologize to them if a bad situation arose and they had to work extra hours. It was an emotional turmoil for me. But after you've had a number of employees walk out on you, steal from you, or let you down by not showing up, you begin to realize that the reason you're making more money than they are is that you're working late and they are at home.

The key is to try and stay objective about your business, your employees, and your role as boss. Remember that employees seek a leader, not a friend. You should strive to earn their respect, not their love. Your role as the boss is to keep your eye on the future, build an entrepreneurial team that works well together, plan the strategies, and instill the inspiration that will spur this team to play well and win at the entrepreneurial game. To perform all these tasks, you must acquire the ability to plan, communicate, direct, and coordinate your player efforts.

As your business grows, you must be able to relinquish your position as captain of the team and take up the position of coach. This move to the sidelines can be difficult when you are used to the smell and touch of the game and the everyday activities of the business. But unless you learn to delegate responsibility effectively, your company will remain small and you will have difficulty retaining good people. Delegation of responsibility is critical to both your company's growth and the professional development of your staff. If a person has initiative, she or he will get dissatisfied unless some responsibility is given to them.

Delegating Authority

Most business owners will tell you that learning to delegate authority was one of the most difficult tasks that they had to learn. As Mary Vinton, of Georgetown Leather Design, puts it, "You have to define the job in an adequate way and then not totally wash your hands of it, but not look over their shoulders too much either. Part of my problem was that I've always felt that I could do anything. Of course, I had a lot more motivation as the owner, but it's very difficult to let things go and see them done less efficiently, or not quite as well." Beverly Jackson, co-owner of Jackson/Summers Associates, agrees that business owners tend to be very possessive. "You don't mind losing control if you know the job is done right; but that means finding someone who'll do it just like you do it, but at a much lower price because that is all you can pay. That's impossible, and that is the dilemma." That dilemma is what an entrepreneurial personality can create when it comes time to move from those entrepreneurial and managerial skills. The extreme self-reliance and high standards of performance, which were a positive factor at the beginning, can become a negative factor later on if you become intolerant of employee differences and find it difficult for you to delegate authority.

The key is to remember that employees are not like you. If they were, they would be starting businesses. All people are motivated differently. Some people are motivated by pay, whereas others are motivated by challenging opportunities. A good manager learns to read these signals, hire the type of people who will fit best in her organization, and offer the types of opportunities that match these needs. Nancy Lang, owner of a real estate firm in Burlington, Vermont, offers some good advice in this regard: "You have to remember that you cannot instill the entrepreneurial spirit in your staff. They will not be you. It's important to realize that management means managing from the bottom up, not the top down."

But no matter who the employee is, everyone needs to feel powerful and in control of some aspect of their lives. By delegating the responsibility and accountability for certain tasks to key employees, you will enable them to exercise their initiative, while assuring you that you are building a company that can function well in your absence. However, delegation of authority does not mean that you abandon authority. When you manage through others, it is essential that you keep control. Although you have made a subordinate responsible and accountable for a certain task, you will need periodic feedback to check the results of the actions she or he takes. The key to good delegation is to—

- delegate only those tasks for which there is some way to measure results so that you can hold the employee accountable,
- communicate clearly the specifics of the task,
- outline the parameters of the authority,
- detail the way that each person's area of responsibility and authority interacts with the other players.

One way to ensure effective delegation is to put in writing the person's function and the extent of her or his authority. This statement can include a list of specific actions they are free to take the initiative on and others that require approval from the front office. You must learn to stand back and let the person you have given the authority to perform the job in her or his way. You should measure your employees not by whether they perform a particular task exactly as you would do it, but by whether the methods used produce the desired results.

To check and see if you are effectively delegating, take a close look at your operations. Are you becoming the bottleneck in your business? Are you bogged down in paperwork? Does everyone come to you for decisions? Are you spending more time at routine tasks than at the planning and management of your business? If you feel that you could not be absent from the office for a day, a week, or a month, you are walking on dangerous ground and have not built an organization that is using its talent to the fullest extent.

Building a Participatory Climate

Suzanne Mendelssohn—president of Fundraising in the Public Interest, Inc., a New York City firm that consults with nonprofit groups who need help financing their programs—is a good example of a woman who knows the benefits of delegation and is using her staff to its fullest potential. Mendelssohn started her business in 1972 but began in 1976 an experiment in cooperative employee management, which has proven a boon for her company. It leaves her more time to do the planning and reflective thinking she thinks a boss should be doing. She hopes her experiment will lead to the eventual employee ownership, which would give her a ready market for her business and the ability to move on to other ventures she would like to start.

Part of Mendelssohn's arrangement includes eliminating all titles, developing a functional assignment of responsibilities, and training employees for employee management. An eight-member management committee now shares many of the previous burdens she once faced alone. Mendelssohn feels that the experiment has created a growing and vibrant enterprise.

> The benefits to me have been enormous. In exchange for the diffusion of authority which my lawyer had cautioned me about, I was given a more efficient operation. The conventional wisdom notwithstanding, I have found that over the past few years that ten or fifteen heads are better than 1 in business. One of the most important advantages of employee participation, as far as I'm concerned, is that it allows me to operate without the fear that troubles most owners in my industry: that good people, found and trained at great cost, will leave, taking valued clients with them. Because of the team system with which we operate, I have found that no one, myself included, is indispensable.[8]

The heart of Mendelssohn's plan to turn over her company to employees and move onto other ventures is to develop a situation in which she can sell the stock in the company to the corporation, which will then be run and managed by employees. Employees will not own shares individually but can become members of the corporate ownership after three years with the firm. They will participate in the management of the company on a one-person, one-vote basis. They will share in both the control and the profits of the firm, setting salary levels, vacations, performance evaluations, and the like.

Mendelssohn is reaping the rewards of creating an organizational environment in which workers can feel a part of the business and have the opportunity to live up to their own potential. Although you may not want to go so far as to copy her experiment with employee participation, you should remember that people rarely work up to full capacity unless they are motivated to do so by their bosses and the work environment. Your goal in managing your organization should be to create a climate that will develop and make maximum use of the career aspirations, talents, and creativity of your employees.

Some simple guidelines can help you maximize the potential of your employees: Remember to match your employees' jobs with their abilities, give them training and development opportunities, give them a reasonable opportunity to participate, and reward them in proportion to their contribution to the business. Although praise is an important motivator, pay is still the reason most people work for a living. You should reward people for the work they do, not the time they put in. Productivity and impact on profits, not seniority, should be the cornerstone of your compensation and promotion system. Some questions to ask yourself about your management of your employees are listed on page 208.

MANAGING YOURSELF

Coping with Stress

There is one person in the organization who always seems to get ignored. This person is the boss. Being the boss can be a lonely, stressful, and demanding job. The job you thought would give you freedom can sometimes bring you slavery. Although you may start your business to get away from having to answer to a boss, you will soon find that you have five bosses: your customers, your employees, your banker, the government, and yourself. You will also find that being the boss means having no one else to blame mistakes on or to ask to make decisions.

Learning how to cope with the stress and strain that this role can bring is as important to your success as anything else you will do in your business. We spend a lot of time and energy managing the other resources in our business, but we tend to forget about that one most critical resource—ourselves. However, making sure that you are keeping your own life in balance is one of the most important things you can do. In a small business, you are the organization. If you are having a bad day, everyone knows it. Therefore, it's important that you learn to manage your own limited resource—time—as effectively as you do your other resources.

Kandra Driggs, owner of Wing Conferences, feels that the most important thing a woman business owner can do for herself is to learn how to balance both her professional and her personal lives. When you own a business, there is a tendency to let your business become your whole life. Driggs, who is in the business of providing communications and career counseling for women, has seen hundreds of women who fail to do this and are miserable. She feels that building "stroking" time into your workweek is imperative if you are to both survive under the strain of ownership and be successful. Stroking can be anything that you personally like to do, from soaking in a bathtub to playing a game of tennis. Kandra believes that if a woman structures twenty hours of stroking time for every forty hours she works, she will be not only more efficient and productive on the job but also a lot happier about her life.

Brooke Mahoney echoes Driggs's feelings. Mahoney, a Harvard Business School graduate, directs the Volunteer Urban Consulting Group in New York City, an organization that provides professional management assistance to nonprofit organizations and minority enterprises. She knows many women who are now having second thoughts about their lack of dimension, after having spent the last five to ten years pouring their energies into their careers. "A woman needs to live out all sides of her personality, so that she doesn't end up burnt out and dried up." Mahoney thinks it is harder for a woman to switch gears between work and home than it is for a man. She finds herself still churning about what happened at the office, whereas men seem to switch all that off.

QUESTIONS TO ASK YOURSELF REGARDING MANAGEMENT OF YOUR EMPLOYEES

- Do employees in your firm know to whom they each report, and are they initially supervised?
- Do you meet frequently with your key employees to coordinate their efforts?
- Do you delegate as much authority as you can to those immediately responsible to you, freeing yourself from unnecessary operating details?
- Do you give employees reasonable freedom to work out the way they feel their jobs can best be done, let them make the day-to-day decisions necessary to carry out their work, and avoid limiting any of them to repetitive, routine tasks?
- Do you seek your employees' opinions, and do you have an employee suggestion system?
- Do you apply the concept of "management by objective"—that is, do you set work goals for yourself and for each employee for the month or season ahead and at the end of each period check the actual performance against these goals?
- Is each new person given adequate job training?
- Are your wage and salary scales externally fair and competitive with local firms?
- Are your wages and other forms of compensation internally fair and suited to the differences in your employees' jobs?
- Are raises and promotions pegged to performance, rather than to seniority?
- Do you have an incentive plan to reward unusually productive and innovative employees?
- Is your overtime policy clear and carefully controlled?
- Do you have an adequate fringe benefit system in terms of medical care and pension plans?
- Do you keep all the personnel records required by federal and state authorities and union contracts?
- Do you have a written personnel policy that governs all matters of employee interests and an operational manual that provides the information you feel essential for the operation of your business?

SOURCE: Adapted from *Management Audit for Small Retailers*. 3rd ed. John W. Wingate and Elmer O. Schaller. Small Business Management Series No. 31. Washington, D.C.: Small Business Administration, 1977.

Juggling Priorities: Time Management

Learning how to handle the many hats you will wear as business owner, woman, wife, and mother can be difficult. According to Lynn Lively, a consultant in Seattle, Washington, the techniques of time management can help.

Lively believes it is important to budget time each day for three things: business, personal matters, and exercise. She adds exercise to the normal business-personal needs because she feels it helps to dissipate the tension that business ownership can bring. She points out that time management, which has nothing to do with clock-watching, means setting priorities, budgeting your time, and learning to use every minute effectively.

Lively started to get interested in time management after she went into an unstructured job situation, where she learned that if she didn't manage herself, no one else would. She has found that the reward of good time management is being able to live two lives a day: her personal and her professional.

Time is like any other resource that must be budgeted. Unfortunately, it exists in limited twenty-four-hour periods, and nothing we can do can stretch it out or replace it once we have used it up. The first step in learning to manage your time is to ask yourself the basic question of how you want to spend your life and what is important to you. If hobbies or sports are important, you have to build these activities into your time management system and be as diligent about making yourself do them as you are about your work activities.

Time management is controlling what you do, not letting time demands control you. Lively believes that the question you must continually ask yourself is, Am I making the best use of my time, or is there someone else who could do this better than I can? It helps to set an hourly rate for yourself and then assess if you could not use your time more wisely working at the things you are really good at, rather than typing your own letters or doing other things that a lower paid employee could do. You should think of time management as a system, just as you develop systems to manage your paperwork, records, and other aspects of your business. The payoff will be more time to do those things that you really should be doing, rather than working to the "squeaky wheel syndrome," which makes you jump to do things that may be unimportant but are making the most noise.

Two excellent books to read on this subject are Alan Lakein's *How to Get Control of Your Time and Your Life* and Alex MacKenzie's *The Time Trap— Managing Your Way Out*. These books suggest that you list all the things that you want to accomplish in a day at random and then rearrange them according to a list of priorities, putting the most important things first. You then need to work from this list, completing each task before you go on to the next. You should work smarter not harder, and you should learn not to worry if you never complete your list. Other suggestions are to plan your hardest tasks at the time of day when your energy level is highest, to handle papers only once, to delegate work to subordinates, to work systematically, rather than jumping from activity to activity.

A system that works for Lynn Lively is to keep a stenographer's notepad on which she lists the activities she needs to accomplish each day. She categorizes them under headings of "write, call, and do" and then tries to attack the tasks in a systematic way. She breaks down large tasks into smaller tasks that can be accomplished easily. A good way to learn time-savers is to ask other busy women what they do. One suggestion is to block off times in your day when you will not be disturbed by interruptions and then return all your telephone calls at the same time, rather than sporadically. Kandra Driggs has found that leaving messages indicating what time people can find you in the office is a way to channel your incoming calls.

Lively feels that women have more difficulty than men in learning to manage their time. The fact that we are socialized to be caring and nurturing and to work around other people's time makes it harder for us to be ruthless about our own time. She points out that it is important to stick to your priorities and keep a schedule, but you must also be realistic about what you can do in a day, remembering that it is human nature to want to do more than you have time for.

The Importance of a Balanced Life

As the women in this book illustrate, owning a business does not mean that you have to become some kind of business machine that has no feelings and no life outside of your business. In fact, if you are that type of woman, chances are you will have less of a chance for success than if you have a well-rounded life. Contrary to popular belief, studies have shown that it is not the "workaholic" who is the successful executive, but the person who can set priorities, work hard, and still juggle all aspects of her or his life. This conclusion is supported by the women who participated in the study done by the American Management Associations for the Task Force. The American Management Associations researchers were amazed to find the number of women who juggled both highly successful businesses and their responsibilities to their families. The responses in the study showed that many perceived themselves successful in terms of not only their financial success but also other aspects of their lives. One participant said she runs a good business, has a happy marriage and a happy home, cooks dinner every night, and is very active in politics. Another divulged that she is successful in her career as well as in the way she has been able to pull everything together, including a very active life in which her husband and children are an important part.

American Management Associations interviewers found the high energy levels of some of these women remarkable. Many seemed to perform exceptionally well in all aspects of their lives and to have an uncanny ability to integrate many activities into their life structure, without neglecting either job or family. The family situation was presented most dramatically by two participants. One noted that besides being active in many other things, she took care of two young children when their mother died. "They were and still are very close to my husband and me and have been a great part of our lives." The other presented a remarkable story of juggling and dedication to family and business.

We had a baby daughter when I was forty-one and my husband was fifty-nine. She was a perfect specimen. We decided that we did not want to raise a child alone, so we adopted a baby boy. Previously, I helped to raise my husband's eleven-year-old child from a previous marriage, as well as various foster children.

We received help from a grandmother and honorary aunties. Then as my husband became semiretired and worked at home, we decided to raise our own children. Now that he's home, he does errands and so forth. I feel that I am a total woman. For example, I love to cook. I guess I have always been a workhorse. I truly believe that the busy person squeezes in the things she or he wants to do.

The women interviewed in this book expressed equally strong commitments to their enterprises, their husbands, and their children and credited the supportiveness of their families as being as critical an ingredient to their success as their ability to set priorities. Also key was their ability to not feel guilty about their dual roles.

Joyce Huber, co-owner of Georgetown Employment Service, is a single parent. She doesn't believe that working, taking care of children, running a house, and handling all of the thousands of things that have to be done is easy as a single parent. "It doesn't flow smoothly, and the responsibilities can be overwhelming. I am amazed day after day that I do it. People who do not have children and work look at what I do and are amazed." Huber doubts that many men could handle it. She concludes that people who set priorities in their lives and stick to them will be a lot happier, and her priorities are her children and her work.

Carla Massoni, Huber's partner, shares child-rearing responsibility with her husband. She says that she misses having other working mothers to share her experiences with, since the women in her neighborhood do not work. Massoni, who has had three children during the nine years that she has worked, feels that the quality of the time she spends with her family makes up for the quantity. "I don't think I have ever felt guilty. I have wished that there was more time to spend, but I have never felt that my children have ever, ever suffered from my working. As a matter of fact, I think they benefit by it because all day they have people with them who want to be with them." When she comes home at the end of the day, she's very happy to be with her children.

Vicki Smith Downing, owner of International Venture Capital and Equity, has been married eighteen years and has two children, ages seven and ten. She maintains that women are now learning that they can have both a career and a family and that women refuse to put the parenting of a family behind the parenting of a business, the way that men have done in the past. "I remember when you used to be told that you could do one or the other. Now I know you can do both." She also thinks it helps children to grow up knowing—rather than wondering—what grown-ups do, as women tend to talk to children more than men will about their work. Downing points out that her children know what she does is tough and that she doesn't work for fun or because she wants to get away from them. "I think it's particularly important for female children to see this. The economic realities mean that they aren't going to grow up and 'be taken care of,' and they need to know what grown-ups do to make a living."

What the women interviewed for this book have found is that business ownership, contrary to popular myth, is both compatible with, and contributes to a woman living out all the dimensions of her spirit. Women do not have to lose their femininity to be successful in the business game, and they can lead full, happy lives at the same time.

Epilogue

The preceding chapters have outlined the nature of the entrepreneurial game and some of its rules. However, it's important to remember that business is a very individualistic game: There is no one or right way to play. What wins is what works. The important thing is to know yourself, your competitors, your business, and some of the basic principles and to then develop your own strategies for winning. Only by playing will you truly begin to learn the entrepreneurial game.

The women interviewed for this book would like you to know that there is nothing mysterious about business, and that it is basically common sense. Only our upbringing has cloaked it in mystery and filled us with fear. They point out that there is humanity in the business community. You are not necessarily jumping into a shark tank when you put up your shingle. People will refer customers to you, customers will respond to the personal touch, colleagues will be helpful.

Although ownership is hard work and involves taking a risk, you will find that you are not alone and that you do not need to know everything. Knowledge can be hired—in the form of advisers—or gained through colleagues. Any business owner will tell you that each day presents a new problem and a new learning experience. You have to be prepared to work at your business full-time, not part-time, and to give it a 100 percent commitment. Sandy Hancock, owner of Sandy Hancock Enterprises, summarizes what the beginning can be like: "I want women to know that starting a business can be a rough time. You have to work 12-, 14-, 16-hour days, 7 days a week. Never did a day end before 10 p.m., and that happened only when I was exhausted. My social life that first year consisted of having a beer at midnight with the construction guys."

Yet all except one said that they would never do anything else other than own a business. Marjorie O'Connell Amey, the owner of a Washington, D.C., law firm, says it's the best thing she ever did. "Even when you are in your office at 11:00 at night, with the calculator in one hand and the dictaphone in the other, and the phone has the nerve to ring, there is a pleasant solace about it. . . . I don't know what it is exactly . . . I guess you could call it pride."

Pride, a sense of self-fulfillment, and self-confidence that you can pit your wits and creativity with the best and win are what women say business ownership is all about. As Martha Stuart puts it, it is the difference between working for something outside of yourself and working for something inside of yourself, and it makes all the difference in the world. "It can make you go to bed at 1:00 a.m. exhausted, and wake up at 6:00 a.m. fully rested and anxious to start a new day."

It has been hard, in a book designed to teach you the basic rules of the entrepreneurial game, to share some of the excitement, spunk, courage, and vision these women have about their businesses.

- The excitement of women like Rosemary Tucker, who, after seventeen years of running Tucker Tire Company out of necessity, attended an executive seminar and found at last that she could acknowledge that she was a boss. She found that it was all right to be a good one and that she *liked* it. She is now opening a new branch and received the Small Business Administration's Small Business Person Award of 1978.
- The spunk of Pauline Hogan, owner of Designs by Pauline's, who faces the double jeopardy of being a minority and a woman and says "kiss my grits" to those blocking her success. She communicates a sense that anyone who is committed can go into business with not much more than a knowledge of the field, two months rent, and a Dome bookkeeping book.
- The courage of Elizabeth Haynes, who, among others, faced the necessity of survival. Elizabeth Haynes stepped in and took over the Baltimore Rigging Company, a nontraditional field for women, when her father died unexpectedly, leaving a large family.
- The vision of women like Martha Stuart (Martha Stuart Communications) and Nancy Lang (Lang Associates, Realtors), who are not only extremely successful businesswomen but are also actively changing their lives, their work environment, and, perhaps eventually, all of our lives.

The women who were interviewed shared their hopes, failures, strengths, and fears. They are strong, alive, joyous, but they are *not* superwomen. In short, they are like you and me. They are mothers, single, young, old, rich, successful, or struggling. Some faced obstacles and some had tragedies. For some, their businesses were a tool for survival, for others a medium for controlling their lives and expressing themselves. But for all, owning a business has been an important step toward realizing self-fulfillment.

Business ownership does not mean giving up something, but it means gaining something. The women in this book break the myth set by societal stereotypes that women who are successful in the business realm are not feminine or have negated the other sides of their personality for a life revolving solely around money and power. Although the women featured in this book are economically successful and powerful in their own right, they have also integrated their work life with their roles as mothers, wives, friends, and individuals. These women live full and balanced lives, in which they have learned that moving yourself up economically does not necessarily mean putting someone else down. They have learned that helping yourself means also helping others, and, as Nancy Lang puts it, that "in order to have 'I' benefits, you must have 'you' benefits."

These women are not tough, heartless, ruthless businesswomen. They are not selfish women but, in the words of Ava Stern (publisher of *Enterprising Women*), self-made women. They are women who were concerned about their businesses, the quality of their products, the well-being of their employees, and the happiness of their families. They are, as Vicki Smith Downing says, women who are refusing to put the parenting of their families behind the parenting of their businesses, and who may have an advantage over men in that they do not carry into the entrepreneurial game many of the negative stereotypes bred in men.

That is not to say that there are not many obstacles placed in a woman's way because of our social upbringing. However, what came through loud and clear in doing this book was that women bring strengths to the entrepreneurial arena. Indeed, although traditional "feminine" values may be held in low esteem in some business sectors, they appear less of a handicap—and sometimes a plus—in owning a business. These were women who asked for personal fulfillment from their work, as well as money and power, and who were not afraid of the necessity of doing things differently from the way it had always been done. Thus, these women felt that their feminine characteristics were not a liability but an asset and they sought to integrate the positive aspects of their female upbringing with the positive aspects of business. Many expressed that for them money was a mechanism by which to get things done and that their businesses offered them the ability to both control their lives and utilize their creativity. Martha Stuart started her business because she did not want to fight for a future job with responsibility. "I want to do it now and prove what can be done. I want the feeling at the end of the day that I've done a lot of loving, and you can't do that without a lot of control."

Indeed while some people view the recent upsurge in interest in business ownership as leading us away from the eventual "greening" predicted by Charles Reich in *The Greening of America*, this does not hold true for women. Reich proposed that man's spirit goes through several levels toward an inevitable "greening." The first level was "Consciousness I"—symbolized by the ruthless entrepreneurial spirit. The second level was "Consciousness II"— symbolized by the Organizational Man, who sublimated his personal goals to the business's goals. The third level was "Consciousness III"—symbolized by a socially concerned person, who had integrated both the personal and economic goals and would eventually grow to the "greening" described in the book.[1]

While it is true that many people are reverting back to Consciousness I, they are doing so with less ruthlessness than the robber barons of the eighteenth and nineteenth centuries. Women, for one, are finding that what is economically freeing is also spiritually freeing. In a sense, starting and running your own company has fit that last piece—the economic piece—into the puzzle that makes up the spiritual whole for most women. It is as if women, rather than going back to Reich's Consciousness I of ruthless entrepreneurship and rugged individualism, have somehow used entrepreneurship to push them to the "greening" that Reich predicted in *The Greening of America:* the integration of personal goals and corporate or organizational goals into their lives.

The women interviewed for this book explode the myth that there is something antithetical about making money, caring, and loving. They embody a new spirit of entrepreneurship, a spirit that

is not contrary but akin to the spirit of the artist—it is to share something of value and to not control the response but live with it. It is to market a product that will make the human condition better, to have the courage to decide what needs to happen, to risk being misunderstood, to enjoy being understood, to use money, even, as a form of communication. For the new entrepreneur has discovered, like the artist, that one person's success doesn't diminish another person's success, that no one does anything the same as anyone else.[2]

APPENDIX 1:

Scoring Sheet and Answer Interpretation:
Do You Have What It Takes to Start Your Own
Business?

After completing the questionnaire provided on page 45, you may use the following scoring sheet to count your correct answers. The accompanying interpretations will illuminate the answers.

SCORING: Count the number of "yes" answers you gave.

Key: 13-16 "yes" = Get going on your business plan—you have the earmarks of entrepreneurship.

    10-12 "yes" = Think twice before taking the plunge.

    6-9 "yes" = The pension you'll get can always be invested by others.

    0-5 "yes" = Have you considered the fact that there are millions of Americans who are not entrepreneurs?

WHAT THE ANSWERS MEAN

1. *Do I have a close relative that is or was in business for herself/himself?*
The available data show that the majority of entrepreneurs had a father or other close relative in business for themselves. The importance of a role model in entrepreneurship is well documented. To make being in business for yourself credible, it is considered important that you see people in action who have also started firms. Strangely, studies on this variable show that a close relative entrepreneur will frequently discourage entrepreneurship in another relative, so don't be dismayed if everyone around you tells you how tough it is and why you shouldn't do it.

2. *Have I ever worked for a small firm where I had close contact with the person who started it?* and

3. *Did I ever work for a small division of a larger firm where I had close contact with the top manager?*

Persons who work in small firms or in small divisions of larger firms get more varied experiences than those who work in very large firms or large divisions of large firms. Because those who work in the smaller firm environment usually get more opportunities to work closely with the top management and/or founders of those firms, their experience pertinent to entrepreneurship is more varied and useful. When you work for such firms, you come to realize that the top manager/entrepreneur is human, and that they make mistakes. One frequently gets the attitude from such experiences that, "if they can do it, so can I."

4. *Is my work experience in a variety of functional areas, such as marketing, finance and production?*

The more functional area experiences, the better. An entrepreneur is a jack of all trades, at least initially. The entrepreneur needs to be conversant with the total functions of the enterprise, and cannot generally afford experts at first. Even if you are wealthy and can afford the experts, you need to understand their functions and how they fit together. This is best gained through education and experience. If you have worked in marketing and finance and know the other important functional areas pertinent to the business you want to start, this is a decided plus for your goal of starting your own firm.

5. *Have I ever had my employer reject my "better mousetrap" idea?*

More companies are started for negative reasons than for positive ones, and the rejection of your idea for the "better mousetrap" is a common negative reason. Large corporations frequently do more to unwittingly encourage entrepreneurship by discouraging creativity than they know. Their reasoning is valid to them—a $5 million market is too small for a $500 million company—but not to you, the entrepreneur. Your "pet rock" may be all right as an independent business, but not within your existing firm.

6. *Am I between the ages of 30 and 40?*

If you are between 30 and 40, that's probably good. These are peak years for energy, vitally necessary for the hard work ahead of you. They are also peak years for having the variety of experience and education that can help you through the difficult first years. Age can give an edge over younger entrepreneurs. At the same time, entrepreneurs in their 30's are not necessarily as accustomed to the comfortable life style that happens in later years, and can do "without" a bit more readily. If you are younger or older than this, don't get too upset—we find the entrepreneurial population is evenly distributed, with people forming their first corporation even in their 60's.

7. *I like to do things, rather than plan things.*

Most entrepreneurs like to *do*, not read, write, think or plan. Entrepreneurs are people of action. This does not mean that you cannot be successful if you like to plan. Indeed, the odds favor a planful approach, but also require action. If you are one of those fortunate persons who is at home both planning and acting, consider yourself a prime candidate for entrepreneurship.

8. *I have lived in three or more cities in my life.*
Mobility is a key factor in the decision to start a company. This relates to flexibility, a necessity in the beginning stages of firms. An openness and receptivity to new ideas and situations can be enhanced by variety, and movement frequently forces this flexibility. In high technology company formations studied, a very large majority of the firms were started by persons who moved around a great deal. Entrepreneurship is also related to being the "new man in town"—the lack of roots and ties found among immigrants and minorities, the displacement of people, creates the need for entrepreneurship—one of the few avenues for upward economic mobility and status.

9. *I have been fired before.*
Most entrepreneurs rebel at working for others—if you answered no to this question, and you think you are entrepreneurial material anyway, you probably quit before you got fired.

10. *(If I am married) my spouse is supportive of my work.*
Entrepreneurs get very much married to their firms. Their families usually suffer in the start-up years and even beyond. This is very important—can your spouse/family withstand the competition of your new spouse and family (the firm) and the time/ financial demands imposed by it? If not, which is more important, the firm or your family? A large percentage of entrepreneurs end up in divorce court sooner or later, but a surprising number of them are very happily married. Entrepreneurship will probably not enhance a shaky marriage, and could take a happy marriage into dissolution. Before you start, talk this over very seriously at length with your spouse and family.

11. *What generally happens to me is something I make happen, not something that is due to luck, good and otherwise.*
Successful entrepreneurs operate in the middleground between pure chance and luck, where *they,* not chance or luck, influence what happens to them and their firms. If you feel you make things happen, this is called an internal locus of control. If you feel other forces (luck, chance, other people's actions) make things happen to you, this is called an external locus of control. There is a quiz for testing the internal/external locus of control felt by an individual, and entrepreneurs consistently score in the direction of being internally focused. If you buy lottery tickets it doesn't mean that you are externally oriented, but you should realize that the odds are not in your favor and you won't have that dollar to invest in growing your firm.

12. *If I had to make a choice between working for a firm which I do not own for twice the money I make now and running my own firm at my present compensation, I would choose to start my own firm.*
Most entrepreneurs desire the independence of owning and managing their own firms far more than the financial security of working for someone else. Non-entrepreneurs cannot understand that desire. Ask your spouse, if you have one, which position he/she would take. This does not mean that entrepreneurs don't desire financial independence, and most entrepreneurs start companies with the anticipation of making and

retaining more money—eventually—than they are now making. That's not the overriding consideration, though, and if you and your spouse/family are at odds on this point, see the discussion about question #10 again.

13. *When a problem comes up that everyone around me says is unsolvable, I usually try to figure out ways to solve it.*
Entrepreneurs are usually inventive, inquisitive, and aggressive. They like challenges. Solving the "unsolvable" when everyone around you gives up makes for fortunes and also for a valuable employee (which may or may not be recognized/rewarded by your present employer). Solving the unsolvable is a capability few have, and can be useful in your own firm. However, be careful—you may be the best inventor or mechanic in the firm, but the way not to grow a successful enterprise is to spend your time inventing. Inventors are not necessarily good entrepreneurs. Inventors have a hard time giving up personal control of "pet" projects where they know everything, and find their firms don't necessarily reach their full economic potential.

14. *As a child, I sold lemonade or had a paper route or similar activities.*
Developmental psychologists maintain that personality and other traits are developed quite early in life. If you did have a paper route, sold lemonade or ran your own band, that's a positive, but not conclusive entrepreneurial sign. Many successful entrepreneurs never did an independent venture prior to starting their firms, but a majority did.

15. *I get along well with other people* and

16. *My subordinates respect me and work hard for me, even if they don't necessarily like me.*
Entrepreneurs are often described as "doers" by many researchers. Successful entrepreneurs, however, recognize that the way to independent business financial success is through coordinating the work of others. If you are a potentially successful entrepreneur and you don't get along well with other people, you can still be successful, but you'll certainly have a most difficult time starting the next Xerox or Itel. It does help, however, if you command the respect and dedication of your employees, even if they don't necessarily like you and your manner. This is called leadership, and the ability to get others to do what you want them to do seems little related to pay, fringe benefits and other material amenities of life. It is related to an ability to attract and retain people who will work hard for and with you, as you build your enterprise. Without this quality, you should probably resign yourself to a small independent business of limited potential; with it, and a good product/service/market, and supportive financing, the potential for you and your enterprise to be successful is enormous.

Copyright, Jeffrey C. Susbauer and the Entrepreneurship Institute, Worthington, Ohio, 1978.

APPENDIX 2:

Tools for Financial Analysis

For the owner of a business, financial analysis is a very useful tool in determining how the business has performed in the past, how the business is performing presently, how the business can be expected to perform in the future, and how the business compares with similar businesses. Through financial analysis, the owner of a business can gain insight regarding the factors that contribute to the profitability or un-profitability of the business. The operations of the business can then be adjusted for optimum profitability. The two key tools of financial analysis are the balance sheet, which will enable you to calculate financial ratios, and the profit and loss (income) statement, which will give you a picture of what factors impact profitability.

UNDERSTANDING FINANCIAL RATIOS

Financial ratios reflect the monetary health of a company. They can provide a valuable tool to allow a manager to compare the operations of her or his business with its past performance and with industry standards to see if expenses are in line. The following is a description and discussion of the ten major financial ratios a small business person should learn how to use. Also included is a sample of a typical balance sheet. The following discussion is excerpted from the Small Business Administration's 1977 booklet *Ratio Analysis for Small Business* (SBMS No. 20), by Richard Sanzo. The figures in the examples are taken from the Balance Sheet and Condensed Profit and Loss Statement of the ABC Company shown on pages 227 and 228.

1. Current assets to current liabilities. Commonly known as the current ratio, the ratio of current assets to current liabilities is one test of solvency, measuring the liquid assets available to meet all debts falling due within a year's time.

$$\frac{\text{current assets}}{\text{current liabilities}} = \frac{\$302,936}{\$153,936} = \quad 1.97 \text{ times}$$

Current assets are those normally expected to flow into cash in the course of a merchandising cycle, including cash, notes and accounts receivable, inventory, and, at times, short-term and marketable securities listed on leading exchanges at current realizable values. Although some concerns may consider such current items as cash-surrender value of life insurance, the tendency is to treat them as noncurrent. Noncurrent assets are those items not readily convertible to cash, such as plant and equipment.

Current liabilities are short-term obligations for the payment of cash due on demand or within a year. Such liabilities ordinarily include notes and accounts payable for merchandise, open loans payable, short-term bank loans, taxes, and accruals. Other short-term obligations, such as maturing equipment obligations and the like, also fall within the category of current liabilities.

Generally, it's considered advisable for a small business to maintain a current ratio of at least 2:1 or close to it for the sake of sound cash flow and healthy financial condition. An exception would be if a major part of the current assets is in cash and readily collectible receivables.

2. Current liabilities to tangible net worth. Like the current ratio, the ratio of current liabilities to tangible net worth is another means of evaluating financial condition by comparing what's owned to what's owed. If this ratio exceeds 80 percent, it's considered a danger sign.

$$\frac{\text{current liabilities}}{\text{tangible net worth}} = \frac{\$153,936}{\$271,760} = \quad 56.6\%$$

Tangible net worth is the worth of a business, minus any intangible items in the assets—such as goodwill, trademarks, patents, copyrights, leaseholds, treasury stock, organization expenses, or underwriting discounts and expenses. In a corporation, the tangible net worth would consist of the sum of all outstanding capital stock—preferred and common—and surplus, minus intangibles. In a partnership or proprietorship, it could be made up of the capital account or accounts, less the intangibles.

Intangibles frequently have a great but undeterminable value. Until these intangibles are actually liquidated by sale, it is difficult for an analyst to evaluate what they might bring. In some cases, they have no commercial value, except to those who hold them—for instance, an item of goodwill. To a profitable business up for sale, the goodwill conceivably could represent the potential earning power over a period of years and actually bring more than the assets themselves. On the other hand, another business might find itself unable to realize anything at all on goodwill. Since the real value of intangible assets is frequently difficult to determine and evaluate, intangibles are customarily given little consideration in financial-statement analysis.

3. Net sales to tangible net worth. Often called turnover of tangible net worth, the ratio of net sales to tangible net worth shows how actively invested capital is being put to

work by indicating its turnover during a period. Both overwork and underwork of tangible net worth are considered unhealthy.

$$\frac{\text{net sales}}{\text{tangible net worth}} = \frac{\$1,518,032}{\$\ \ 271,760} = 5.6 \text{ times}$$

There is no particular norm for this ratio. Each line of business tends to establish its own, according to studies made by Dun & Bradstreet, Robert Morris Associates, trade associations, and others.

4. Net sales to working capital. Also known as turnover of working capital, the ratio of net sales to working capital measures how actively the working cash in a business is being put to work in terms of sales. Working capital is assets that can readily be converted into operating funds within a year. It does not include invested capital. A low ratio shows unprofitable use of working capital; a high one, vulnerability to creditors.

$$\frac{\text{net sales}}{\text{working capital}} = \frac{\text{net sales}}{\text{current assets} - \text{current liabilities}}$$

$$\frac{\$1,518,032}{\$\ \ 149,000} = \frac{\$1,518,032}{\$302,936 - \$153,936} = 10.2 \text{ times}$$

To derive working capital, deduct the sum of the current liabilities from the total current assets. A business with $900,000 in cash, receivables, and inventories and no unpaid obligations would have $900,000 in working capital. A business with $900,000 in current assets and $300,000 in current liabilities also would have $600,000 in working capital. Obviously, however, items like receivables and inventories cannot usually be liquidated overnight. Hence, most businesses require a margin of current assets over and above current liabilities to provide for stock and work-in-process inventory and also to carry ensuing receivables after the goods are sold and until the receivables are collected.

The importance of maintaining an adequate amount of working capital in relation to the amount of annual sales being financed cannot be overemphasized. And it is this degree of adequacy that the ratio of net sales to working capital measures.

5. Net profits to tangible net worth. As the measure of return on investment, the ratio of net (after-tax) profits to tangible net worth—the return on capital—is increasingly considered one of the best criteria of profitability, often the key measure of management efficiency. Net profits are widely looked on as the final source of payment on investment, plus a source of funds available for future growth. If the return on capital is too low, the capital involved could be better used elsewhere.

$$\frac{\text{net profits}}{\text{tangible net worth}} = \frac{\$\ 47,536}{\$271,760} = 17.5\%$$

This ratio relates profits actually earned in a given length of time to the average net worth during that time. Profit here means the revenue left over from sales income and allowing for payment of all costs, including cost of goods sold, write-downs, charge-offs, federal and other taxes accruing over the period covered, and whatever miscellaneous adjustments may be necessary to reduce assets to current, going values. The ratio, which is expressed as a percentage, is determined by dividing tangible net worth at a given period into net profits for a given period.

6. Average collection period of receivables. The collection-period ratio shows how long in terms of days the money in a business is tied up in credit sales. The average collection received represents the number of days' sales tied up in trade accounts and notes receivable. In comparing this figure with net maturity in selling terms, many consider a collection period excessive if it is more than 10 to 15 days longer than those stated in selling terms. To derive the collection-period figure, first determine average daily credit sales—net credit sales for the year divided by 365 days—and then divide that figure into the sum of notes and accounts receivable.

$$\frac{\text{net (credit sales for year)}}{365 \text{ days a year}} = \text{daily (credit) sales}$$

$$\frac{\$1,518,032}{365 \text{ days}} = \$4,158$$

$$\text{Average collection period} = \frac{\text{notes and accounts receivable}}{\text{daily credit sales}}$$

$$= \frac{\$215,120}{\$\ \ \ 4,158} = 51.7 \text{ days}$$

The receivables discounted or assigned with recourse are included in the average collection received because they must be collected directly by the borrower or lender; if uncollected, they must be replaced by cash or substitute collateral. A pledge with recourse makes the borrower just as responsible for collection had the receivables not been assigned or discounted. Aside from this, the likely collectibility of all receivables must be analyzed, regardless of whether they are discounted. Hence, all receivables are included in determining the average collection period.

7. Net sales to inventory. Known also as the stock-to-sales ratio, the ratio of net sales to inventory, a hypothetical average inventory turnover, is valued purely and solely for purposes of comparing one company's performance with itself from one period to another, with that of another company, or with the industry.

To derive this ratio, divide the average inventory into the net sales over a given period. The result is the number of times the inventory has turned over in the period selected.

$$\frac{\text{net sales}}{\text{average inventory}} = \frac{\$1,518,032}{\$\ \ \ 83,080} = 18.3 \text{ times}$$

A manufacturer's inventory is the sum of finished merchandise on hand, raw material, and material in process. It does not include supplies unless they are for sale. For retailers and wholesalers, it is simply the stock of salable goods on hand. It is expected that inventory will be valued conservatively on the basis of standard accounting methods of valuation—such as its cost or its market value, whichever is the lower.

This ratio is not an indicator of physical turnover. The only accurate way to obtain a physical turnover figure is to count each type of item in stock and compare it with the actual physical sales of that particular item.

Some people compute turnover by dividing the average inventory value at cost into the cost of goods sold for a particular period. However, this method still gives only an average. A hardware store stocking some ten thousand items might divide its dollar inventory total into cost of goods sold and come up with a physical average, but this figure would hardly define the actual turnover of each item from paints to electrical supplies.

8. Fixed assets to tangible net worth. The ratio of fixed assets to tangible net worth shows the relationship between investment in plant and equipment and the owner's capital, indicating the liquidity of net worth. The higher this ratio, the less the owner's capital is available for use as working capital—to meet debts and payrolls, pay bills, or carry receivables.

$$\frac{\text{fixed assets}}{\text{tangible net worth}} = \frac{\$122,760}{\$271,760} = 45.2\%$$

Fixed assets are the sum of assets such as land, buildings, leasehold improvements, fixtures, furniture, machinery, tools, and equipment, less depreciation. The ratio is obtained by dividing the depreciated fixed assets by the tangible net worth. Generally, it is inadvisable for a small business to have more than 75 percent of its tangible net worth represented by fixed assets.

9. Total debt to tangible net worth. The ratio of total debt to tangible net worth measures what's owed to what's owned. As this figure approaches 100 percent, the creditors' interest in the business assets approaches that of the owner.

$$\frac{\text{total debt}}{\text{tangible net worth}} = \frac{\$153,936}{\$271,760} = 56.6\%$$

Total debt includes both current and long-term debt. It is the sum of all obligations owed by the company, such as accounts and notes payable, bonds outstanding, and mortgages payable. The ratio is obtained by dividing the total of these debts by tangible net worth. In the example above, since there is no long-term debt for the ABC Company, the result is the same as the ratio of current liabilities to tangible net worth.

10. Net profit on net sales. The ratio of net profit to net sales is the rate of return on net sales. The resulting percentage indicates the amount of each sales dollar remaining, after considering all income items and excluding taxes.

$$\frac{\text{net profits}}{\text{net sales}} = \frac{\$\ \ \ 47,536}{\$1,518,032} = 3.1\%$$

The ratio of net operating profit to net sales reveals the profitability of sales—that is, the profitability of the regular buying, manufacturing, and selling operations of a business.

Many business owners consider a high rate of return on net sales as necessary for successful operation. This view is not always sound. To evaluate properly the significance of the ratio, consideration should be given to such factors as the value of sales, the total capital employed, and the turnover of inventories and receivables. For example, low rate of return accompanied by rapid turnover and large sales volume may result in satisfactory earnings.

ANALYZING THE PROFIT AND LOSS (INCOME) STATEMENT

Data taken from the profit and loss statement can be used to develop operating ratios, which show the percentage relationships of each item to a common base of net sales. These percentages may be compared with those of previous periods to measure a firm's performance. They also can be compared with the typical percentages of businesses in similar trades or industries when they are available. Such comparisons will indicate the competitive strengths and weaknesses of a business.

The items included in profit and loss statements vary from business to business. For example, some businesses break down their sales expense to show the costs of salesmen's salaries and commissions, advertising, delivery costs, supplies, and so forth; some do not. Only major items are included in the following explanation of profit and loss items. A condensed profit and loss statement accompanies this discussion.

Net sales. Net sales represent gross dollar sales less merchandise returns and allowances. Some accountants also deduct cash discounts granted to customers on the theory that these are actually a reduction of the net selling price; others credit the discounts to "other" expense. Trade and quantity discounts are, of course, concessions off the price and should be deducted from the gross sales.

Cost of goods sold. For retailers and wholesalers, this figure is the inventory at the beginning, plus purchases and "freight in" and minus inventory at the end of the period. "Freight out" is generally shown as delivery expense. For manufacturers, various additional items are considered, including supervision, power, supplies, the direct costs of manufacturing labor (including social security and unemployment taxes on factory employees), that portion of depreciation which enters into cost production, and many others.

Gross profit on sales. The gross profit on sales is obtained by deducting the cost of goods sold from net sales.

Selling expenses. Selling expenses include such items as salaries of salesmen and sales executives, wages of other sales employees, commissions, travel expense, entertainment expense, and advertising.

Operating profit. Operating profit is the difference between the gross profit on sales and the sum of the selling expenses.

General and administrative expenses. General and administrative expenses include officers' salaries, office overhead, light, heat, communication, salaries of general office and clerical help, cost of legal and accounting services, "fringe" benefits payable on administrative personnel, sundry types of franchise and similar taxes, and other expenses.

Financial expenses. Financial expenses include interest, doubtful accounts, and discounts granted if not already deducted from sales.

Other operating expenses and income. The category of other operating expenses and income might include various unusual expense items not elsewhere classified—for

ABC COMPANY
BALANCE SHEET AS OF DECEMBER 31, 1978

Assets

Current assets	
Cash on hand and in banks	$ 34,560
Notes receivable	38,560
Less: notes discounted	24,000
Total notes	$ 14,560
Accounts receivable	$176,560
Less: reserve for bad debts	16,000
Total accounts receivable	$160,560
Inventories	83,080
Prepayment of expenses	10,176
Total current assets	$302,936
Plant and equipment	
Land and building	$115,960
Equipment, fixtures, and furniture	38,400
Less: allowances for depreciation	31,600
Total plant and equipment	$122,760
Intangibles	
Goodwill	4,000
Patents	4,000
Total intangibles	$ 8,000
Total assets	$433,696

Liabilities

Current liabilities	
Notes payable (bank)	$ 32,000
Accounts payable (trade)	82,576
Taxes payable	28,800
Other payables	10,560
Total current liabilities	$153,936
Long-term debt	0
Total liabilities	$153,936

Capital

Capital stock	$200,000
Surplus	79,760
Total equity or net worth	$279,760
Total liabilities and capital	$433,696

example, moving expenses, against which might be credited income from investments and miscellaneous credits and debits.

Extraordinary charges. Extraordinary charges, which do not occur very often, would include such items as losses on sale of unused fixtures and equipment.

Net profit before taxes. Net profit before taxes is the profit after deducting regular and extraordinary business charges.

Taxes. The tax item includes all federal, state, and local taxes paid out of earnings.

Net profit after taxes. Net profit after taxes, the final figure, shows earnings available for distribution or retention.

ABC COMPANY
CONDENSED PROFIT AND LOSS STATEMENT, 1978

	Amount	As a Percentage of Sales
Gross sales	$1,547,776	
Less: returns, allowances and cash discounts	29,744	
Net sales	$1,518,032	100.00%
Cost of goods sold	1,178,784	77.65
Gross profit on sales	$ 339,248	22.35%
Selling expenses	$ 83,832	5.52%
Administrative expenses	56,020	3.69
General expenses	100,060	6.59
Interest and other expenses	10,496	0.69
Total expenses	$250,408	16.49%
Operating profit	$ 88,840	5.86%
Extraordinary expenses	2,400	0.16
Net profit before taxes	$ 86,440	5.70%
Federal, state, and local taxes	39,084	2.57
Net profit after taxes	$ 47,536	3.13%

APPENDIX 3:

Resources

This appendix provides a brief overview of some of the types of resources available to the individual contemplating entrepreneurship or presently in business. These resources supplement those noted in the text and chapter notes of the book. Because it would not be possible to present a comprehensive list of all available sources of aid and encouragement, the resources here should be used as a first step leading to others.

The number of associations comprised of women business owners is growing rapidly, both locally and nationally. These associations should be a fertile source of information and assistance.

GENERAL SOURCES OF INFORMATION

A wide variety of groups and organizations exist to assist owners of small businesses. These groups can generally be divided into educational institutions, chambers of commerce, trade associations, women's associations, and government agencies. All these groups may periodically offer workshops on relevant topics.

EDUCATIONAL INSTITUTIONS. Colleges and universities are becoming more responsive to the special needs of women regarding business management and financial skills. Small business development centers (SBDCs) are located in some state universities. These centers serve as one-stop sources of business information and educational materials. They operate similarly to the agriculture extension service. Check with your regional Small Business Administration office for the one nearest you. Also, graduate students are often a source of information concerning problems you may be having.

CHAMBERS OF COMMERCE. Chambers of commerce are voluntary associations of business owners organized to promote the welfare of their communities. The activities of these organizations vary widely. Some offer a full range of services to the business community and consumers, and many will furnish economic statistics on their communities and will help businesses locate sites for factories and stores within their towns.

TRADE ASSOCIATIONS. Trade associations are membership organizations whose members belong to a single trade or business. They can offer information on opportunities within their field. Membership is one way of keeping up with your field and also of making contacts.

WOMEN'S ASSOCIATIONS.   The following organizations direct themselves specifically to those issues of concern to women.

American Women's Economic Development Corporation
Beatrice Fitzpatrick, Executive Director
1270 Avenue of the Americas
New York, NY 10020

Business and Professional Women's Federation
Irma Finn Brosseau, Executive Director
2012 Massachusetts Avenue, NW
Washington, DC 20036

Hispanic Business and Professional Women
Gloria Muguerza, President
3621 Newark Street, NW
Washington, DC 20016

National Association for Female Executives
Wendy Rue, President
160 East 56th Street
New York, NY 10017

National Association of Bank Women, Inc.
Ruth I. Smith, President
111 East Wacker Drive
Chicago, IL 60601

National Association of Minority Women in Business
Inez Kaiser, President
906 Grand, Suite 2705
Kansas City, MO 64106

National Association of Negro Business and Professional Women
Robin Owens, President
843 Cleveland Street
Flint, MI 48503

National Association of Women Business Owners
2000 P Street, NW
Washington, DC 20036

National Association of Women in Construction
Marcella Curry, National President
Betty Kornegay, Executive Director
2800 West Lancaster Avenue
Fort Worth, TX

National Conference of Puerto Rican Women's Associations
Carmen Delgado Votaw, President
6717 Loring Court
Bethesda, MD 20034

National Women's Business Development Corporation
Wynona Lake, Executive Director
1413 K Street, NW
Washington, DC 20005

Women's Banks—Offices
Women's Bank
P.O. Box 647
Richmond, VA 23205

Western Women's Bank
235 Front Street
San Francisco, CA 94111

First Women's Bank of Maryland
P.O. Box 2022
Rockville, MD 20852

The Women's National Bank
1627 K Street, NW
Washington, DC 20006

The First Women's Bank of New York
111 East 57 Street
New York, NY 10022

First Women's Bank of California
12301 Wilshire Blvd.
Los Angeles, CA 90025

Women's Bank, N.A.
Equitable Building
724 17 Street
Denver, CO 80202

Connecticut Women's Bank
100 Mason Street
Greenwich, CT 06830

GOVERNMENT AGENCIES.   Federal government agencies provide vast amounts of assistance to prospective and existing entrepreneurs. This information ranges from the regulations and licenses required for starting up your business to advice on management and obtaining contracts with the federal government. Some agencies of special interest to business owners and the specialized areas of information which these agencies provide are listed below.

Agency	*Information*
Department of Commerce	
Bureau of Business Development Room 3826 14th and E Sts, NW Washington, DC 20230	Reference materials, markets, industry data, franchising
Bureau of the Census Federal Office Bldgs. 3 and 4 Suitland, MD 20233	Business census, trade statistics
Bureau of International Commerce Library, 7th Fl, Main Commerce Washington, DC 20230	Exporting, trade opportunities programs
National Technical Information Service 5285 Port Royal Rd. Springfield, VA 22161	Technical data, reports, mag tapes, periodicals
Economic Development Administration 14th and E Sts., NW Washington, DC 20230	Business development loans; special women's pilot projects
Office of Minority Business Enterprise 14th and E Sts., NW Washington, DC 20230	Minority business enterprise
Ombudsman Special Assistant to the Secretary Department of Commerce Washington, DC 20230	Help with federal government
Patent Office 2021 Jefferson Davis Highway Arlington, VA 20231	Patents, trademarks

Department of Agriculture
Business and Industrial Loan Division
U.S. Department of Agriculture
Farmers Home Administration
South Building
Washington, DC 20250

Business loans in rural areas

Interagency Committee on Women's Business Enterprise
Executive Director
Small Business Administration
1441 L St., NW
Washington, DC 20417

Information on special women's programs

Department of Defense
Office of Under Secretary of Defense
Pentagon, Room 2A340
Washington, DC 20301

Federal procurement procedures (ask for *Selling to the Military* and *Small Business and Labor Surplus Area Specialists Designated to Assist Small, Minority, and Labor Surplus Area Businesses*)

Department of Labor
Wage and Hour and Public Contracts Division, Room 904
6525 Belcrest Rd.
Hyattsville, MD 20782

Federal minimum wage–hour law

Department of the Treasury
Bureau of Customs
Customs District Director and Customhouse
3180 Blandensburg Rd., NE
Washington, DC 20018

Custom rates, import requirements, quotas

Internal Revenue Service
Room 701
1201 E St., NW
Washington, DC 20226

Taxpayer service for new businesses (ask for *Your Business Tax Kit*)

Federal Trade Commission
Pennsylvania Ave. and 6th Sts., NW
Washington, DC 20580

Office of Public Information

(Ask for *List of Publications*)

Bureau of Consumer Protection

Consumer complaints

Division of Legal and Public Records

Trade practices and regulations, franchises (ask for *FTC Buyer's Guide 4: Franchise Business Risks*)

General Services Administration
Business Service Center, Reg. 3
Room 1050, 7th and D Sts., SW
Washington, DC 20407

(Ask for *Doing Business with the Federal Government, Federal Buying Directory, SF 129: Bidders Mailing List Application*)

Government Printing Office
710 N. Capitol St., NW
Washington, DC 20402

Government publications—sales and distribution

Interstate Commerce Commission
12th and Constitution Ave., NW
Washington, DC 20423

Information, regulations

Library of Congress
National Referral Center
Thomas Jefferson Bldg. - A 5227
2nd and Independence Sts., SE
Washington, DC 20540

Referral service

Register of Copyrights
Copyright Office, Bldg. 2
1921 Jefferson Davis Highway
Arlington, VA 20540

Copyrights

Securities and Exchange Commission
500 North Capitol St., NW
Washington, DC 20549

Public information, consumer affairs

Small Business Administration
1441 L St., NW
Washington, DC 20417

The Small Business Administration offers many services for the small business person. Assistance programs fall primarily into three areas: financial, management and technical, and procurement. Its financial assistance programs include both guaranteed and direct loans, although the bulk of this assistance is in the area of guaranteed loans through regular commercial lending institutions. Its management and technical assistance programs include a wide range of publications, seminars, clinics, and consulting. Its procurement assistance programs include an automated procurement list (the PASS System), which tries to match purchasing opportunities in the federal government with small businesses. In addition to assisting all small businesses, the SBA also has programs for socially and economically disadvantaged persons under its Minority Enterprise Program. A listing of selected publications of interest to small business owners and addresses of SBA regional field offices follows.

SMALL BUSINESS ADMINISTRATION PUBLICATIONS

SMALL BUSINESS MANAGEMENT SERIES (SBMS).   The booklets in this series provide discussions of special management problems in small companies. The management assistance booklets on this list are published by the Small Business Administration and are sold by the Superintendent of Documents, U.S. Government Printing Office, and not by the Small Business Administration. Submit your order (with stock number) with check or money order to Superintendent of Documents, U.S. Government Printing Office, Washington, D.C. 20402. Make check or money order payable to Superintendent of Documents. Minimum order is $1.00. The following is a partial list of booklets available.

No.	Title	Stock No.	Price
3	*Human Relations in Small Business* (Discusses human relations, including finding and selecting employees and developing and motivating them.)	045-000-00036-2	$1.60
15	*Handbook of Small Business Finance* (Written for the small business owner who wants to improve financial management skills. Indicates the major areas of financial management and describes a few of the many techniques that can help the small business owner.)	045-000-00139-3	1.50
20	*Ratio Analysis for Small Business* (A discussion of ratio analysis, which is the process of determining the relationship between certain financial or operating data of a business to provide a basis for managerial control. The purpose of the booklet is to help the owner/manager in detecting favorable or unfavorable trends in the business.)	045-000-00150-4	1.80
25	*Guides for Profit Planning* (Guides for computing and using the break-even point, the level of gross profit, and the rate of return on investment. Designed for readers who have no specialized training in accounting and economics.)	045-000-00137-7	0.85
26	*Personnel Management Guides for Small Business* (An introduction to the various aspects of personnel management as they apply to small firms.)	045-000-00126-1	1.10
30	*Insurance and Risk Management for Small Business* (A discussion of what insurance is, the necessity of obtaining professional advice on buying insur-	045-000-00037-1	1.90

No.	Title	Stock No.	Price
	ance, and the main types of insurance a small business may need.)		
31	*Management Audit for Small Retailers* (Designed to meet the needs of the owner/manager of a small retail enterprise; 149 questions guide the owner/manager in a self-examination and a review of the business operation.)	045-000-00149-1	1.80
32	*Financial Recordkeeping for Small Stores* (Written primarily for the small store owner or prospective owner whose business doesn't justify hiring a full-time bookkeeper.)	045-000-00142-3	1.55
34	*Selecting Advertising Media—A Guide for Small Business* (Intended to aid the small business person in deciding which medium to select for making the product, service, or store known to potential customers and how best to use advertising money.)	045-000-00154-7	2.75
35	*Franchise Index/Profile* (Presents an evaluation process that may be used to investigate franchise opportunities. The index tells what to look for in a franchise, and the profile is a worksheet for listing the data.)	045-000-00125-3	0.85
37	*Financial Control by Time-Absorption Analysis* (A profit control technique that can be used by all types of business. A step-by-step approach shows how to establish this method in a particular business.)	045-000-00134-2	1.60
38	*Management Audit for Small Service Firms* (A do-it-yourself guide for owner/managers of small service firms to help them evaluate and improve their operations. Brief comments explain the importance of each question in 13 critical management areas.)	045-000-00143-1	0.90
39	*Decision Points in Developing New Products* (Provides a path from idea to marketing plan for the small manufacturing or R&D firm that wants to expand or develop a business around a new product, process, or invention)	045-000-00146-6	0.90

NONSERIES PUBLICATIONS. The following nonseries publications are published by the Small Business Administration but are available from the Superintendent of Documents, U.S. Government Printing Office, Washington, D.C. 20402. Make check or money order payable to Superintendent of Documents.

Managing for Profits   045-000-00005-2   1.90
(Ten chapters on various aspects of small busi-
ness management, marketing, production, and
credit.)

Buying and Selling a Small Business   045-000-00003-6   2.30
(Deals with the problems that confront buyers
and sellers of small businesses. Discusses the
buy-sell transaction, sources of information for
buyer-seller decision, the buy-sell process,
using financial statements in the buy-sell transaction, and analyzing the market position of the
company.)

MANAGEMENT AIDS. The Management Aid, Small Marketers Aid, and Small
Business Bibliography leaflets are available without charge. Submit your order (with
publication number, your name, address, and zip code) to the Small Business
Administration, P.O. Box 15434, Fort Worth, Texas 76119. Or call toll free (800)
433–7212; Texas only, call (800) 792–8901.

These leaflets deal with functional problems in small businesses and are of interest to
executives. The following is a partial list of Management Aid pamphlets available.

No.	*Title*
170	*The ABC's of Borrowing*
171	*How to Write a Job Description*
176	*Financial Audits: A Tool for Better Management*
186	*Checklist for Developing a Training Program*
187	*Using Census Data in Small Plant Marketing*
190	*Measuring the Performance of Salesmen*
191	*Delegating Work and Responsibility*
192	*Profile Your Customers to Expand Industrial Sales*
193	*What Is the Best Selling Price?*
194	*Marketing Planning Guidelines*
195	*Setting Pay for Your Management Jobs*
197	*Pointers on Preparing an Employee Handbook*
201	*Locating or Relocating Your Business*
203	*Are Your Products and Channels Producing Sales?*
205	*Pointers on Using Temporary-Help Services*
206	*Keep Pointed Toward Profit*
208	*Problems in Managing a Family-Owned Business*
220	*Basic Budgets for Profit Planning*
222	*Business Life Insurance*
223	*Incorporating a Small Business*
224	*Association Services for Small Business*
225	*Management Checklist for a Family Business*
226	*Pricing for Small Manufacturers*
229	*Cash Flow in a Small Plant*
233	*Planning and Goal Setting for Small Business*
234	*Attacking Business Decision Problems with Breakeven Analysis*

SMALL MARKETERS AIDS. These leaflets provide suggestions and management guidelines for small retail, wholesale, and service firms.

No.	Title
118	*Legal Services for Small Retail and Service Firms*
121	*Measuring the Results of Advertising*
124	*Knowing Your Image*
126	*Accounting Services for Small Service Firms*
128	*Building Customer Confidence in Your Service Shop*
130	*Analyze Your Records to Reduce Costs*
142	*Steps in Meeting Your Tax Obligations*
144	*Getting the Facts for Income Tax Reporting*
146	*Budgeting in a Small Service Firm*
147	*Sound Cash Management and Borrowing*
148	*Insurance Checklist for Small Business*
152	*Using a Traffic Study to Select a Retail Site*
153	*Business Plan for Small Service Firms*
154	*Using Census Data to Select a Store Site*
155	*Keeping Records in Small Business*
156	*Marketing Checklist for Small Retailers*
158	*A Pricing Checklist for Small Retailers*
160	*Advertising Guidelines for Small Retail Firms*
163	*Public Relations for Small Business*
164	*Plan Your Advertising Budget*

SMALL BUSINESS BIBLIOGRAPHIES. These leaflets furnish reference sources for individual types of businesses.

No.	Title
9	*Marketing Research Procedures*
10	*Retailing*
12	*Statistics and Maps for National Market Analysis*
13	*National Directories for Use in Marketing*
20	*Advertising—Retail Store*

The Small Business Administration puts out several booklets if you want to find out more about contracting with the federal government. Some suggested publications are *U.S. Government Purchasing and Sales Directory* ($4.50), *Selling to the U.S. Government,* and *SBA's Procurement and Technical Assistance Programs.* You may obtain further information about these and similar booklets by writing to the Small Business Administration, 1441 L Street, NW, Washington, DC 20416.

SMALL BUSINESS ADMINISTRATION FIELD OFFICES

Region I

60 Battery March, 10th Floor, Boston, MA 02110
150 Causeway Street, 10th Floor, Boston, MA 02114
302 High Street, 4th Floor, Holyoke, MA 01040
Federal Building, 40 Western Avenue, Room 512, Augusta, ME 04330
55 Pleasant Street, Room 213, Concord, NH 03301
One Financial Plaza, Hartford, CT 06103
Federal Building, 87 State Street, Room 204, Box 605, Montpelier, VT 05602
57 Eddy Street, 7th Floor, Providence, RI 02903

Region II

26 Federal Plaza, Room 3214, New York, NY 10007
425 Broad Hollow Road, Room 205, Melville, NY 11746
Chardon and Bolivia Streets, P.O. Box 1915, Hato Rey, PR 00919
U.S. Federal Office Building, Veterans Drive, Room 283, St. Thomas, VI 00801
970 Broad Street, Room 1635, Newark, NJ 07102
1800 East Davis Street, Camden, NJ 08104
Federal Building, Room 1073, 100 South Clinton Street, Syracuse, NY 13260
111 West Huron Street, Room 1311, Federal Building, Buffalo, NY 14202
180 State Street, Room 412, Elmira, NY 14901
99 Washington Avenue, Twin Towers Building, Room 921, Albany, NY 12210
Federal Building, 100 State Street, Rochester, NY 14614

Region III

231 St. Asaphs Road, 1 Bala Cynwyd Plaza, Suite 646 West Lobby, Bala Cynwyd, PA
   19004
1500 North Second Street, Harrisburg, PA 17102
Penn Place, 20 N. Pennsylvania Avenue, Wilkes-Barre, PA 18702
844 King Street, Federal Building, Room 5207, Wilmington, DE 19801
Oxford Building, 8600 LaSalle Road, Room 630, Baltimore, Towson, MD 21204
109 North 3rd Street, Room 301, Lowndes Building, Clarsburg, WV 26301
Charleston National Plaza, Suite 628, Charleston, WV 25301
Federal Building, 1000 Liberty Avenue, Room 1401, Pittsburgh, PA 15222
Federal Building, 400 North 8th Street, Room 3015, Box 10126, Richmond, VA 23240
1030 Fifteenth Street, NW, Suite 250, Washington, DC 20417

Region IV

1375 Peachtree Street, NE, Atlanta, GA 30309
1720 Peachtree Street, NW, 6th Floor, Atlanta, GA 30309
908 South 20th Street, Room 202, Birmingham, AL 35205

230 S. Tryon Street, Suite 700, Charlotte, NC 28202

215 S. Evans Street, Room 206, Greenville, NC 27834

1801 Assembly Street, Room 131, Columbia, SC 29201

Providence Capitol Building, Suite 690, 200 E. Pascagoula Street, Jackson, MS 39201

111 Fred Haise Blvd., Gulf National Life Insurance Bldg., 2nd Floor, Biloxi, MS 39530

Federal Building, 400 West Bay Street, Room 261, P.O. Box 35067, Jacksonville, FL 32202

Federal Building, 600 Federal Place, Room 188, Louisville, KY 40202

2222 Ponce De Leon Blvd., 5th Floor, Coral Gables, FL 33134

1802 - 700 Twiggs Street, Suite 607, Tampa, FL 33602

404 James Robertson Parkway, Suite 1012, Nashville, TN 37219

502 South Gay Street, Room 307, Fidelity Bankers Building, Knoxville, TN 37902

Federal Building, 167 North Main Street, Room 211, Memphis, TN 38103

Federal Building, 701 Clematis Street, Room 229, West Palm Beach, FL 33402

Region V

Federal Building, 219 South Dearborn Street, Room 838, Chicago, IL 60604

One North, Old State Capital Plaza, Springfield, IL 62701

1240 East 9th Street, Room 317, Cleveland, OH 44199

Federal Building, U.S. Courthouse, 85 Marconi Boulevard, Columbus, OH 43215

Federal Building, 550 Main Street, Cincinnati, OH 45202

477 Michigan Avenue, McNamara Building, Detroit, MI 48226

540 W. Kaye Avenue, Don H. Bottum University Center, Marquette, MI 49855

575 North Pennsylvania Street, Room 552, New Federal Building, Indianapolis, IN 46204

122 West Washington Avenue, Room 713, Madison, WI 53703

Federal Building, Room 246, 517 East Wisconsin Avenue, Milwaukee, WI 53202

500 South Barstow Street, Room B9AA, Federal Office Bldg./Courthouse, Eau Claire, WI 54701

12 South 6th Street, Plymouth Building, Minneapolis, MN 55402

Region VI

1720 Regal Row, Regal Park Office Building, Room 230, Dallas, TX 75235

1100 Commerce Street, Room 3C36, Dallas, TX 75242

100 South Washington Street, Federal Building G-12, Marshall, TX 75670

5000 Marble Avenue, NE, Patio Plaza Building, Room 320, Albuquerque, NM 87110

One Allen Center, 500 Dallas Street, Houston, TX 77002

611 Gaines Street, Suite 900, Little Rock, AR 72201

1205 Texas Avenue, 712 Federal Office Building/Courthouse, Lubbock, TX 79401

4100 Rio Bravo, Suite 300, El Paso, TX 79901

222 East Van Buren Street, Box 2567, Harlington, TX 78550 (Lower Rio Grande Valley)

3105 Leopard Street, Corpus Christi, TX 78408

1001 Howard Avenue, Plaza Tower, 17th Floor, New Orleans, LA 70113

Fannin Street, U.S. Post Office and Courthouse Building, Shreveport, LA 71101

Federal Building, 200 N.W. 5th Street, Suite 670, Oklahoma City, OK 73102

727 E. Durango, Room A-513, Federal Building, San Antonio, TX 78206

Region VII

911 Walnut Street, 23rd Floor, Kansas City, MO 64106
1150 Grand Avenue, 5th Floor, Kansas City, MO 64106
New Federal Building, 210 Walnut Street, Room 749, Des Moines, IA 50309
Nineteenth and Farnum Streets, Empire State Building, Omaha, NE 68102
Suite 2500, Mercantile Tower, One Mercantile Center, St. Louis, MO 63101
110 East Waterman Street, Main Place Building, Wichita, KS 67202

Region VIII

Executive Tower Building, 1405 Curtis Street, 22nd Floor, Denver, CO 80202
721 - 19th Street, Room 426A, Denver, CO 80202
Federal Building, Room 4001, 100 East B Street, Box 2839, Casper, WY 82602
Federal Building, 653 Second Avenue, North, Room 218, Fargo, ND 58102
618 Helena Avenue, Box 4819, Helena, MT 59601
Federal Building, 125 South State Street, Room 2237, Salt Lake City, UT 84138
National Bank Building, 8th and Main Avenue, Room 402, Sioux Falls, SD 57102
515 Ninth Street, Federal Building, Room 246, Rapid City, SD 57701

Region IX

450 Golden Gate Avenue, Box 36044, San Francisco, CA 94102
211 Main Street, 4th Floor, San Francisco, CA 94105
1229 N Street, P.O. Box 828, Fresno, CA 93712
2800 Cottage Way, Sacramento, CA 95825
301 E. Stewart, Box 7527, Downtown Station, Las Vegas, NV 89101
50 South Virginia Street, Room 308, Box 3216, Reno, NV 89505
300 Ala Moana, P.O. Box 50207, Honolulu, HI 96850
Pacific Daily News Building, Room 507, Agana, Guam 96910
350 S. Figueroa Street, 6th Floor, Los Angeles, CA 90071
112 North Central Avenue, Phoenix, AZ 85004
880 Front Street, Federal U.S. Building, Room 4-S-33, San Diego, CA 92188

Region X

710 Second Avenue, 5th Floor, Dexter Horton Building, Seattle, WA 98104
915 Second Avenue, Federal Building, Room 1744, Seattle, WA 98174
1016 West 6th Avenue, Suite 200, Anchorage Legal Center, Anchorage, AK 99501
Federal Building & Courthouse, P.O. Box 14, 101 Twelfth Avenue, Fairbanks, AK
    99701
1005 Main Street, 2nd Floor, Continental Life Building, Boise, ID 83701
1220 S.W. Third Avenue, Federal Building, Portland, OR 97204
Court House Building, Room 651, Box 2167, Spokane, WA 99210

Bibliography

Books and Pamphlets

STARTING A BUSINESS

Acquisitions, Mergers, Sales and Takeovers. Charles A. Scharf. Englewood Cliffs, N.J.: Prentice-Hall, 1971.

The Business of Acquisitions and Mergers. Ed. George Scott Hutchison. New York: Presidents Publishing House, 1968.

Franchise Opportunities Handbook. U.S. Department of Commerce, Bureau of Domestic Commerce. Washington, D.C.: Superintendent of Documents, U.S. Government Printing Office, 1972.

Going Into Business: How to Do It by the Man Who Did It. Eugene Ferkauf. New York: Chelsea House, 1977.

How to Organize and Operate a Small Business. 5th ed. Pearce C. Kelley, Kenneth Lawyer, and Clifford M. Baumback. Englewood Cliffs, N.J.: Prentice-Hall, 1973.

How to Prepare a Business Plan: Guidelines for Entrepreneurs. Rev. ed. Belmont, Mass: Institute for New Enterprise Development, 1976.

How to Start a Money-Making Business at Home. Laura Robertson. New York: Frederick Fell, 1969.

How to Start a Small Business. Larry Lackey. New York: Exposition Press, 1971.

How to Start and Manage Your Own Small Business. Gardiner G. Greene. New York: McGraw-Hill, 1975.

How to Start, Finance, and Manage Your Own Small Business. Joseph R. Mancuso. Englewood Cliffs, N.J.: Prentice-Hall, 1978.

How to Start Your Own Business. Ed. William D. Putt. Cambridge: M.I.T. Press, 1974.

Small Business Survival Kit. New York: Artemis Publications, 1977.

Small Time Operator: How To Start Your Own Small Business, Pay Your Taxes, and Stay Out of Trouble—A Guide and Workbook. Bernard Kamoroff. Laytonville, Calif.: Bell Springs Publishing, 1976.

Starting and Succeeding in Your Own Small Business. Louis L. Allen. New York: Grosset and Dunlap, 1968.

Successful Small Business Management. Rev. ed. Curtis E. Tate, Jr. Dallas: Business Publications, 1978.

The Woman's Guide to Starting a Business. Claudia Jessup and Genie Chipps. New York: Holt, Rinehart and Winston, 1976.

FINANCES

Accounting for Managerial Analysis. James M. Fremgen. Homewood, Ill.: Richard D. Irwin, 1972.

Borrowing Basics for Women. New York: Citibank, Public Affairs Department, 1978.

Building Economy. 2nd ed. P. A. Stone. Oxford, New York: Pergamon Press, 1976.

Businessman's Information Guide. Rev. ed. New York: American Institute of Certified Public Accountants, 1975.

Consumer and Commercial Credit Management. 5th ed. Robert H. Cole. Homewood, Ill.: Richard D. Irwin, 1976.

Credit Management Handbook. 2d ed. Credit Research Foundation. Homewood, Ill.: Richard D. Irwin, 1965.

The Eternal Triangle: Management—Sales—Credit. Kenneth J. Forshee. New York: National Association of Credit Management, 1975.

Everyday Credit Checking: A Practical Guide. Sol Barzmane. New York: T. Y. Crowell in association with the National Association of Credit Management, 1973.

Financial Management: Theory and Techniques. George C. Philippatos. San Francisco: Holden-Day, 1973.

Financial Manager's Handbook. J. H. Henessy, Jr. Englewood Cliffs, N.J.: Prentice-Hall, 1977.

Financial Studies of the Small Business. Arlington, Va.: Financial Research Associates, 1976.

Financing for Small and Medium-Sized Businesses. Harry Gross. Englewood Cliffs, N.J.: Prentice-Hall, 1969.

Financing the Dynamic Small Firm. Roland I. Robinson. Belmont, Calif.: Wadsworth Publishing, 1968.

Financing Your Business. Egon W. Loffel. New York: David McKay, 1977.

Guide to Venture Capital Sources. 4th ed. Stanley M. Rubel. Chicago: Capital Publishing, 1977.

How to Build Profits by Controlling Cost. New York: Dun & Bradstreet, Public Relations and Advertising, 1959.

How to Control Accounts Receivable for Greater Profits. Rev. ed. New York: Dun & Bradstreet, Public Relations and Advertising, 1978.

How to Raise and Invest Venture Capital. Stanley M. Rubel and Edward G. Novotny. New York: Presidents Publishing House, 1971.

How to Win Profits and Influence Bankers—The Art of Practical Projecting. Richard C. Belew. New York: Van Nostrand-Reinhold, 1973.

Managerial Cost Accounting. Harold Bierman, Jr., and Thomas R. Dyckman. New York: Macmillan Co., 1971.

The Modern Accountant's Handbook. Ed. James Don Edwards and Homer A. Black. Homewood, Ill.: Dow Jones–Irwin, 1976.

Modern Developments in Financial Management. Ed. Stewart C. Myers. New York: Praeger, 1976.

Organizing and Financing Business. 6th ed. Joseph H. Bonneville, Lloyd E. Dewey, and Harry M. Kelly. Englewood Cliffs, N.J.: Prentice-Hall, 1959.

Practical Accounting for Small Business. Lyn Taetzsch and Laura Taetzsch. New York: Petrocelli/Charter, 1977.

Practical Operating Budgeting. Lawrence M. Matthews. New York: McGraw-Hill, 1977.

Profit and Cash Flow Management for Non-Financial Managers. John Welsh and Jerry White. Dallas: Caruth Institute of Owner-Managed Business, School of Business Administration, Southern Methodist University, 1974.

Understanding Accounting—Fast. Robert C. Peterson. New York: McGraw-Hill, 1976.

Venture Capital: A Guidebook for New Enterprises. Albert J. Kelley, Frank B. Campanella, and John McKiernan. Boston: Management Institute, Boston College, 1973.

What You Should Know about Reducing Credit Losses. John H. Burns and John E. Cook. Dobbs Ferry, N.Y.: Oceana Publications, 1966.

MARKETING AND PUBLIC RELATIONS

Advertising Graphics. 2d ed. William H. Bockus, Jr. New York: Macmillan Co., 1974.

Advertising and Marketing Research: A New Methodology. B. Stuart Tolley. Chicago: Nelson-Hall, 1977.

Advertising Manager's Handbook. Richard H. Stansfield. Chicago: Dartnell Corp., 1969.

Advertising Today and Tomorrow. W. A. Evans. Brooklyn, N.Y.: Beekman Publishing, 1974.

Do-It-Yourself Marketing Research. George Edward Breen. New York: McGraw-Hill, 1977.

Do's and Don'ts in Advertising Copy. Monthly supplements (first published in 1949). New York: Council of Better Business Bureaus.

The Entrepreneur's Manual. Richard M. White, Jr. Radnor, Pa.: Chilton Publishing, 1977.

Getting Big Results from a Small Advertising Budget. Cynthia S. Smith. New York: Hawthorne Books, 1973.

Growth Opportunity Analysis. John A. Weber. Reston, Va.: Reston Publishing, 1976.

Handbook of Public Relations. 2d ed., H. Stephenson. New York: McGraw-Hill, 1971.

How to Handle Your Own Public Relations. H. Gordon Lewis. Chicago: Nelson-Hall, 1976.

How to Make Advertising Work. Burton R. Durkee. New York: McGraw-Hill, 1967.

Marketing for Business Growth. 2d ed. Theodore Levitt. New York: McGraw-Hill, 1974.

Marketing Management: Analysis, Planning, and Control. Philip Kotler. Englewood Cliffs, N.J.: Prentice-Hall, 1977.

Professional's Guide to Public Relations Services. 3d ed. Richard Weiner. New York: Richard Weiner, 1975.

Selecting and Evaluating Distributors. Roger N. Pegram. New York: National Industrial Conference Board, Studies in Business Policy No. 116, 1965.

Strategy in Advertising. Leo Bogart. New York: Harcourt Brace & World, 1967.

What You Should Know about Advertising. Joel Amstell. Dobbs Ferry, N.Y.: Oceana Publications, 1969.

What You Should Know about Advertising Copywriting. Shirley Milton. Dobbs Ferry, N.Y.: Oceana Publications, 1969.

What You Should Know about Public Relations. Edward Starr. Dobbs Ferry, N.Y.: Oceana Publications, 1968.

What You Should Know about Small Business Marketing. Eugene H. Fram. Dobbs Ferry, N.Y.: Oceana Publications, 1968.

MANAGEMENT

Administrative Office Management. Herbert Webster Johnson and William G. Savage. Reading, Mass.: Addison-Wesley, 1968.

Analyzing Performance Problems or "You Really Oughta Wanna." Robert Mager and Peter Pipe. Belmont, Calif.: Fearon, 1970.

The Art and Skill of Delegation. Lawrence L. Steimetz. Reading, Mass.: Addison-Wesley, 1976.

Bargaining: Formal Theories of Negotiation. Ed. Oran R. Young. Urbana, Ill.: University of Illinois Press, 1975.

Business Management Handbook. Jacob Kay Lasser. New York: McGraw Hill, 1968.

Compensating Employees: Lessons of the 1970's. David A. Weeks. New York: Conference Board, 1976.

Complete Guide to Financial Management for Small and Medium-Sized Companies. Donald S. Brightly and the Prentice-Hall editorial staff. Englewood Cliffs, N.J.: Prentice-Hall, 1971.

Developing Teams and Organizations: A Practical Handbook for Managers and Consultants. Uri Merry and Melvin E. Allerhand. Reading, Mass.: Addison-Wesley, 1977.

The Effective Entrepreneur. Charles Swayne. Morristown, N.J.: General Learning Press, 1973.

The Effective Executive (The Key Handbook for the Key Executive). Peter Drucker. New York: Harper and Row, 1967.

Elements of Modern Management. Eugene J. Benge and the editors of Alexander Hamilton Institute. New York: AMACOM, 1976.

General Office Practice. 2d ed. Fred Coleman Archer. New York: McGraw-Hill, Gregg Division, 1968.

How to Conduct a Meeting. New York: Dun & Bradstreet, Business Education Division, 1969.

How to Manage by Objectives. John William Humble. New York: American Management Associations, 1973.

How to Manage by Results. 3d ed. Dale D. McConkey. New York: American Management Associations, 1976.

How to Run a Small Business. 4th ed. Jacob Kay Lasser. New York: McGraw-Hill, 1974.

The Human Side of Enterprise. Douglas McGregor. New York: McGraw-Hill, 1960.

Management of Organizational Behavior: Utilizing Human Resources. Paul Hersey and Kenneth Blanchard. Englewood Cliffs, N.J.: Prentice-Hall, 1972.

Management of Small Enterprises: Cases and Readings. 2d ed. William Rotch. Charlottesville, Va.: University Press of Virginia, 1967.

The Managerial Woman. Margaret Hennig and Anne Jardim. Garden City, N.Y.: Doubleday, Anchor Press, 1977.

Managing New Enterprises. Richard H. Buskirk and Percy J. Vaughn. St. Paul, Minn.: West Publishing Company, 1976.

Managing the Small Business. Rev. ed. Donald P. Stegall, Laurence Steinmetz, and John Kline. Homewood, Ill.: Richard D. Irwin, 1976.

Managing with Style: and Making It Work for You. Henry O. Golightly. New York: AMACOM, 1977.

Monitoring the Human Resource System: Based on a Panel Session at the Conference, April 20, 1976, New York City. New York: Conference Board, 1977.

Motivational Theories and Applications for Managers. Donald Sanzotta. New York: AMACOM, 1977.

Office and Administrative Management: Systems Analysis, Data Processing, and Office Services. 3d ed. Cleatice L. Littlefield. Englewood Cliffs, N.J.: Prentice-Hall, 1970.

Patterns for Success in Managing a Business. New York: Crowell Dun & Bradstreet, Business Education Division, 1969.

Person to Person Managing: An Executive's Guide to Working Effectively with People. Thomas L. Quick. New York: St. Martin's Press, 1977.

Personnel Management: Principles, Practices, and Point of View. 6th ed. Walter Dill Scott et al. New York: McGraw-Hill, 1961.

The Pitfalls in Managing a Small Business. New York: Dun & Bradstreet, Public Relations and Advertising, 1977.

The Practice of Supervising: Making Experience Pay. Martin Broadwell. Reading, Mass.: Addison-Wesley, 1977.

Small Business Management. 3d ed. Halsey N. Broom and J. G. Longenecker. Cincinnati, Ohio: Southwestern Publishing Co., 1971.

Small Business Management: A Casebook. Windsor Arnold Hosmer, Frank L. Tucker, and Arnold C. Cooper. Homewood, Ill.: Richard D. Irwin, 1966.

Sure Fail: The Art of Mismanagement. Raymond Dreyfack. New York: William Morrow & Co., 1976.

Survival and Growth: Management Strategies for the Small Firm. Theodore Cohn and Roy A. Lindberg. New York: AMACOM, 1974.

What the Manager Should Know about the Computer. Rev. ed. New York: Crowell Dun & Bradstreet, Business Education Division, 1970.

GOVERNMENT

Business, Government, and the Public. Murray L. Weidenbaum. Englewood Cliffs, N.J.: Prentice-Hall, 1977.

Internal Revenue Code. Chicago: Commerce Clearing House, January 1979.

Tax Choices in Organizing a Business. Chicago: Commerce Clearing House, 1969.

Tax Factors in Business Decisions. Dan Throop Smith. Englewood Cliffs, N.J.: Prentice-Hall, 1968.

Tax Guide for Small Businesses. 1979 ed. Publication No. 334. Washington, D.C.: Department of the Treasury, Internal Revenue Service, 1978.

Tax Planning Opportunities. Gerald F. Richards. New York: David McKay, 1977.

U.S. Master Tax Guide. Chicago: Commerce Clearing House, December 1978.

GENERAL

The Achieving Society. David C. McClelland. New York: John Wiley, Irvington Publishers, Halstead Press, 1976.

The Bottom Line: (Un)Equal Enterprise in America. Report of the President's Task Force on Women Business Owners. Washington, D.C.: U.S. Government Printing Office, 1978.

Business Planning Guide. Rev. ed. David H. Bangs, Jr., and William R. Osgood. Business Assistance Monograph Series. Portsmouth, N.H.: Upstart Publishing Company, 1978.

Employee Savings Plan: The Coming Trend in Retirement Planning. Bion H. Francis. Chicago: Advertising Publications, 1969.

The Entrepreneur's Manual: Business Start-ups, Spin-offs, and Innovative Management. Richard M. White, Jr. Radnor, Pa.: Chilton Publishing, 1977.

Entrepreneurship and the Corporation. William Copulsky and Herbert W. McNulty. New York: AMACOM, 1974.

An Introduction to Business Law. Rafe A. Howell. Hinsdale, Ill.: Dryden Press, Division of Holt, Rinehart and Winston, 1974.

Law for the Businessman. Bernard D. Reams. Dobbs Ferry, N.Y.: Oceana Publications, 1974.

Legal Guidelines for Business Enterprise Planning. Portland, Maine: New Enterprise Institute, University of Maine, 1977.

Legal Handbook for Small Business. Marc J. Lane. New York: AMACOM, 1977.

New Business Venture and the Entrepreneur. Patrick R. Liles. Homewood, Ill.: Richard D. Irwin, 1974.

New Venture Creation, a Guide to Small Business Development. Jeffry A. Timmons, Leonard E. Smollen, and Alexander L. M. Dingee, Jr. Homewood, Ill.: Richard D. Irwin, 1977.

Pre-Retirement Planning System. Elmer Otte. Appleton, Wis.: Retirement Research, 1975.

Protecting Your Business. Egon W. Loffel. New York: David McKay, 1977.

Retirement Dollars for the Self-Employed. New York: Dun & Bradstreet, Business Education Division, 1972.

Social Security. Robert James Myers. Homewood, Ill.: Richard D. Irwin, 1975.

Understanding Business Law. 4th ed. Arnold Edward Schneider. New York: McGraw-Hill, Gregg Division, 1967.

Why S.O.B.'s Succeed and Nice Guys Fail in a Small Business. San Diego, Calif.: Financial Management Associates, 1976.

Women-Owned Businesses 1972. U.S. Department of Commerce, Bureau of the Census, Office of Minority Business Enterprise. Publication No. 003-024-01171-9. Washington, D.C.: Superintendent of Documents, U.S. Government Printing Office, 1976.

DIRECTORIES

Analysis of the 25,000 Leading U.S. Corporations. New York: News Front, Year, Inc., 1971.

Directory of Largest Corporations. New York: Fortune, May 1978.

Everything You Can Get from the Government for Free—or Almost for Free. Craig T. Norback and Peter Norback. New York: Van Nostrand-Reinhold, 1975.

Franchise Directory. Lewiston, N.Y.: International Franchise Opportunities, 1979.

Franchise Investigation and Contract Negotiation. Harry Gross and Robert S. Levy. New York: Pilot Books, 1967.

Guide to American Directories. Ed. Bernard Klein. New York: McGraw-Hill, 1978.

Middle Market Directory. New York: Dun & Bradstreet, 1978.

Million Dollar Directory. New York: Dun & Bradstreet.

1979 Directory of Franchising Organizations. New York: Pilot Industries, 1979.

1979 Directory of Women-Owned Businesses: Washington/Baltimore Metropolitan Area. Washington, D.C.: National Association of Women Business Owners, 1979.

Register of Corporations, Directors, and Executives. New York: Standard and Poor's, 1978.

Small Business Information Sources (An Annotated Bibliography). Joseph C. Schabacker. Milwaukee, Wis.: National Council for Small Business Management Development, 1976.

Thomas Register of American Manufacturers and First Hands in All Lines. Published annually. New York: Thomas Publishing Co., 1979.

Venture Capital. Leroy W. Sinclair. New York: Technimetrics, Inc., 1973.

Periodicals

Advertising Age. Crain Communications, 740 N. Rush St., Chicago, Ill.

Black Enterprise. Earl G. Graves Publishing Co., Inc., 295 Madison Ave., New York, N.Y.

Business Horizons. Business Horizons, School of Business, Indiana University, Bloomington, Ind.

Business Monthly. United Media International, Inc., 306 Dartmouth St., Boston, Mass.

Business Week. McGraw-Hill Publications, 1221 Ave. of the Americas, New York, N.Y.

Dun's Review. Dun-Donnelley Publishing Corp., 666 Fifth Ave., New York, N.Y.

Enterprising Women. c/o Ava Stern, ed., 525 West End Ave., New York, N.Y.

Finance: The Magazine of Money. Finance Publishing Corp., Box G, Lenox Hill Station, New York, N.Y.

Forbes. Forbes, Inc., 60 Fifth Ave., New York, N.Y.

Fortune. Time Inc., 541 N. Fairbanks Court, Chicago, Ill.

Harvard Business Review. Subscription Service Department, Graduate School of Business Administration, P.O. Box 9730, Greenwich, Conn.

Human Resource Management. University of Michigan Business Review, Graduate School of Business Administration, University of Michigan, Ann Arbor, Mich.

Journal of Business. Graduate School of Business, University of Chicago Press, 5801 Ellis Ave., Chicago, Ill.

Journal of Marketing. American Marketing Association, 222 S. Riverside Plaza, Chicago, Ill.

Journal of Marketing Research. American Marketing Association, 222 S. Riverside Plaza, Chicago, Ill.

Journal of Small Business Management. National Council of Small Business Management Development, West Virginia University, Bureau of Business Research, Morgantown, W. Va.

Management Review. American Management Associations, Box 319, Saranac Lake, N.Y.

Office. Office Publications, Inc., 1200 Summer St., Stamford, Conn.

Personnel. American Management Associations, Box 319, Saranac Lake, N.Y.

Personnel Psychology. Personnel Psychology, Inc., P.O. Box 6965, College Station, Durham, N.C.

Sales and Marketing Management. Sales Management Inc., 633 Third Ave., New York, N.Y.

Successful Business Magazine: The Magazine for Independent Business. Successful Business, 505 Market St., Knoxville, Tenn. Attention: Bill Schultz.

Survey of Current Business. Superintendent of Documents, U.S. Government Printing Office, Washington, D.C.

Taxes. Commerce Clearing House, Inc., 4025 W. Peterson Ave., Chicago, Ill.

Venture. Venture Magazine Inc. 35 West 45th St., New York, N.Y.

Notes

INTRODUCTION

1. *The Bottom Line: (Un)Equal Enterprise in America*. Report of the President's Task Force on Women Business Owners. Washington, D.C.: U.S. Government Printing Office, 1978, p. 23.
2. "Women's Employment." Teresa J. Odendahl and Leslie E. Smith. *Comment* 2, no. 1 (September 1978): 1.
3. Public service announcement regarding the Equal Credit Opportunity Act, February 1979. U.S. Federal Trade Commission.
4. "Women's Employment," p. 1.
5. *The Bottom Line: (Un)Equal Enterprise in America*, p. 29.
6. Ibid, p. 40.

CHAPTER 1

1. Speech before the National Chamber of Commerce Convention, May 2, 1978. Anne Wexler.
2. *Entrepreneurship and the Corporation*. William Copulsky and Herbert W. McNulty. New York: AMACOM, 1974, p. 40.
3. *The Bottom Line: (Un)Equal Enterprise in America*. Report of the President's Task Force on Women Business Owners. Washington, D.C.: U.S. Government Printing Office, 1978, p. 23.
4. Ibid, p. 24.
5. Ibid, p. 40.
6. Ibid, p. 29.
7. From a forthcoming book by Ava Stern. New York: Doubleday, Anchor Press, in press.

CHAPTER 2

1. *The Bottom Line: (Un)Equal Enterprise in America*. Report of the President's Task Force on Women Business Owners. Washington, D.C.: U.S. Government Printing Office, 1978. These statistics defined a business as "woman-owned" if it was 50 percent owned by a woman or women. They did not include corporations with more than ten shareholders.
2. Selected services include hotels and other lodging places; personal (such as laundry and cleaning, beauty shops, shoe repair); business; automotive repair and garages; miscellaneous repair (such as electrical, watch and jewelry, welding); motion pictures; amusement and recreation; health and education; social; and miscellaneous (such as noncommercial research organizations, accounting, and auditing).
3. *The Bottom Line: (Un)Equal Enterprise in America*, p. 168.
4. Ibid, p. 175.
5. Ibid, p. 168.
6. "The Application of Psychological Testing to Entrepreneurial Potential." Michael Palmer. *California Management Review* 13, no. 3 (1971): 32–38.
7. *The Achieving Society*. David C. McClelland. New York: John Wiley, Irvington Publishers, Halstead Press, 1976, p. 229.

8. Ibid, p. 12.
9. *New Venture Creation: A Guide to Small Business Development*. Jeffry A. Timmons, Leonard E. Smollen, and Alexander L. M. Dingee, Jr. Homewood, Ill.: Richard D. Irwin, 1977, p. 95.
10. Ibid.
11. Ibid, p. 96.
12. *The Achieving Society*, p. 212.
13. *The Bottom Line: (Un)Equal Enterprise in America*, p. 32.
14. Ibid.
15. Ibid, p. 33.
16. Ibid.
17. Ibid, p. 34.
18. Ibid.
19. Ibid.
20. Ibid, p. 216.

CHAPTER 3

1. *Ratio Analysis for Small Business*. R. Sanzo. Small Business Management Series No. 20. Washington, D.C.: Small Business Administration, 1977.
2. *The Business Failure Record, 1976*. New York: Dun & Bradstreet, 1977, p. 12. The major causes of business failure listed by order of incidence are incompetence, unbalanced experience, lack of experience in the line, lack of managerial experience, unknown reasons, disaster, neglect, and fraud.

CHAPTER 5

1. *The Pitfalls in Managing a Small Business*. New York: Dun & Bradstreet, Public Relations and Advertising, 1977.
2. *The Joy of Money: The Guide to Women's Financial Freedom*. Paula Nelson. New York: Bantam Books, 1975, p. 45.
3. *The Bottom Line: (Un)Equal Enterprise in America*. Report of the President's Task Force on Women Business Owners. Washington, D.C..: U.S. Government Printing Office, 1978, p. 209.
4. "The Care and Feeding of Bankers." Kathleen Ross. *Enterprising Women: A Business Monthly* 4, no. 2 (October 1978): 3–7.

CHAPTER 6

1. "Marketing When Things Change." Theodore Levitt. *Harvard Business Review* 55 (November–December 1970): 107.

CHAPTER 7

1. *Motivation and Personality*. Abraham Harold Maslow. New York: Harper and Row, 1970.

CHAPTER 8

1. *Overcoming Math Anxiety*. Sheila Tobias. New York: W. W. Norton, 1978, pp. 95–96.

CHAPTER 9

1. *Entrepreneurship and the Corporation*. William Copulsky and Herbert W. McNulty. New York: AMACOM, 1974, p. 58.
2. *The Business Failure Record, 1977* New York: Dun & Bradstreet, 1978.

3. *The Managerial Woman*. Margaret Hennig and Anne Jardim. Garden City, N.Y.: Doubleday, Anchor Press, 1977, p. 25.
4. *Making It in Management: A Behavioral Approach for Women Executives*. Margaret Fenn. Englewood Cliffs, N.J.: Prentice-Hall, 1978, pp. 48–56.
5. "Women: Born to Manage." M. L. Johnson. *Industry Week*, August 4, 1975, pp. 22–26.
6. Women were found superior in aptitudes for accounting, basic to statistical and actuarial work; verbalization, critical to persuasion capability; silograms, which is a measure of memory for languages and professional terminology; the ability to form associations easily between words that are known or unknown; abstract visualizations, which are related to the ability to deal with abstract problems, ideas, and principles; observations; and finger dexterity. The two aptitudes men rated higher on were structural visualization, which is basic to technical and scientific progressions, and basic handgrip strength.
7. "Supervision, Management, and Administration." William Dinsmore. *Personnel Magazine*, July-August 1962, pp. 77–80.
8. "How Well Could They Manage If You Weren't There to Work the Strings?" Suzanne Mendelssohn. *Small Business*, October–November 1978, pp. 4–10.

EPILOGUE

1. *The Greening of America: How the Youth Revolution Is Trying to Make America Livable*. Charles A. Reich. New York: Random House, 1970.
2. "The Entrepreneur Who Is the Artist." Martha Stuart. *Executive* 4, no. 1 (1977): 35.

Index

accountants, business use of, 48, 63, 64,
85–88, 100, 103, 104, 175, 186–87
advertising, 142
advisers for businesswomen, 85–90
(*see also* accountants, lawyers)
Age Discrimination Act, 168
American Management Association
study of women entrepreneurs, 25–27,
45–47, 52, 85, 87, 104, 107–09, 203,
210
American Women's Economic Development Corporation, 21–22, 26, 53, 62,
85, 94, 110, 116, 127, 173
Amey, Margorie O'Connell, 75, 87–88,
153, 214
Ash, Mary Kay, 30
assets, 37, 65, 178–79

balance sheets, 37, 64, 71, 177–79
Bandle, Luke, 133, 137, 141
Bangs, David H., Jr., and William
Osgood, *Business Planning Guide* 101
Bank of America studies on starting a
business, 57
banks: credit arrangements, 115
(*see also* loans); ratio analysis by,
56–57; use of, by businesswomen,
47–48, 57–58, 87–94, 103–05, 110–11,
121–22; for women, 14, 106–07
Barnard, Lynn, 83
Barnett, Judith, 119–20
Bender, Henry, 25–27, 107, 203
Berman, Aline, 203
Bissell, Patricia, 85, 88, 89, 174–75, 187
bonuses for employees, 166
break-even point, 99, 136–37
Burks, Juanita, 23

Business Administration degrees
awarded to women, 23
business failures, 24–25, 32–33, 59, 93,
193
business jargon, 172–73, 182
business organization, types of, 70–74;
tax considerations, 186, 189
business plans, 100–103, 195–96
buying into a business, 60–67

capital: equity (net worth), 111–14,
178–79; estimating amount needed,
57–58, 98–100, 110; raising of, 57–58,
71–72, 93–98, 100–07, 109, 111–23 (*see
also* loans)
cash crisis, 173–74, 185, 186
cash-flow management, 115, 177, 182–86
Cavanaugh, Denise, 38, 83, 108, 142, 191
census data, use of, 57, 132–33
Chamber of Commerce, 63, 91–92
Civil Rights Avt, 168
Clayton Act, 143, 144
Cloherty, Patricia, 21, 116
Cohen, Charlotte, 20–21
Commerce Business Daily, 145, 146
commercial law, 143
communication skills, 193–204
competitors, 36, 129, 132; as source of
help, 59
consumer market statistics, 132–33
Consumer Product Safety Act, 144
Cook, Dottie Bruce, 82
Copulsky, William, and Herbert
McNulty, *Entrepreneurship and the
Corporation*, 20, 192
corporation as form of business, 70–75,
186, 189

costs of operation, 57–58, 98–100, 136–37; in cash flow statement, 182–83; for personnel, 149, 152, 154, 162, 167; in profit and loss statement, 180–82
credit rating, 119–21
Cunane, Nora, 155
customers, 36–37, 48, 131, 132; as source of financial help, 109–10

dealerships, 68
debt, nature of, 96–97
debt financing, 111–12, 115–17, 183 (*see also* loans)
decision-making ability, 197–98
Deming, Janet, 98
depreciation, 186
directories: on government purchasing and sales, 145; of industries and associations, 132; of lawyers, 87
Disability Benefits Law, 169
discounting, 136
discrimination against businesswomen, 47–48, 87, 94, 103–08, 128; laws prohibiting, 156, 168
Downing, Vicki Smith, 24, 28, 49, 54, 62, 211, 215
Driggs, Kandra, 54, 149, 163, 207, 210
Dun & Bradstreet: on business failure, 32–33; 56, 59, 93, 193; publications of, 56, 132, 182

Economic Development Administration, 22
educational system, brainwashing of women by, 16
Employee Retirement Insurance Security Act (ERISA), 167–70
employees: compensation of, 149, 152–54, 162–67, 200; contract, 152; government regulations on, 167–70; job descriptions for, 155–61, 205; management of, 25, 26, 162, 193, 196–206; motivation of, 162–63, 202, 205–06; part-time, 152–54; planning for, 150–53; productivity of, 164–65, 180; recruitment and hiring, 80, 150, 153, 155, 156; shared ownership by, 80, 206; temporary, 152–53; withholding tax payments for, 189
employment agencies, 154
Enterprising Women, 24, 26, 33, 86, 121, 215
entrepreneurial personality characteris-
tics, 39–48, 192–93, 204
entrepreneurial role requirements, 44, 191–92
Entrepreneurship Institute, 42, 134
Equal Credit Opportunity Act, 103, 104, 119
Equal Employment Opportunity Commission, 156, 168
Equal Pay Act, 168
Essman, Pansy, 76–77

factoring companies, 117
Fair, Carrie, 107–08
Fair Labor Standards Act, 163
family responsibilities and business ownership, 210–12
Federal Trade Commission, 68–69, 143, 144
Fenn, Margaret, 34, 197
finance company loans, 117
financial management, 86–89, 171; of cash flow, 182–86; estimating expenses, 98–99; language of, 172–73; obtaining capital (*see* capital, raising of); planning, 86–89; use of records in, 173–74, 195
financial records, 37, 171, 173–77, 195
financial statements, 177–86
Finch, Christi, 59, 122
First Women's Bank of Maryland, 106, 120, 139
First Women's Bank of New York, 14, 61, 86, 95, 103, 106
Fitzpatrick, Beatrice, 21–22, 26, 53, 62, 94, 173
franchises, 60, 69–70
Friday, Nancy, 83–85
fringe benefits for employees, 153, 162, 165–66
Furstenburg, Diane von, 23

goals of business ownership, 37–39, 52–55
goodwill as business asset, 37, 66
Graham, Betty, 30, 93
Green, Pamela, 99
Grover, Eve, 106, 120, 139
growth, management of, 191–96

Hancock, Sandy, 135–36, 213–14
Handman, Barbara, 82–83, 99
Hardwick, Cathy, 41–42
Haslett, Brian, 59, 79, 109

256 *Index*

Haynes, Elizabeth, 23, 48, 214
Henning, Margaret, and Anne Jardim, *The Managerial Woman*, 197
Hindall, Genie, 63, 67
Hogan, Pauline, 214
Holloman, J. Herbert, 33
home-based businesses, 139–40
Huber, Joyce, 31, 35, 49, 81–82, 84, 176–77, 211
Hyatt, Carole, 49, 123, 126–27, 142

income: of women-owned firms, 29–30, 55; of women vs. men, 15
Institute for New Enterprise Development, 42
insurance: for employees, 167, 169; liability, 98
Internal Revenue Service: auditing by, 187; publications of, 167, 169, 189 (*see also* taxes)
International Franchise Association, publications of, 69, 70
inventory management, 89, 175–76, 193; loans for, 115
Ives, Suzanne, 39, 85, 139

Jackson, Beverly, 49, 82, 140, 204
job descriptions, 155–61, 205
Johnson O'Conner Research Foundation, 198

Kenney, Constance, 62, 96
Keogh plans, 167, 170
Kovner, Sarah, 81–83, 99

Lakein, Alan, *How to Get Control of Your Time and Your Life*, 209
Lang, Nancy, 102–03, 204, 214, 215
Lanham Trademark Act, 144
Lawrence, Mary Wells, 23
lawyers: as business advisers, 64, 70, 85–86, 103, 112–13, 168; discrimination against women by, 48, 87, 164; selection of, 85–90
leveraging, 37, 118
Levitt, Theodore, 133
liabilities, 37, 72–73, 178–79
liability insurance, 98
licensing of business, 75
liquidity position, 178
Lively, Lynn, 208–10
loans: bank criteria for, 53–54, 57, 61; collateral for, 117–18; repayment of, 99, 115, 117–18; short- and long-term, 115; size of, 53–54, 57–58, 98–99; Small Business Administration, 115–16; strategy for obtaining, 57–58, 93–98, 100–108, 110
location of business, 138–40, 193
Loeseur, Norma, 199–200
logo, 136 (*see also* trademark)

McClelland, David, 39–41
MacKenzie, Alex, *The Time Trap— Managing Your Way Our*, 209
McRea, Bill, 134
Mahoney, Brooke, 207
managerial jobs, percent of women in, 22
managerial skills, 192–99; delegation of authority, 204–06; employee supervision, 196–04; handling stress, 207; planning and organizing, 193–98
Mapel, Virginia, 83–84, 139
marketing strategy: 125, 128; competition in, 129–30; location in, 138–40; market dislocations in, 130–31; market research in, 131–33; packaging in, 137–38; pricing in, 136–37; products in, 135–36; promotion in, 140–42
Marmoll, Helen E., 72, 74
Marshall, Miriam, 105–06
Martindale-Hubbell Law Directory, 87
Maslow, Abraham, *Motivation and Personality*, 162
Massoni, Carla, 82, 211
Maynard, Virginia, 61, 86, 92, 95, 103
Mendelssohn, Suzanne, 205–06
Miller-Tydings Act, 143
Minority Business Enterprise office, 145
minority-enterprise small business investment companies (MISBIC), 113, 114
minority preferences in government contracts, 147
Mitchell, Isabel, 129, 138
Molloy, Jim, 99, 129, 133, 193
money: as business capital (*see* capital); business concept of, 96–98; feminine approach to, 62, 94–97
Morris, Robert, Associates: publications of, 132, 182; ratio studies of, 56
motivation of employees, 162–63 202, 205–06; of entrepreneurs, 29–40, 48–49, 61–62
myths about businesswomen, 46

National Association of Women Business
Owners, 91, 144
National Cash Register Company,
Expenses in Retailing, 56–57
National Center for Educational Statis-
tics, 23
Nelson, Paula, *Joy of Money*, 96

Occupational Safety and Health Administration, 168, 170
Olsen, Karen, 74
overtime, 152

packaging, 137–38
Pallie, Anne, 113
partnerships as form of business, 70–75,
80–84, 189
Patinkin, Barbara, 133, 134
pension plans, 166–70
Person, Anne, 30
Petery, Mary Ann, 202–03
Pingree, Diane, 122
Pitlor, Joel, 41, 130
pricing strategies, 136–37
Procurement Automated Purchasing System, 145
product safety legislation, 144
product strategies, 135–36
professional and technical jobs, percent
of women in, 22
professional and trade associations, businesswomen in, 90–91
profit and loss statements, 37, 171, 177,
179–82
profit objectives, 137
profits, taxation of, 73–74
profit-sharing plans, 166
promotion, 104, 128, 138, 140–42
public relations, 141

ratio analysis, use of, 56–57
Reich, Charles, *The Greening of America*, 215–16
Reid, Jean, 85, 110, 127
renting business space, 139
retailing: location of business in, 138;
women-owned businesses in, 29–31
risk taking in business ownership, 32–35,
40–41, 97, 192
Ross, Kathleen, 121
Rotary Club, attitude toward women of,
91–92

sales personnel, 152, 164–65
Salvage, Lynn, 14, 61
Schifter, Sandy and Mel, 129
Schubert, Edith, 67, 203
Self-Employed Retirement Act of 1962,
167, 170
self-employment of women,
statistics on, 15–16, 24
selling skills, 126–28
Shaffer, Peg, 138, 140, 153, 196
Sherman Anti-Trust Act, 143
size of business: as factor in success, 53;
women-owned, 53–55, 114
Small Business Administration, 21, 22,
90, 111, 113, 116; loans, 115–16; publications, 57–58, 67, 69, 101, 137, 139, 142,
145, 148, 156, 175, 200; Small Business
Person Award, 24, 214
small business investment companies
(SBIC), 113, 114
Social Security Act, 169, 190
sole proprietorships as form of business,
70–75, 189
Spain, Jayne, 201–202
Statistical Abstract of the United States,
132
Stern, Ava, 24, 26, 33, 86, 215
stock options for employees, 166
strategy skills in business, 37–39
stress, coping with, 207
Stuart, Martha, 20, 214
Stutz, Geraldine, 106
Summers, Sheila, 82
suppliers, 48, 53; as source of credit,
109, 116–17

Tarvin, Marie, 104, 128
Task Force on Women Business Owners,
17, 19, 30; 1979 survey, 16, 24, 45, 53,
55, 60, 70, 90, 95, 104, 109, 114, 116,
127–28, 144
taxes on business, 73, 89–90, 168, 169,
180, 186–90; excise, 190; payroll deductions, 74, 187, 189–90
teamwork, need for in business ventures,
36, 79–80
time management, 207–10
Timmons, Jeffrey A., Leonard Smollen,
and Alexander Dingee, *New Venture
Creation: A Guide to Small Business
Development*, 42–44
Tobias, Sheila, *Overcoming Math Anxiety*, 173

trade associations and publications, 132
trademarks, 68, 69, 144 (*see also* logo)
trade names, 76
Travis, Corrine, 135, 136
Tucker, Rosemary, 24, 198, 214

undercapitalization, 93
unemployment insurance, 169, 190
Uniform Commercial Code, 143
U.S. Bureau of the Census, *Survey of Women-Owned Businesses, 1972,* 29, 45, 55, 70
U.S. government contracts, 127–28, 144–48
U.S. government publications for business: census reports, 141–33; on government contracts, 145; on labor-management relations, 167–69; market reports, 132, on taxes, 167, 169, 189
venture capital firms, 113–14
Venture Founders, 41, 42, 59, 79, 109, 130
Vinton, Mary, 86–88, 93, 116–17, 136, 142, 194–95, 203, 204

wages and salaries: incentive arrangements, 162–65; legislation on, 167–68; ss operating cost, 74, 149, 152; taxation of, 74, 187–90; types of payments, 164–65
Wall Street Journal, business opportunity listings in, 63
wealth, ownership of, by women, 14
Weinberg, Eileen, 59, 122
Welsh, John, 177
Wexler, Anne, 19–20
Wolmach, Emily, 121
women's liberation movement and entrepreneurial spirit, 14
Women's National Bank of Washington, D.C., 121
work flow, management of, 152–53
work life of women, length of, 15
workmen's compensation, 169

Young, Frances, 200

Zulalian, Mary, 66–67, 127, 196